Studies in Jewish and Christian Literature

Messiah and the Throne, Timo Eskola
Father, Son, and Spirit in Romans 8, Ron C. Fay

FATHER, SON, AND SPIRIT IN ROMANS 8

Father, Son, and Spirit in Romans 8

The Roman Reception of Paul's Trinitarian Theology

Ron C. Fay

Fontes

Father, Son, and Spirit in Romans 8:
The Roman Reception of Paul's Trinitarian Theology

Copyright © 2020 by Ron C. Fay

ISBN-13: 978-1-948048-26-2 (hardback)
ISBN-13: 978-1-948048-27-9 (paperback)

All rights reserved. No part of this publication may be reproduced, stored in a retrieval system, or transmitted in any form or by any means—electronic, mechanical, photocopy, recording, or any other—except for brief quotations in printed reviews, without the prior permission of the publisher.

FONTES PRESS
DALLAS, TX
www.fontespress.com

Contents

Abbreviations ix

1 Introduction 1
   1.1 Problem and Thesis 2
   1.2 Methodology 4
   1.3 Limitations 6
   1.4 Looking Ahead 11

2 Greco-Roman Concepts of Deity 13
   2.1 The Greatest God: Jupiter 14
   2.2 Gods and Mystery Cults 17
   2.3 Humans as Gods 26
      2.3.1 Religious and Historical Foundation 26
      2.3.2 Emperors as Gods Outside of Rome 30
      2.3.3 Emperors as Gods in Rome: Caligula, Nero,
         and Domitian as Case Studies 32
      2.3.4 Summary 35
   2.4 Conclusion 36

3 God and Mankind 39
   3.1 The Context of Romans 8: God's Gospel 39
   3.2 God and Creation 46
   3.3 God and Recreation 53
      3.3.1 God and Adoption 54
      3.3.2 God and Glory 63
   3.4 God and Salvation 73
   3.5 Summary 79

4 God and the Son and the Spirit 81
   4.1 Son, Spirit, and Sin 82
      4.1.1 The Law 82
      4.1.2 Law and Sin 89
   4.2 Son, Spirit, and Recreation 95
      4.2.1 Son, Spirit, and Adoption 95
      4.2.2 Son, Spirit, and Glory 100
      4.2.3 Son, Spirit, and Creation 107
   4.3 Son, Spirit, and Salvation 108
      4.3.1 "In Christ" and "In the Spirit" 108
      4.3.2 Life 117
   4.4 Son, Spirit, and God 121
      4.4.1 Son and Father 121
      4.4.2 Son and Spirit 128
   4.5 Triunity? 132

Conclusion 139

Bibliography 145

Index 165

Abbreviations

AB	Anchor Bible Commentary
ABD	*Anchor Bible Dictionary.* Edited by D. N. Freedman. 6 vols. Doubleday, 1992.
ABR	*Australian Biblical Review*
AnBib	Analecta biblica
ANRW	*Aufstiegund Niedergang der römischen Welt: Geschichte und Kultur Rom sim Spiegel der neuren Forschung.* Edited by H. Temporini and W. Haase. Berlin, 1972–
ATANT	Abhandlungen zur Theologie des Alten und Neuen Testaments
BDAG	Bauer, W., F. Danker, W. F. Arndt, and F. W. Gingrich. *Greek-English Lexicon of the New Testament and Other Early Christian Literature.* 3rd ed. University of Chicago Press, 1999.
BECNT	Baker Exegetical Commentary on the New Testament
BI	*Biblical Illustrator*
BJRL	*Bulletin of the John Rylands University Library of Manchester*
BZ	*Biblische Zeitschrift*
BR	*Biblical Research*
CBQ	*Catholic Biblical Quarterly*
DNTB	*Dictionary of New Testament Background.* Edited by C. A. Evans and S. E. Porter. IVP, 2000.
EKKNT	Evangelisch-katholischer Kommentar zum Neuen Testament
EPRO	Etudes préliminaires aux religions orientales dans l'empire romain

ExpTim	*Expository Times*
FoiVie	*Foi et Vie*
Greg.	*Gregorianum*
HNTC	Harper New Testament Commentary
ICC	International Critical Commentary
ISFCJ	International Studies in Formative Christianity and Judaism
ITQ	*Irish Theological Quarterly*
IVPNTCS	IVP New Testament Commentary Series
JBL	*Journal of Biblical Literature*
JETS	*Journal of the Evangelical Theological Society*
JPT	*Journal of Pentecostal Theology*
JRS	*Journal of Roman Studies*
JSNT	*Journal for the Study of the New Testament*
JSNTSup	Journal for the Study of the New Testament: Supplement Series
JSOTSup	Journal for the Study of the Old Testament: Supplement Series
JTS	*Journal of Theological Studies*
KEK	Kritisch-exegetischer Kommentar über das Neue Testament
LEC	Library of Early Christianity
L&N	*Greek-English Lexicon of the New Testament: Based on Semantic Domans.* Edited by J. P. Louw and E. A. Nida. 2nd ed. Fortress, 1989.
MNTC	Moffat New Testament Commentary
NAC	New American Commentary
NCBC	New Century Biblical Commentary
NICNT	New International Commentary on the New Testament
NICOT	New International Commentary on the Old Testament
NIGTC	New International Greek Testament Commentary
NovT	*Novum Testamentum*
NovTSup	Novum Testamentum Supplements, Supplements to Novum Testamentum
NSBT	New Studies in Biblical Theology
NTS	*New Testament Studies*
OTL	Old Testament Library
PNTC	Pillar New Testament Commentary
ResQ	*Restoration Quarterly*
RevExp	*Review and Expositor*
RTR	*Reformed Theological Review*

SBLDS	Society of Biblical Literature Dissertation Series
SBLMS	Society of Biblical Literature Monograph Series
SBLRBS	Society of Biblical Literature Resources for Biblical Study
SJT	*Scottish Journal of Theology*
SNTSMS	Society for New Testament Studies Monograph Series
ST	*Studia theologica*
TPINTC	TPI New Testament Commentaries
TDNT	*Theological Dictionary of the New Testament.* Edited by G. Kittel and G. Friedrich. Translated by G. W. Bromiley. 10 vols. Eerdmans, 1964-1976.
TLNT	*Theological Lexicon of the New Testament.* C. Spicq. Translated and edited by J. D. Ernst. 3 vols. Hendrickson, 1997.
TNTC	Tyndale New Testament Commentary
TynBul	*Tyndale Bulletin*
WBC	Word Biblical Commentary
WUNT	Wissenschaftliche Untersuchungen zum Neuen Testament
ZNW	Zeitschrift für die neutestamentliche Wissenschaft und die Kunde der älteren Kirche

Chapter 1

Introduction

The role of Jesus in Paul's theology has long been a topic of debate, yet rarely does the question of the Trinity surface with respect to Paul's view of God.[1] Some commentaries mention portions of a passage or might have a brief essay speaking of Trinitarian thought, yet few take the time to explore the concept of God offered by an author or book.[2] Though scholarship has been urged to consider the place of God in New Testament studies,[3] this type of study does not occur often.[4] Some approach the problem as a Biblical Theology problem, taking a tour through a specific author (in this case Paul) and bringing together various themes, elements, and verses in order to construct a Trinitarian theology for said author.[5] Some focus on God and his character.[6]

---

[1] E.g. James D. G. Dunn, *The Theology of Paul the Apostle* (Eerdmans, 1998), 27–50. Dunn cogently begins with the Paul's starting point, God, but then never addresses the issue of the Trinity in Paul, focusing only on Jewish monotheism. This has started to be rectified, however, as seen in Ron C. Fay, "Was Paul a Trinitarian? A Look at Romans 8," in *Paul and His Theology* (ed. Stanley E. Porter; Brill, 2006), 327-345, Andrew K. Gabriel, "Pauline Pneumatology and the Question of Trinitarian Presuppositions," in *Paul and His Theology* (ed. Stanley E. Porter; Brill, 2006), 347-362, and Wesley Hill, *Paul and the Trinity: Persons, Relations, and the Pauline Letters* (Eerdmans, 2015).

[2] This is not the case, however, in the Gospel of John. See, for example, Andreas J. Köstenberger and Scott R. Swain, *Father, Son and Spirit: The Trinity and John's Gospel* (NBST; InterVarsity, 2008).

[3] Nils Alstrup Dahl, "The Neglected Factor in New Testament Theology," in *Jesus the Christ: The Historical Origins of Christological Doctrine* (ed. Donald H. Juel; Fortress, 1991), 153-162. Dahl's challenge appears on 155.

[4] A rare counterexample is found in Larry W. Hurtado, *God in New Testament Theology* (Library of Biblical Theology; Abingdon, 2010).

[5] E.g. Gordon Fee, "Christology and Pneumatology in Romans 8:9-11 — and Elsewhere: Some Reflections on Paul as a Trinitarian," in *To What End Exegesis? Essays Textual, Exegetical, and Theological* (Eerdmans, 2001), 218–239, and Francis Watson, "The Triune Divine Identity: Reflections on Pauline God Language, in Disagreement with J. D. Dunn," *JSNT* 80 (2000): 99-124.

[6] Paul-Gerhard Klumbies, *Die Rede von Gott bei Paulus in ihrem zeitgeschichtlichen Kontext* (Vandenhoeck & Ruprecht, 1992).

Some concentrate on the relationship between God and Christ, neglecting the Holy Spirit.[7] Some focus on the Holy Spirit in exclusion to everything else.[8] Rather than building a composite picture by a proof-texting method,[9] a better approach would be to concentrate specifically on a single text and show the way an author views God, Jesus, and the Holy Spirit. After one examines the author's understanding of each, then one can begin to build an accurate picture of whether or not the author has a Trinitarian theology, a proto-Trinitarian theology, or not a Trinitarian theology at all.

1.1 Problem and Thesis

Paul makes reference to God, Jesus, and the Spirit many times, yet rarely together. Paul is certainly focused on God in terms of his letters and thus theology. The epistle to the Romans in particular harbors much information on Paul's thoughts about God. In the epistle, Paul develops the idea of God as the Father of all who believe.[10] At the same time, Jesus as God's son appears throughout the book as well.[11] Of all his letters, Paul's epistle to the Romans also includes the most theologizing about the Holy Spirit.[12] Romans 8 in particular often carries the title of "life in the Spirit,"[13] a section in which Paul discusses the Holy Spirit more than in any of his other writings.

The problem comes across in a very nuanced way. Paul writes occasional literature, not systematic works.[14] Therefore, what Paul writes is his approach to an issue or an answer to a problem; it is not his theology laid out in a systematic or even necessarily logically ordered format, since he could be an-

---

7 E.g. Christopher Cowan, "The Father and Son in the Fourth Gospel: Johannine Subordination Revisited," *JETS* 49 (2006): 115–135.

8 E.g. Gordon Fee, *God's Empowering Presence: The Holy Spirit in the Letters of Paul* (Hendrickson, 1994). To be fair, he also has a companion volume *Pauline Christology: An Exegetical–Theological Study* (Hendrickson, 2007).

9 E.g. Bill Thrasher, *The Attributes of God in Pauline Theology* (Wipf & Stock, 2001). Thrasher describes God in Paul based solely upon Paul's descriptive terms for God. Thus, he can call God good simply because Paul uses the term of God.

10 E.g. Marianne Meye Thompson, "'Mercy Upon All': God as Father in the Epistle to the Romans," in *Romans and the People of God: Essays in Honor of Gordon D. Fee on the Occasion of His 65th Birthday* (ed. Sven K. Soderlund and N. T. Wright; Eerdmans, 1999), 203–216.

11 E.g. Larry W. Hurtado, "Jesus' Divine Sonship in Paul's Epistle to the Romans," in *Romans and the People of God: Essays in Honor of Gordon D. Fee on the Occasion of His 65th Birthday* (ed. Sven K. Soderlund and N. T. Wright; Eerdmans, 1999), 217–233.

12 Cf. C. E. B. Cranfield, *Romans* (2 vols; ICC; T&T Clark, 1975; repr., T&T Clark 2003), 2:840–844.

13 Or identity in the Spirit, as in Philip F. Esler, *Conflict and Identity in Romans: The Social Setting of Paul's Letter* (Fortress, 2003), 243.

14 Karl P. Donfried, "False Presuppositions in the Study of Romans," in *The Romans Debate* (ed. Karl P. Donfried; Hendrickson, 1991), 102–125, here 124–125.

swering a set of questions in the order he received them. This is the difference between Paul's theologizing (meaning his writing discrete answers containing theological truth) and Paul's theology (what Paul lets govern his spiritual life and understanding of God).[15] It is through Paul's theologizing that glimpses of his theology can be found.

What is Paul's theology of God? More specifically, how does Paul explain the presence of the Holy Spirit in theological terms and what is the identity of Jesus Christ, and who are both Jesus and the Spirit in relationship to God? J. D. G. Dunn responds by separating Christology from theology proper throughout his theology of Paul.[16] He then decides that Christology points to theology proper, yet there is no reciprocal relationship.[17] He denies that Paul could ever attach significant divine titles to Jesus due to his strict monotheism.[18] Francis Watson counters Dunn by calling this "a characteristic *Arian* move" in that Jesus points to God without in any way being part of God's identity.[19] Dunn's problem is one of methodology in that he looks for explicit terms that demonstrate Paul literally calling Jesus "God," as can be seen by his conclusion of the matter when discussing Rom 9:5 as the only place where "the issue hangs" with respect to Jesus being considered divine.[20] This accords with Dunn's denial of any sort of preexistence of Jesus as well, since he denies "sending" language in Paul can describe such a characteristic of Jesus Christ.[21] Cranfield takes exception to Dunn's comments, pointing out the flaws in Dunn's arguments and occasionally his methodology (e.g. Dunn not commenting on the juxtaposition of Christ and God in 8:9).[22]

Who in this debate is correct? If Dunn is correct, then Paul had a concept of Christ as greater than human or approaching divine status as found in Paul's theologizing. If Watson and Cranfield are correct, Paul had a Trinitarian conceptualization, delineating different functions of each person while

---

15 Cf. James D. G. Dunn, "In Quest of Paul's Theology: Retrospect and Prospect," in *Pauline Theology Volume IV: Looking Back, Pressing On* (ed. E. Elizabeth Johnson and David M. Hay; Scholars Press, 1997), 95–115. Dunn makes a distinction between Paul's theology and Paul's theologizing; the latter is his writing and the former can be found within his letters but at a deeper level.

16 Cf. Dunn, *Theology of Paul*, 27–50, 163–315.

17 Dunn, *Theology of Paul*, 255.

18 Dunn, *Theology of Paul*, 256–257.

19 Watson, "The Triune Divine Identity," 117.

20 Dunn, *Theology of Paul*, 257.

21 James D. G. Dunn, *Christology in the Making: A New Testament Inquiry into the Origins of the Doctrine of the Incarnation* (2nd ed.; Eerdmans, 1989), 38–46.

22 C. E. B. Cranfield, "Some Comments on Professor J. D. G. Dunn's *Christology in the Making* with Special Reference to the Evidence of the Epistle to the Romans," in *The Glory of Christ in the New Testament* (ed. L. D. Hurst and N. T. Wright; Clarendon Press, 1987), 267–280, here 270–273.

holding to an essential unity, even though none can point to a systematic formulation within Paul's writings.

The question becomes one of Paul's theologizing, namely would Paul's readers[23] have understood him as promoting a triunity understanding of God? By "triunity understanding of God," this book refers not to Nicean standards of the Trinity, rather the reference is to a monotheistic faith expressed in the simultaneous work of the Father, Son, and Holy Spirit as separate yet unified actants. Dunn's work points toward a proto-Trinitarian theology within the letters of Paul while Watson and Cranfield believe that Paul already held to the concept of the Trinity. This work intends to solve this dispute, arguing for the position that Paul held a triune concept of God. *When taking into account his Jewish background and the Romans context into which he was writing, Paul communicates the Father, Son, and Spirit as a triunity to his readers in Romans 8.*

1.2 Methodology

In order to prove this thesis, two main questions need to be answered. First, did Paul hold to a triune concept of God in the first place? Second, if he held a triune concept of God, would his readers have understood his letter as advocating or originating from such a view?

The book will begin by surveying the concept of God in Rome during the first century and earlier in order to draw on the data and conclusions while exegeting Romans 8. This includes reviewing inscriptions, archeology, poetry, and history in order to formulate a general definition of the term θέος for first-century Rome. Each culture has an underlying story or collection of stories that helps form the identity of that culture (e.g. the *Iliad* for Greece or the OT for Jews).[24] The stories of Rome centered on one overarching principle: religion.[25] Due to the influence of the emperor upon religion (e.g. Augustus as *pontifex maximus*), much of the field of politics in Rome during the empire overlapped and blended with religion in the first century, and even more so thereafter due to the tradition of divine status accorded the emperor.[26] Therefore, the issue of emperor worship inside and outside of Rome is pertinent

---

23 "Readers" and "recipients" will be used interchangeably throughout this work to refer to the original intended recipients who were most likely hearing this read to them rather than reading it themselves.

24 The recognition of the place of story in cultural identification has become stronger in recent years in Biblical studies. See especially N. T. Wright, *The New Testament and the People of God* (Christian Origins and the Question of God 1; Fortress, 1992), 47–80.

25 One need only look at Virgil's *Aeneid*.

26 See 2.3 below.

to understanding the religious nature of Rome. Before moving in that direction, however, a general introduction to Roman deities and beliefs will set the stage for understanding the mindset of a first-century resident of Rome. All of these findings will be limited to the first century, as this is the time when Paul was writing.

This project also involves using grammatical and historical methods to analyze what Paul was conveying to his readers in the book of Romans. The basic methods employed will be historical-grammatical and religious-historical. The main idea is to canvas what the text says by utilizing grammatical, syntactical, and historical research. Instead of working through the text in a verse by verse commentary format, this project intends to bring questions and topics to the text and then answer them according to what the text states, often times with the text raising further questions. While this work focuses on Romans 8, it will also draw upon both the context of Romans and other portions of the Pauline corpus in order to clarify certain words, phrases, or concepts in the text. This book will note how Paul speaks from both of his cultural heritages, Jewish and Greco-Roman, as neither should be downplayed since the culture of a writer and his recipients need to be taken into consideration.[27] However, the Old Testament will not figure prominently within the work as the main focus will intentionally be placed upon the pagan worldview of the Romans. Paul does use the Old Testament throughout Romans, yet Romans 8 has only one explicit quotation with a few allusions sprinkled in, most of which occur in the doxological section of the chapter (Rom 8:31–39).

The most important aspect in this work is the focus upon the Roman recipients of the letter and thus on Paul's arguments which fit into such a context. Much literature on Paul emphasizes his apostolic authority, his Jewish heritage, or both while neglecting to highlight his Diaspora roots, as he claims to be from outside the land of Israel while still being a Jew.[28] Even though Paul was ethnically Jewish, he was also culturally and legally a Roman. One cannot have an accurate picture of Paul or his works without recognizing the special character of Diaspora Judaism.[29] As Paul writes occasional literature,

---

27 Wright, *People of God*, 81–144.
28 F. F. Bruce, *Paul: Apostle of the Heart Set Free* (Eerdmans, 1977) covers all three, but only mentions Tarsus as his place of birth and does not consider the significance of this for Paul's self-understanding.
29 For the divergences between Jerusalem Judaism and Diaspora Judaism, see John M. G. Barclay, "Diaspora Judaism," in *Religious Diversity in the Graeco-Roman World* (The Biblical Seminar 79; ed. Dan Cohn-Sherbok and John M. Court; Sheffield Academic Press, 2001), 47–64.

understanding his work within its cultural and ethnic setting is the only way to comprehend fully his arguments.[30]

1.3 Limitations

The text chosen for this investigation is Romans 8. The most important reason for this choice lies in the content and use, especially by Francis Watson, of the chapter. Romans 8 contains the most references to the Holy Spirit out of any chapter in the Pauline corpus. At the same time, it has become a battleground over the nature of Christ and Paul's theology proper in general.[31] Within Romans 8, Paul speaks of God, Jesus, and the Holy Spirit while also describing specific functions for each that relates in some sense to the others. For example, both the Spirit and Jesus are said to intercede (8:27 and 8:34 respectively). Jesus is related to God as son (8:2, 29, 32). The Spirit enables believers to call upon God as *Abba* (8:15). The Spirit is called both the πνεῦμα θεοῦ and πνεῦμα Χριστοῦ within the same verse (8:9).

Romans has been classified as different sub-genres of literature within the genre of epistle or letter. G. Bornkamm sees Romans as Paul's will or testament before he sets off to die.[32] G. Klein thinks of Romans as a theological treatise written to underscore the need for every church to have an apostolic foundation, and Paul as the apostle to the Gentiles is claiming jurisdiction over Rome.[33] Aune posits Paul's letter as a *logos protreptikos*, which is a letter written to intentionally promote a specific philosophical viewpoint by noting the shortcomings in opponents' positions while strengthening its own position.[34] None of these various classifications end up being helpful in describing the argumentation of Romans; for that, one must look at rhetorical criticism. Some scholars compare Paul's work to that of ancient authors'.[35] A useful technique is to look at how various elements of Greek or Roman rhet-

---

30 Leander E. Keck, "What Makes Romans Tick?" in *Pauline Theology Volume III: Romans* (ed. David M. Hay and E. Elizabeth Johnson; SBL, 2002), 3–29, here 20–23.

31 See especially Dunn, *Christology in the Making*, 44–45 and the response in Cranfield, "Evidence in the Epistle to the Romans," 270–272, 275, 278–279. Cf. Watson, "The Triune Divine Identity," 115–117, 122.

32 Günther Bornkamm, "The Letter to the Romans as Paul's Last Will and Testament," in *The Romans Debate* (ed. Karl P. Donfried; Hendrickson, 1991), 18–28.

33 Günther Klein, "Paul's Purpose in Writing the Epistle to the Romans," in *The Romans Debate* (ed. Karl P. Donfried; Hendrickson, 1991), 29–43.

34 David E. Aune, "Romans as Logos Proptreptikos," in *The Romans Debate* (ed. Karl P. Donfried; Hendrickson, 1991), 278–296.

35 E.g. Joachim Classen, "St. Paul's Epistles and Ancient Greek and Romans Rhetoric," in *Rhetoric and the New Testament: Essays from the 1992 Heidelberg Conference* (ed. Stanley E. Porter and Thomas H. Olbricht; JSNTSup 90; Sheffield Academic Press, 1993), 265–291.

oric appear in Paul's letters in order to understand the flow of those letters,[36] though some try to be overly precise in terms of argumentative flow.[37] Paul's rhetoric, however, enables the exegete to see both his Jewish and Roman sides in his work.[38] Reed is most likely correct what he summarizes all of the relevant data and concludes that Paul uses an epistolary style and some rhetorical methods within the letter, but finalizing a sub-genre within the category of epistle does not do credit to the letter and the originality of Paul.[39]

The diatribe as a sub-genre within Romans has become a popular choice for certain sections of the letter. Diatribe is defined as a rhetorical technique fulfilling some or all of these four "markers"[40]: (1) dialogues with interlocutors, (2) the rhetorical use of the second person plural and occasionally the third person, (3) μὴ γένοιτο as a rejection phrase, and (4) the use of vocatives. Stanley Stowers' dissertation[41] and subsequent publications[42] have been the leading edge in reevaluating Romans along these lines. He sets the diatribe within the realm of Greco–Roman letter writing in general,[43] while still taking a cautious approach to the issues in Romans. Changwon Song takes a bolder stance, advocating the position that the entire letter (apart from the epistolary introduction and concluding greeting list) is written as diatribe, including Romans 8.[44] This does not, however, fit the context or import of Romans 8. Though Romans 7 is diatribe in form, Romans 8 responds to the diatribe with

---

36 E.g. David Hellholm, "Amplificatio in the Macro-Structure of Romans," in *Rhetoric and the New Testament: Essays from the 1992 Heidelberg Conference* (ed. Stanley E. Porter and Thomas H. Olbricht; JSNTSup 90; Sheffield Academic Press, 1993), 123–151.

37 E.g. Ira J. Jolivet Jr., "An Argument from the Letter and Intent of the Law as the Primary Argumentative Strategy in Romans," in *The Rhetorical Analysis of Scripture: Essays from the 1995 London Conference* (ed. Stanley Porter and Thomas H. Olbricht; JSNTSup 146; Sheffield University Press, 1997), 309–335.

38 Marc Schonei, "The Hyperbolic Sublime as a Master Trope in Romans," in *Rhetoric and the New Testament: Essays from the 1992 Heidelberg Conference* (ed. Stanley E. Porter and Thomas H. Olbricht; JSNTSup 90; Sheffield Academic Press, 1993), 171–192.

39 Jeffrey T. Reed, "Using Ancient Rhetorical Categories to Interpret Paul's Letters: A Question of Genre," in *Rhetoric and the New Testament: Essays from the 1992 Heidelberg Conference* (ed. Stanley E. Porter and Thomas H. Olbricht; JSNTSup 90; Sheffield Academic Press, 1993), 292–324, here 324.

40 Taken from Changwon Song, *Reading Romans as a Diatribe* (Studies in Biblical Literature 59; Peter Lang, 2004), 16.

41 Stanley K. Stowers, *The Diatribe and Paul's Letter to the Romans* (SBLDS 57; Scholars Press, 1981). He bases his work on Rudolf Bultmann, *Der Stil der paulinischen Predigt und die kynisch–stoische Diatribe* (Vandenhoeck & Ruprecht, 1910).

42 Stanley K. Stowers, "The Diatribe" in *Greco–Roman Literature and the New Testament* (SBLRBS 21; ed. David E. Aune; Scholars Press, 1988), 71–83, and *Rereading of Romans: Justice, Jews, and Gentiles* (Yale University Press, 1994).

43 Stanley K. Stowers, *Letter Writing in Greco-Roman Antiquity* (LEC 5; Westminster, 1986).

44 Song, *Reading Romans as Diatribe*, especially 46, 56–82, 101.

Paul's solution rather than extending the diatribe format, especially since 8:31–39 forms a rhetorical climax with a prose doxology.

This book will not defend Paul's monotheistic beliefs but will assume them. Scholarship has essentially agreed that Paul's epistles display implicitly and explicitly that he has not left behind Jewish monotheism.[45] Watson has noted that the tendency is to embrace Paul's monotheism to the extent that his Trinitarian leanings are denied.[46] Richard Bauckham has argued that NT authors understood their Christology within the stream of Jewish monotheism.[47] Thus, it is taken as a given that Paul holds to monotheism in his theology proper, no matter how one wants to define or redefine the term.[48]

Since Romans is the major topic of study, this work will interact with the major commentaries on Paul's letter. Among those this book will interact the most with are the works of Cranfield,[49] Fitzmyer,[50] Moo,[51] and Schreiner.[52] Fitzmyer approaches the text as a Roman Catholic and the other three as Reformed Protestants. Fitzmyer provides a balanced view of the text, though his work can be uneven as he concentrates on some minor points and overlooks some larger ones. Cranfield tends to look more deeply into the grammatical issues in the text while Moo and Schreiner concentrate on the theological aspects. Wilckens,[53] Käsemann,[54] Michel,[55] and Lagrange[56] also contribute greatly to the study of Romans. Wilckens provides an in–depth study of Romans, though he overemphasizes the eschatological aspects of the letter. Käsemann tends to paint over the text in broad strokes, finding themes and tying to-

---

45 See especially James D. G. Dunn, "Was Christianity a Monotheistic Faith from the Beginning?" *SJT* 35 (1982): 303–335; C. H. Giblin, "Three Monotheistic Texts in Paul," *CBQ* 37 (1975): 527–547. Cf. Richard Bauckham *God Crucified: Monotheism and Christology in the New Testament* (Eerdmans, 1998) updated as *Jesus and the God of Israel: God Crucified and Other Studies on the New Testament's Christology of Divine Identity* (Eerdmans, 2009).

46 Watson, "The Triune Divine Identity," 123. He calls it "a broad consensus about the nature of Pauline theology."

47 Bauckham, *God Crucified*.

48 Cf. R. W. L. Moberly, "How Appropriate is 'Monotheism' as a Category for Biblical Interpretation?" in *Early Jewish and Christian Monotheism* (JSNTSup 263; ed. Loren T. Stuckenbruck and Wendy E. S. North; T&T Clark, 2004), 216–234.

49 Cranfield, *Romans*.

50 Joseph A. Fitzmyer, *Romans: A New Translation with introduction and Commentary* (AB 33; Doubleday, 1993).

51 Douglas J. Moo, *The Epistle to the Romans* (NICNT; Eerdmans, 1996).

52 Thomas J. Schreiner, *Romans* (BECNT 6; Baker, 1998).

53 Urlich Wilckens, *Der Brief an die Römer* (3 vols.; EKK 6.1-6.3; Neukirchener Verlag, 1978–1982).

54 Ernst Käsemann, *Commentary on Romans* (ed. And trans. Geoffrey W. Bromiley; Eerdmans, 1980).

55 Otto Michel, *Der Brief an die Römer* (KEK; 4h ed.; Vandenhoeck & Ruprecht, 1966).

56 Marie–Joseph Lagrange, *Saint Paul Épitre aux Romains* (Études Biblique; Gabalda, 1916).

gether parts of Paul's arguments that others might have missed, yet he speculates too often in making decisions on interpretation. Michel looks for the flow of thought more than the detail, though he can pick up on small details others overlook. The commentary by Lagrange tends to be a theological work, yet some grammatical and syntactical issues are covered. One major study on Romans 8 deserves mention as well, that by Osten–Sacken.[57] He uses the "hymn" of Rom 8:31–39 as his starting point in discussing soteriology yet undervalues the significance of Rom 8:1–4 in Paul's arguments within the chapter.

James D. G. Dunn[58] deserves special mention in this list of commentators, as his various works come back time and again to Romans. Dunn has examined both Christology[59] and pneumatology[60] in the works of Paul, never afraid to be controversial or to go where he believes the text leads him. Dunn has also tried to give an overall expression of Paul's theology of Romans,[61] an act that demonstrates his continued scholarly interest in Paul's most famous epistle. Dunn functions as a foil in this book, as he denies any development towards Trinitarian thought in Paul, instead relying upon Paul's monotheistic tendencies. Dunn also has a penchant for finding Adam Christology in unlikely places in Romans, especially considering that Adam is only mentioned explicitly once in the book (5:14).

To whom was the letter of Romans written? While Schmithals[62] believes the text-critical problems in Rom 1:7 and 15 rule out Rome as a destination and pushes for Ephesus as the intended target, most other scholars believe that Rome was in deed the intended goal, with some slight variations.[63] Though the beginnings of the church in Rome tends to be a historical mystery, there is no real doubt that there was a sizable Jewish population in Rome even early in the first century.[64] As for the appearance of Christians there, some scholars

---

57 Peter von der Osten–Sacken, *Römer 8 als Beispiel paulinischer Soteriologie* (Vandenhoeck & Ruprecht, 1975).

58 James D. G. Dunn, *Romans* (2 vols.; WBC 38A–B; Word, 1988).

59 In addition to his previously noted works, see also James D. G. Dunn, "Christology as an Aspect of Theology," in *The Future of Christology: Essays in Honor of Leander E. Keck* (ed. Abraham J. Malherbe and Wayne A. Meeks; Fortress, 1993), 202–212.

60 James D. G. Dunn, "Spirit Speech: Reflections on Romans 8:12–27," in *Romans and the People of God: Essays in Honor of Gordon D. Fee on the Occasion of His 65th Birthday* (ed. Sven K. Soderlund and N. T. Wright; Eerdmans, 1999), 82–91.

61 Dunn, "In Quest of Paul's Theology," and *Theology of Paul*.

62 Walter Schmithals, *Der Römerbrief: Ein Kommentar* (Gerd Mohn, 1988) and *Der Römerbrief als historisches Problem* (Gerd Mohn, 1975).

63 E.g. Chamgwon Song theorizes that Romans was written for use in a Pauline school for converts, but had an epistolary introduction and conclusion added in order to turn it into a letter. See his *Reading Romans as Diatribe*, 121–122.

64 E.g. Harry J. Leon, *The Jews of Ancient Rome* (updated ed.; Hendrickson, 1995); F. F. Bruce, "Christianity Under Claudius," *BJRL* 44 (1962): 309–326, especially 313–314.

hypothesize they came from the conversions in Acts 2[65] and others link them to the movement of Christians (and others) from Jerusalem to other parts of the empire in a natural geographic progression.[66] The Christians probably gathered together focused around the synagogues[67] at first and then began to expand beyond them.[68] The churches likely originated with a large Jewish population to begin with,[69] including some god–fearers or proselytes.[70] As time progressed, and especially due to Claudius' expulsion of the Jews from Rome[71] and his decree to not let them immigrate from Egypt and Syria,[72] the churches moved from predominantly Jewish to overwhelmingly Gentile, at least until the death of Claudius. Afterwards, since the Jews would be able to come back, there was some sort of mix.[73] Thus, when Paul wrote to Rome, he wrote to a church that was mostly Gentile yet had a number of Jews as well.[74]

Due to the mixed ethnic nature of the recipients of Romans and the date of composition, this work will focus on first-century sources with respect

---

65 For a summary of the issues, see Eckhard J. Schnabel, *Early Christian Mission* (2 vols.; InterVarsity, 2004), 801–814. For the issues surrounding the list of peoples, see E. Güting, "Der geographische Horizont der sogennanten Völkerliste des Lukas (Acta 2:9–11)," *ZNW* 66 (1975): 149–169.

66 Peter Lampe, *From Paul to Valentinus: Christians at Rome in the First Two Centuries* (Fortress Press, 2003), 9–11. Lampe argues they likely just followed the major trade routes already in place.

67 On the existence and layout of synagogues in Rome, see Peter Richardson, "Augustan–Era Synagogues in Rome," in *Judaism and Christianity in First–Century Rome* (ed. Karl P. Donfried and Peter Richardson; Eerdmans, 1998), 17–29.

68 So Peter Stuhlmacher, "The Purpose of Romans," in *The Romans Debate: Revised and Expanded Edition* (ed. Karl P. Donfried; Hendrickson, 1991), 231–242.

69 Cf. Romano Penna, "Les Juifs à Rome au Temps de l'Apôtre Paul," *NTS* 28 (1982): 321–347.

70 The distinction, or the lack of, between these two terms is not relevant for this discussion. For more information, see A. T. Kraabel, "The Disappearance of the 'God–fearers'," *Numen* 28/2 (1981): 113–126; Thomas M. Finn, "The God–fearers Reconsidered," *CBQ* 47 (1985): 74–84; J. Andrew Overman, "The God–fearers: Some Neglected Features," *JSNT* 32 (1988): 17–26; Graydon F. Snyder, "The Interaction of Jews with Non–Jews in Rome," in *Judaism and Christianity in First–Century Rome* (ed. Karl P. Donfried and Peter Richardson; Eerdmans, 1998), 69–90. Cf. Lawrence H. Schiffman, *From Text to Tradition: A History of Second Temple and Rabbinic Judaism* (Ktav Publishing, 1991), 82–86.

71 On the congruity or lack thereof with respect to Dio Cassius, *Roman History*, 60.6.6 and Seutonius, *Claud.*, 25.4, see Helga Boterman, *Das Judenedikt des Kaisers Claudius: Römischer Staat und Christiani im 1. Jarhundert* (Hermes Einzelschriften 71; Steiner, 1996), especially 103–140; Rainer Reisner, *Paul's Early Period: Chronology, Mission, Strategy, Theology* (Eerdmans, 1998), 167–179.

72 H. Dixon Slingerland, *Claudian Policymaking and the Early Imperial Repression of Judaism at Rome* (USF Studies in the History of Judaism; Scholars Press, 1997), 100–101.

73 Cf. Paul Keresztes, *Imperial Rome and the Christians: from Herod the Great to about 200 A.D.* (vol. 1; University Press of America, 1989), 45–66.

74 See the summary in Robert Jewett, *Romans: A Commentary* (Hermeneia; Fortress Press, 2007), 70–72. Cf. Stuhlmacher, "The Purpose of Romans," 235. Contra T. Fahy, "St. Paul's Romans Were Jewish Converts," *ITQ* 26 (1959): 182–191.

to the Roman world. Occasionally earlier data will be included in order to demonstrate historical and theological development. For example, one cannot understand the importance of the emperor cult in Rome unless one discusses Julius Caesar.[75] It is his life that sets the foundation for Octavian and all the following rulers to name themselves Caesar and to begin taking divine honors both post- and pre-mortem. In addition, one cannot understand first-century Roman religion without tracing some historical roots in borrowing from both local paganism in addition to Greek and other foreign deities and cults, including those from Persia (Mithras) and Egypt (Isis). The concept of Jupiter changed in local areas and often either accrued new characteristics for Jupiter or else combined him with someone else.[76] Any letter dealing with God, Jesus, and the Holy Spirit sent to those who had been pagan would need to take into account how the readers would understand the language employed by the author. Since Paul always wrote to a particular audience (e.g. greeting lists and specific anecdotes), he would also fashion his arguments with his intended recipients in mind.

1.4 Looking Ahead

Chapter two will introduce Roman religion. The purpose of the chapter is to give a brief introduction to some of the major theological realities of the first century. Certain themes in Roman religion are present in the general religion of the day (e.g. Jupiter and Mars), in the individual mystery cults (e.g. Isis and Mithras), and in emperor worship. In order to explore these themes, the chapter will first look at the characteristics and theological development of Jupiter, taken as an example of all gods and because he is the specific deity of Rome and the Romans (as opposed to Roma, who is Rome personified). The chapter will then describe two major mystery cults and the impact they had upon their adherents. The chapter will end with a description of the imperial cult and the implications drawn from these discussions.

Chapter three will begin the exegesis of Romans 8, specifically focusing on God the Father. The chapter will open by giving the context of Romans 8 both with respect to the entire book and with respect to Romans 5 and 7, emphasizing the problem of sin in 7. Romans 8 is an outworking from both of those chapters. The book will then focus on God in Romans 8, looking particularly at how God works. God is the one who created, so he has a relationship to this

---

75 Cf. Stefan Weinstock, *Divius Julius* (Clarendon, 1971).
76 John Ferguson, *The Religions of the Roman Empire* (Aspects of Greek and Roman Life; Thames and Hudson, 1970), 37–43.

world and the people in it as their creator. God does not work directly in the lives of humanity in Romans 8, instead he sends Jesus and the Holy Spirit as his agents. He uses both of them to bring about re-creation (recreation from here on) through adopting children to whom he will give glory in order to remove the affects of the curse found in Genesis 3. God saves, but he does so through Christ and the Spirit.

Chapter four will detail the functions of the Son and Spirit as found in Romans 8 in relation to each other, to the Father, and to the created order. The chapter will begin with a brief section on sin and the law in order to delineate the complementary functions of the Son and Spirit in overcoming sin. The issues of adoption, glory, and recreation with respect to the Son and the Spirit will then be discussed. God's solution to sin comes in the form of salvation, and the Son and Spirit participate through the "in" language ("in Christ" and "in the Spirit") and by enabling life for believers. It is due to the convergence of the functions of the Son and Spirit that they must be discussed together. Finally, the chapter draws together the separate strands of conversation into a completed whole.

Chapter five concludes the book with a brief summary of the various arguments used to arrive at the conclusion that Paul holds to a triune theology and that his original readers would understand that. The major contributions of this work will be discussed. The chapter will end with areas of further study suggested by this work.

Chapter 2

Greco-Roman Concepts of Deity

The concept of deity is culturally defined, and what needs to be understood for each culture is the importance of the cultus in identifying key characteristics for a particular people.[1] In the case of first-century Rome, the Roman people define themselves and their world through the gods and goddesses they worship. While sharing between the Greek and Roman cultures occurred, especially with respect to the nature and function of the gods, first-century Rome held a unique blend of Greek and Roman thought such that only the term "Greco-Roman" could encapsulate the true nature of the culture. S. Perowne describes this mixture as the older, rough Roman gods being adapted to fit their more human and yet more divine Greek counter parts, such as Juno taking on the traits of Hera.[2] This chapter will describe the Greco-Roman concept of what is meant by "god," or θεός. In order to set boundaries on the term, this chapter will describe a statue to give a pictorial rendering from Rome about the associated cult while also reflecting the theology of the people. This chapter will then turn to look at how the various myths of Rome shape what the people believed about the nature of the gods, the issue of worship, the idea of triads, the questions surrounding salvation (what it is and when it is), and the nature of sin. These topics were chosen due to their influence on the worldview of typical people from Rome and their intersection with Christianity. After looking at these areas, the issue of heroes becoming gods

---

1 A different version of this chapter, though broader in appeal but narrower in scope, can be found in Ron C. Fay, "Greco-Roman Concepts of Deity," in *Paul's World* (ed. Stanley Porter; Pauline Studies 4; Brill, 2008), 51-80. Special thanks to Brill for allowing this to be reused with just some minor changes. Many of the discussions are the same but the aims of the chapters are different.

2 Stewart Perowne, *Romans Mythology* (Library of the World Myths and Legends; Peter Bedrick Books, 1984), 12–17.

and the Imperial Cult will conclude the discussion. All of these sections will be limited to descriptions based upon occurrences or items from the first century or earlier in order to avoid anachronistic findings. These discussions will paint a picture of what the Greco-Roman concept of deity was in first-century Rome, the first step in understanding the argument of Romans 8 as the original recipients would have.

2.1 THE GREATEST GOD: JUPITER

Crowning Capitoline Hill was the temple of Jupiter Optimus Maximus (Jupiter best and greatest). This hill of the temples lies in the heart of Rome, surrounded by the Circus Maximus, the great statue of Nero, and later the Flavian amphitheater (more commonly called the Coliseum). This area constituted the public face of Rome, both to her enemies and to her citizens. The major temple held the altars to Jupiter and his two consorts, Juno and Minerva. A statue of Jupiter dominated the main hall of the temple, being the focus of the place of worship. This statue mirrored the statue of Zeus at Olympia, with the great god seated on his throne.[3] In his right hand he held a thunderbolt, ready to strike down any opposition. He wore a purple toga with designs of gold, signifying his royal or imperial status as ruler of the gods. He also wore a tunic covered in palm branches, indicating victories. Upon his head he wore a wreath, which illustrated the title of Jupiter Victoris and spawned the later association of the wreath with victory in various games or in war. During various festivals, his face would be painted red.[4] Typically the greatest god wore sandals, with the ties around the lower ankle. His hair hung in curls around his head, matching the beard which covered his face. In other statues, such as the one found at the Villa Albani in Rome, Jupiter often holds a rod or staff in his right hand and a bolt of lightning in his left.[5] He is depicted with an eagle as his totem animal, a symbol that derives from Zeus.[6] The great deity who rules the sky goes by the name of "Dyaus Pitar, Dies-piter,"[7] or Jupiter. The

---

[3] For a full description of both the statue and the temple, see Samuel Ball Platner, *A Topographical Dictionary of Ancient Rome* (rev. by Thomas Ashby; Oxford University Press, 1929), 297–302. See also the picture in Perowne, *Roman Mythology*, 14.

[4] Ovid, *Fasti*, 1.201–202; and Pliny the Elder, *Natural History*, 33.111–112; 35.157.

[5] See Perowne, *Roman Mythology*, 19.

[6] Possibly the image of the eagle derives from Zeus' abduction of Ganymede, as in *Iliad* 20.267–272. However, the eagle can also be the symbol of sovereignty. See the discussion on Jupiter borrowing from Zeus below.

[7] John Ferguson, *The Religions of the Roman Empire* (Aspects of Greek and Roman Life; Thames and Hudson, 1970), 33. Cf. Walter Burkert, *Greek Religion* (Harvard University Press, 1985), 125–126. Burkert discusses the various common roots of these titles or names.

people of Rome attributed him with various names including "Tonans (Thunderer), Fulgur (Lightening), Fulgurator (Sender of Lightening),"[8] and Sky-Father. A rock that fell from the sky had been placed centuries before Paul's time in Jupiter's temple, perhaps considered a physical representation of him, and thus the name Lapis was added to Jupiter. He is the king of the gods, reigning from on high, and so his name became used for oaths and treaties.[9] Typically the covenant document would include his name as the witness and executer of punishment if the terms were not met or kept. Due to the mix of cultures, many attributes and stories about Zeus accreted to Jupiter. Ferguson lists the numerous associations:

> As the culture of Greece spread in the Hellenistic age it was natural to find Zeus identified with numbers of supreme local gods . . . Thus already Herodotus can identify Zeus with Amen-Ra. In Syria Zeus was on with the local Ba'al; at Baalbek with Hadad, the consort of Atar-gatis; at Doliche with the old supreme god of the Hittites who had survived in that obscure corner. Here we have two of his most widespread guises under the Roman Empire. Jupiter Heliopolitanus is found in Athens, Pannonia, Venetia, Puteoli, Rome, Gaul and Britan, and Jupiter Dolichenus traveled even more extensively. Philo of Byblus makes explicit the identification with Ba'alshamin, the Lord of Heaven found throughout Phoenicia and Syria.[10]

The main source for common knowledge about Zeus from the fifth century B.C. until the patristic age comes from the Homeric works, though more from the *Iliad* than other sources.[11] The original Jupiter, in terms of Roman mythology, likely ruled over oaths, oath taking, and punished those who broke oaths.[12] Rome originally had gods with little resemblance to humans, but as the Romans grew in knowledge of the wider world, their gods came to resemble humanity just as the neighboring religions taught. By no means does this type of syncretism stand alone, as Zeus often became another name for the ruling

---

8 Ferguson, *Religions*, 33. The name "Sky–Father" is the title of the chapter in Ferguson's book.

9 Strangely enough, it is often by the name of Jupiter Lapis that such treaties are made, as the Romans consider the stone evidence of how he watches over all. See Ferguson, *Religions*, 33–34.

10 Ferguson, *Religions*, 34.

11 See especially the passages in David G. Rice and John E. Stambaugh, *Sources for the Study of Greek Religion* (SBL Sources for Biblical Study 14; Scholars Press, 1979), 1–20.

12 Perowne, *Roman Mythology*, 17.

deity or else the sky-god of other peoples.[13] Rome often borrowed deities or theological concepts from people they conquered or with which they came into contact. One need only look at the various accounts of non-Roman gods being taken into the city[14] or the Roman adoption of various mystery cults.[15] This borrowing did not in any way inhibit the fervency of any of the cults, and in some cases enhanced them. Though Jupiter had Roman roots, most of those roots were below the first-century surface, and only the Greco-Roman tree remained. Much of the description of Jupiter fit the Roman emperors as well. Typically, generals who won major battles or wars would parade into the city wearing a purple toga with traces of gold and wearing the wreath of a victor on their heads. While seen as honoring to the general allowed to so parade, it also honored Jupiter in that his name was invoked with each victory. Just as Jupiter watched over oaths, so did he watch over battles. In this way, the common person in Rome saw the image of Jupiter used as a symbol of victory. Jupiter alone could empower other gods. As Zeus in Homer's *Iliad*, Achilles' mother Thetis acknowledges him greatest of the gods and how none can overcome him once he acts, something that Hera also acknowledges. All the emperors who wanted to be accorded divinity looked to Jupiter as their patron or even ultimate father, since it was he alone who could grant them true divinity. This becomes more explicit with the second-century emperors such as the arch of Trajan depicting Jupiter welcoming the emperor home with open arms and gives him a lightning bolt, thus transferring his divine power and dignity to Trajan.[16] The Stoics went so far as to declare the universe simply the city of Zeus/Jupiter.[17] The only entity ever said to rule over Jupiter/Zeus was fate (or the Fates, when personified), but this was never consistent in the literature. He is the only god who had multiple set festivals every year by Roman law under different names (on September 13 as Jupiter Optimus Maximus, on April 13 as Jupiter Victor, on June 13 as Jupiter Invictus).[18] As seen by this, Jupiter Optimus Maximus lived up to his name in the mythology and ethos of the first century, and the Roman people saw him as the protector of the city and themselves.

---

13 Ferguson, *Religions*, 37–43. In this section, Ferguson relates the different local gods with which Zeus became identified.

14 See the two stories in Jan Bremmer, "The Legend of Cybele's Arrival in Rome," in *Studies in Hellenistic Religion* (ed. M. J. Vermaseren; EPRO 78; Brill, 1979), 9–22.

15 These will be dealt with below, yet note that Isis came from Egypt and Mithra/Mithras originally from Persia.

16 Ferguson, *Religions*, 40.

17 Ferguson, *Religions*, 40.

18 Kurt Latte, *Römische Religionsgeschichte* (Beck, 1960), 80.

Jupiter did not dwell alone on the hill. He was part of a triad, known as the Archaic triad, as the three great gods of Rome all had statues upon the hill. Along with Jupiter, Quirinus and Mars also originally ruled over the city of Rome. Mars had his own temple upon the hill, complete with statues and other cultic accoutrements.[19] Quirinus had less to proclaim his greatness yet still had a presence.[20] This triad was later overtaken in popularity, though not authority, by the Capitoline triad of Jupiter, Minerva, and Juno, as seen in the temple of Jupiter built by Lucious Tarquinius Superbus, the last king before the republic. This triad, however, stood above the rest of the Roman pantheon as the great gods of Rome. Quirinus was the cultic name for Romulus, the founder of Rome and a descendant of Aeneas the Trojan hero.[21] Finally, Mars paralleled Ares as the god of war.[22] Jupiter was the Father of all, parallel to Zeus in Greek thought. Though he was part of two triads, he was considered the greatest of the Roman pantheon by the people whom they invoked as the god of the Roman empire. As seen in Jupiter, the Roman gods borrowed heavily from Greek mythology, but the accumulation of foreign gods did not end there.

2.2 Gods and Mystery Cults

In borrowing from other cultures, cults sprang up around various patrons (those who had enough money) at various times, usually dedicated to specific deities. For example, the cult of Isis built a large following in the Greco-Roman world based upon the universality of her appeal as mother of all, a fertility aspect. Nearly all cultures had some sort of fertility goddess (Artemis of Ephesus, Asherah in the ANE, etc.), and various peoples often assimilated Isis into this role by combining her with their current fertility goddess. Isis, though, did not have much sway in Rome until the time of Caligula.[23] Her cult followed much the same pattern of other mystery cults in terms of membership, function, and goals. Mystery cults forced a person to become initiated into the cult before any of the deeper teachings were divulged.[24] The idea

---

19 Pierre Gros, *Aurea templa: recherches sur l'architecture religeuse de Rome à l'époque d'Auguste* (Palais Farnèse, 1976), 92–94, 142–143, 166–169, and 189–195.
20 Gros, *Aurea templa*, 116–117. See also Bernadette Liou-Gille, *Cultes "Héroïques" romains: Les foundateurs* (Société d'Édition "Les Belles Lettres," 1980), 141–156.
21 Liou-Gille, *Cultes*, 135–208.
22 Latte, *Römische Religionsgeschichte*, 114–116.
23 Hans-Josef Klauck, *The Religious Context of Early Christianity* (Studies of the New Testament and Its World; T&T Clark, 2000), 132–133.
24 John M. Court, "Mithraism Among the Mysteries," in *Religious Diversity in the Greco-Roman World: A Survey of Recent Scholarship* (ed. Dan Cohn-Sherbok and John M. Court;

of joining a cult was not parallel to a conversion, as joining merely meant adding another deity to one's personal worship rather than ignoring all other gods for the cult just joined. For example, when Cybele joined the Roman pantheon in 201 B.C. or when Diocletian made Mithras a formal god of Rome in A.D. 307, neither constituted a break from previous gods.[25] Mystery cults were considered additions to the religious life of an individual rather than a radical change. Mystery cults neither detracted from nor were a substitution for religion in the home. People could choose what type of religious life they wanted simply by choosing to which god or gods they would devote time and resources.

The difference between mystery cults and the formal cults hinged on the function. Burkert defines a mystery religion as being "initiation rituals of a voluntary, personal and secret character that aimed at a change of mind through experience of the sacred."[26] People appeased the normal gods through sacrifices, as keeping the gods from working negatively in the devotee's life remained the primary goal. Offerings for healing or some other benefit also occurred frequently.[27] In the mystery cults, the individuals came together in order to pursue a deeper level of religion. This does not mean the mystery religions ignore these two functions, rather the mystery cults supplement them with additional reasons for worship and offerings.[28] A specific element of the mystery religions, however, is the use of magic. This magic functioned only for those within the cult, as one had to be special (i.e. a member) before one could ask for favors from the deity.[29] The cults were also focused on the afterlife, though not all in the same way. The following discussion will focus primarily on Isis, the Mother of All, and Mithras, a warrior god from Persia, in the city of Rome as both had widespread influence as their cults were adapted in different areas and sectors of life.

Sheffield Academic Press, 2001), 182–195. Court, 187, notes that the rituals "provided" salvation through "what could loosely be termed 'sacramental' means."

25 In fact, Diocletian was combining Mithras with *sol Invictus*. See Gary Lease, "Mithraism and Christianity," in *ANRW* 28.2:13202–1332, cf. especially 1322. Walter Burkert mentions how even the use of the terms "'faith' and 'salvation'...do not imply 'conversion'" (*Ancient Mystery Cults* [Harvard University Press, 1987], 14). In regard to the initiation of Lucius into the Isis cult, see 17.

26 Burkert, *Ancient Mystery Cults*, 11. Burkert's definition is evidently one commonly used by other experts in the field. For example, see Mary Beard, John North, and Simon Price, *Religions of Rome* (2 vols.; Cambridge University Press, 1998), 1:247 n. 3, where they use the same definition.

27 See the helpful work by Burkert, *Ancient Mystery Cults*, 12–15.

28 Burkert, *Ancient Mystery Cults*, 15. He mentions that one of Isis' original cultic functions was to heal disease, especially considering her close ties to Asclepius in the Greek world.

29 Burkert, *Ancient Mystery Religions*, 24–25.

Isis originated as an Egyptian goddess who was the sister and wife of Sarapis/Osiris and the mother of Horus, which directly connected her to the ruling pharaohs of Egypt.[30] Osiris ruled Egypt as the first king, but his brother Set grew jealous and killed him. Set, after a number of other events, finally cut the body of Osiris into pieces, but not until after Osiris had impregnated Isis. Isis gave birth to Horus who defeated Set. Horus went on to rule the country as the first pharaoh. Egypt, therefore, considered Isis the mother of all the pharaohs and the mother of all of Egypt. The Egyptians directly linked her to the Nile itself, and as the Nile brings life to Egypt, so did Isis bring life to all, becoming the mother of all.[31]

The idea of a goddess of motherhood, or one who is mother of all, had only partial parallels in Greek culture, and virtually none in Roman. The worship of other goddesses, such as Venus or Magna Mater, paralleled in some aspects the worship of Isis due to common attributes. Isis played the role of wife and mother *par excellence*.[32] Those who worshipped Isis spoke of her as being worshipped under other names and specifically used those attributes as points of contact.[33] When Cybele became part of the pantheon, for the first time a deity parallel to Isis could be called Roman.[34] Isis was well-known in the Roman world, however, as both the Greeks and the Romans held her in high esteem.[35]

Some inscriptions designate Isis as the upholder of the entire Greco-Roman pantheon,[36] but this was not the norm. Versnel argues for a henotheistic idea, such that Isis is the great goddess and the one most worthy of devotion, but not the only goddess.[37] Admittedly, Octavian disallowed Egyptian gods to be worshipped in Rome proper, and Tiberius worked to eliminate all non-Roman cults (or at least what he considered non-Roman) from the city.[38] Caligu-

---

30 France Le Corsu, *Isis: myth et mystères* (Les Belle Letters, 1977), 7–13. There are two slightly different versions of the tale, one Egyptian and one Roman, but the Roman version is not attested until the time of Plutarch.

31 R. E. Witt, *Isis in the Graeco-Roman World* (Cornell University Press, 1971), especially 30–31.

32 Le Corsu, *Isis*, 15. Cf. Sharon Heyob, *The Cult of Isis Among Women in the Greco-Roman World* (EPRO 51; Brill, 1975).

33 Beard et al., *Religions of Rome*, 1:281.

34 She joined Palatine Hill in 201 B.C., and her temple was dedicated in 191.

35 Ladislav Vidman, *Isis und Sarapis bei den Griechen und Römern: Epigraphische Studien zur Verbreitung und zu den Trägern des ägyptischen Kultes* (Religionsgeshichtliche Versuche und Vorarbeiten; de Gruyter, 1970), 97.

36 Beard et. al., *Reilgions of Rome*, 1:281.

37 H. S. Versnel, *Ter Unus: Isis, Dionysos, Hermes: Three Studies in Henotheism* (Inconsistencies in Greek and Roman Religion 1; Brill, 1990), especially 35–38 and 44–52.

38 See the brief summary in Jack Finegan, *Myth and Mystery: An Introduction to the Pagan Religions of the Biblical World* (Baker, 1989), 196.

la, however, quickly reinstated the Egyptian gods upon attaining the purple after Tiberius and likely not only took part in the cult,[39] but established some of the feasts.[40] Claudius, Vespasian, Titus, and Domitian[41] all showed either direct or indirect support for the Isis cult, with Domitian rebuilding the temples of Isis and Sarapis exemplifying direct support and Vespasian and Titus spending the night in the temple of Isis before their victory processional in Rome exemplifying indirect.[42] Isis did not ascend to a place by the triad of Jupiter, Juno, and Minerva, as though she were conquering Rome and the Roman pantheon.[43] Even in her own temples, other Roman gods, such as Dionysus and Venus, had statues present.[44] The cult did not compete with the Roman gods in general, rather the Emperors and Senate added them to the current list of gods.

As the cult of Isis spread, the function moved from the foundation of a ruler cult (Egypt), to a worldwide celebration of motherhood, to finally allowing various forms of salvation to the adherents. The worship of Isis varied from place to place, and as the cult grew, it became adapted by the regional needs of the cultists.[45] Salvation in the Isis cult was firmly entrenched in the physical world at the beginning.[46] Magic ruled in their conception of the world, and the cultists sought it above all other things with respect to the cult.[47] Part of salvation was the achievement of longer life.[48] Due to the confluence of Isis with the Greco-Roman religiosity of the time, a priest of Isis claimed to have visited the Elysian fields (the Greco-Roman version of paradise) which were evidently promised to him.[49] S. Heyob argues for a future state of salvation, as women looked to escape from this world and enter into the next, basing this conclusion upon the inscription δοίη σοι Ὄσιρις τὸ ψυχρὸν ὕδωρ ("may Osiris

---

39 Suetonius, *Gaius* 54.2; 57.4.

40 This is the conclusion reached by Michel Malaise, *Les conditions de pénétration et de diffusion des cultes égyptiens en Italie* (EPRO 22; Brill, 1972), 221–228.

41 For a complete listing of the various relationships between the cult of Isis and the emperors, see Tran tam Tinh, "Les empereurs romains versus Isis, Sérapis," in *Subject and Ruler: The Cult of the Ruling Power in Classical Antiquity* (ed. Alastair Small; Journal of the Roman Archaeology Supplementary Series 17; Thomson–Shore, 1996), 215–230.

42 Finegan, *Myth and Mystery*, 196–197.

43 Witt, *Isis*, 72.

44 Beard et. al., *Religions of Rome*, 1:281–282. For a more comprehensive discussion and description, see Le Corsu, *Isis*, 182–189.

45 The famous "diffusion" for which Le Corsu argues unconvincingly (*Isis*, 211–278).

46 Although some scholars prefer the term "transformation" to "salvation" (cf. Beard et. al., *Religions of Rome*, 287 n. 119), the notion is close enough to the Christian concept for the term to remain the same.

47 Le Corsu, *Isis*, 192–193.

48 Beard et. al., *Religions of Rome*, 290.

49 Burkert, *Mystery Cults*, 26.

give you fresh water").⁵⁰ She finds this conclusive because of the association of Osiris with water being salvific. The problem is this inscription (or variants⁵¹) occurs only five times, and of those only four refer to women,⁵² plus the link between water and salvation is rather weak. However, Vidman strengthens this case by describing a sarcophagus he had seen.⁵³ The picture on the left side is summarized by Heyob as follows: "A seated woman holds in her left hand the lid of a small box which at the same time a man standing near her holds in his left hand; with his right hand he anoints her left eye."⁵⁴ The woman is named Tetratia Isias, and it is her husband Sosius Iulianus who made the sarcophagus for her. The longer poem names Tetratia as Memphi (or Memphius, depending on the form), since often people are renamed after entering the Isis cult.⁵⁵ The final line written on the side with Latin letters but spelling Greek words reads as "caere calihanes aepoe su plerophoru psyche," which Vidman revises to "caere calliphanes aepoe su plerophoru psyche," giving the Greek sentence of Χαῖρε, χαλλιφανής, εἴποι σοῦ πληροφόρου ψυχῇ.⁵⁶ Festugière amended this to "Χαῖρε, χαλλιφανής," εἴποι σοι "πληροφόρου ψυχή," ("'Greetings, beautiful one,' may he say to you, 'your soul be [ful]filled'")⁵⁷ which implies that Iulianus gave to Memphi the correct secret words needed to gain salvation from Isis when she judges.⁵⁸ Contrary to Vidman's view, Burkert states the following as his conclusion to the matter of salvation and Isis, "The main emphasis, at any rate, is on the power of Isis ruling in this cosmos, changing the fates here and now for her protégé."⁵⁹ This does not answer the evidence from the inscriptions nor from the sarcophagus that Vidman details. In the end, with the majority of the evidence pointing toward little thought of afterlife in the Roman version of the Isis cult, and with the post-first-century dating of the sarcophagus, it is more likely that salvation beyond this life was not an emphasis of the Isis cult in first century Rome.

---

50 Heyob, *The Cult of Isis Among Women*, 61.
51 There is only an extra occurrence of the article in some inscriptions, as seen in Vidman, *Isis und Sarapis*, 13.
52 Moreover, only three occur in Rome. See the listing in Heyob, *The Cult of Isis Among Women*, 61 nn. 33–34.
53 Vidman, *Isis und Sarapis*, 132–138. This description follows the observations of Vidman.
54 Heyob, *The Cult of Isis Among Women*, 62.
55 The name confusion comes from the vocative being the form used. See Vidman, *Isis und Sarapis*, 132–133.
56 Vidman, *Isis und Sarapis*, 135.
57 Thank you to Barry Hofstetter for helping me smooth this translation. All mistakes are still mine.
58 A. J. Festugière, "Initée par l'époux," *Monuments Piot* 53 (1963): 135–146. The problem with this solution is the conjectural nature of it.
59 Burkert, *Mystery Cults*, 27.

Mithras also had his cult in the Greco-Roman world, though it was not as widespread as that of Isis during the first century. Just as Jupiter Lapis ruled over covenants or agreements in Rome, so did Mithras perform the same function in Persia, as evidenced by his name meaning "mediator of a contract."[60] The earliest inscription to Mithras in Rome itself can be dated to A.D. 102, though this points toward an influence during the first century.[61]

Mithras was linked with the sun long before becoming a Roman or even a Greek religious figure.[62] At first, he merely served the sun as the child of Aditi.[63] Later, he was equated with the sun himself.[64] Many Parthian kings bore the name Mithradates, showing the close affinity for Mithras in their cultic system.[65] Especially key in understanding the significance of such a name lies in seeing Mithras as the balance between the good god Ahura Mazda (also called Ormuzd) and Ahriman (also called Angra Mainyu) as the evil, though lesser god.[66] This triad stood above the other deities in the Iranian pantheon.[67] Though it later became a symbol of his role as psychopomp,[68] the link with the sun displays the physicality and this-worldliness of Mithras.

The Mithras cult had two distinguishing characteristics, as laid out by Klauck.[69] First, he had no consort. While Isis was balanced by Osiris (or vice versa), Mithras did not have a comparable mate. Second, his history or back story does not contain some tragic event. Isis wandered looking for Osiris, whom Set murdered, yet Mithras does not have a parallel episode of afflic-

---

60 Klauck, *Religious Context*, 140.

61 Klauck, *Religious Context*, 141.

62 Roger Beck, "Ritual, Myth, Doctrine, and Initiation in the Mysteries of Mithras: New Evidence from a Cult Vessel," *JRS* 90 (2000): 145–180.

63 See Finegan, *Myth and Mystery*, 203.

64 Hugo Gressmann, *Die orientalischen Religionen im hellenistisch–römischen Zeitalter* (de Gruyter, 1930), 139. Lease ("Mithraism and Christianity," 1320 n. 110) translates the appropriate phrase as, "in the tenth *yashta* of the Avesta Mithra has a place equal to Ahura–Mazda, and is also equal to the sun."

65 Eckart Olshausen, "Mithradates VI. Und Rom," in *ANRW* 1.806–815. Olshausen focuses on the skirmishes between Mithradates VI and Rome, though he does devote some time to Mithradates' lineage. Cf. Finegan, *Myth and Mystery*, 203.

66 Finegan, *Myth and Mystery*, 103. The hymn describes how Mithras would cross the sky in his chariot and Ahriman would hide in fear.

67 For more on the Iranian pantheon and the place of Mithras in it, see John R. Hinnells, ed., *Mithraic Studies: Proceedings of the First International Congress of Mithraic Studies* (2 vols; Manchester University Press, 1975), 1:1–248.

68 Bruce Lincoln, "Mithra(s) as Sun and Savior," in *La soteriologia dei culti oriental nell' Impero Romano* (ed. Ugo Bianchi and Maarten J. Vermaseren; Brill, 1982), 505–523.

69 Klauck, *Religious Context*, 141–142. The two items come from Klauck and are reinforced by other scholars as well. Mithraism did later incorporate some suffering aspects, but the dates for such inscriptions, manuscripts, and authors come from after the range of this study, so the ideas run parallel to or after rather than being part of the historical backdrop of apostolic Christianity. See Lease, "Mithraism and Christianity," 1327–1330.

tion. Both of these features are unique among the mystery religions as far as is known, as even Demeter has the tale of Persephone with Hades (covering both consort and suffering).[70]

The worshippers of Mithras slowly began to blend him into the surrounding deities already present. Part of the same dynasty that had kings named as Mithradates also had tombs upon which Mithras was sculpted as the enthroned god Apollo–Mithras.[71] Mithras came to be identified with Perseus, the son of Zeus and Danae who slew Medusa. The link becomes very evident by looking at various depictions of Perseus killing Medusa compared to Mithras killing the bull: both look away from that which they are killing.[72] With Mithras, there is no discernable reason for his turning away from the bull. In fact, any other parallel slaughtering or heroic victory over a foe always has the god or hero watching the accomplishment. Perseus, however, must glance aside lest he be turned to stone by the Gorgon's gaze. This same Perseus fathered Perses, from whom the Persians took their name.[73] Perseus himself became a hero later elevated to god status in Tarsus, as the citizens of the city worshipped him.[74] King Tiridates of Armenia tells Nero that he worships Mithras.[75] The use of symbols in the cult best displays this slow Greco-Romanization of Mithraism. When the Mithras cult purchased or took a building from a different cult, a majority of the old symbols were left alone, such as a thunderbolt, a sistrum, the name of Jupiter-Sarapis, or even a crown of Venus.[76] Unlike Isis, there are no extent occurrences of someone naming Mithras as above the pantheon, and in fact some Mithraic chapels included statues of other gods (e.g. Apollo, Demeter) combined into the worship of Mithras.[77] In the original Iranian version of the cult of Mithras, there is little to no indication of any associated mysteries.[78] This underscores the blurred line between deities and how readily the Romans adapted foreign aspects to their own established gods and heroes.

---

70   For the comparison between Isis and Demeter, see Le Corsu, *Isis*, 58–61.
71   Theresa Goell, "Nirumd Dagh: The Tomb of Antiochus I, King of Commagene," *Archeology* 5 (1952): 136–144.
72   David Ulansey, *The Origins of the Mithraic Mysteries: Cosmology and Salvation in the Ancient World* (Oxford University Press, 1989), 30–31.
73   Finegan, *Myth and Mystery*, 204.
74   Ibid. See also Dio Chrysostom, 33.45.
75   Finegan, *Myth and Mystery*, 205. Finegan dates this occurrence to A.D. 66.
76   Samuel Laeuchli, "Mithraic Dualism," in *Mithraism in Ostia: Mystery Religion and Christianity in the Ancient Port of Rome* (ed. Samuel Laeuchli; Garrett Theological Studies 1; Northwestern University Press, 1967), 46–66, especially 47–53.
77   Beard et. al., *Religions of Rome*, 282–283.
78   Carsten Colpe, "Mithra–Verehrung, Mithras–Kult und die Existenz iranischer Mysterien," in *Mithraic Studies: Proceedings of the First International Congress of Mithraic Studies* (ed. John R. Hinnels; 2 vols; Manchester University Press, 1975), 2.378–405.

An important point in terms of dating the Mithraic mysteries in Roman itself comes from Manfred Clauss, who takes the evidence as pointing toward the mystery cult beginning in Rome and moving outward from there.[79] Clauss notes that the earliest inscriptions found about Mithras in the Roman Empire all occur at about the same time, the end of the first century or the beginning of the second.[80] However, instead of a progression in age of the inscriptions as one approaches Rome, the opposite seems to be true. The inscriptions are all by those who formerly lived in Rome.[81] The expansion shows movement from Rome and toward the provinces, in which case a date of the strong establishment of the cult in the city before the end of the first century becomes likely.

Salvation in the Mithraic rites has stirred some controversy in two respects. First, some scholars have tied salvation and the entire cult to astrological phenomena, noting how the initiates graduate to new levels within the cult (there are seven levels, from initiate to head of the cult) based upon the Zodiac symbols.[82] In fact, the signs of the Zodiac surround the bull-slaying scene that dominates the walls of most Mithraic chapels (often in caves).[83] Brandon argues for salvation being focused on the afterlife based upon the parallels in the ANE and because Zoroastrianism had a salvific bent originally.[84] This overlooks two significant factors. First, the data would only make a case if in fact Roman Mithraism directly followed the original teachings of Zoroaster. This is negated by the mystery cult that Mithraism had become, since in Iran it had been a public religion.[85] Second, while ANE religions may have looked for a salvation for the afterlife, the Romans typically did not. The argument from parallels does not overcome the absence of evidence. Thus, the salvation offered in the Mithraic mysteries offered no transcendent answer. Mithras gave power or help to those in need in this world, not in any world to come.[86] Finegan argues that the movement of the initiate from one grade to the next must be paralleled by the movement of the soul's ascen-

---

79 Manfred Clauss, *The Roman Cult of Mithras: The God and His Mysteries* (Rutledge, 2001).
80 Ibid., 22.
81 Ibid., 21–22. Clauss also notes that there were multiple inscriptions or offerings within a short time span, something he believes points toward the ready acceptance of the cult.
82 This is the main argument of Ulansey, *Origins of the Mithraic Mysteries*. See especially 67–124. Ulansey links the bull-slaying with the rites of the equinoxes.
83 Finegan, *Myth and Mystery*, 207.
84 S. G. F. Brandon, "The Idea of the Judgment of the Dead in the Ancient Near East," in *Mithraic Studies: Proceedings of the First International Congress of Mithraic Studies* (ed. John R. Hinnels; 2 vols; Manchester University Press, 1975), 2.470–478.
85 Contra Roger Beck, "The Mysteries of Mithras: A New Account of Their Genesis," *JRS* 88 (1998): 115–128. Beck is trying to bring back the hypothesis of Franz Cumont which has been out of favor for nearly 25 years.
86 Contra Finegan, *Myth and Mystery*, 208–209.

dance from one planet to the next since the planets each fit a grade of initiation. However, there is little to no evidence backing such a claim, and this seems to be a case of allowing the imagery to overshadow the facts.[87] Often found in the guise of Helios, he never took his flaming chariot beyond this physical reality, and thus a life beyond this one could not be in view for his followers since their god would be absent.

The mystery cults of Isis and Mithras clearly display important traits of Roman religion, traits which convey the religious stance of the residents of first-century Rome. First, there is little concern for the world to come, as most Romans in their religious practices were concerned primarily with earthly life.[88] This is especially noteworthy in the case of Mithras, as the Zoroastrian form of the cult concentrated upon the world to come.[89] Second, these private cults were often combined with the public cults, such that even though one must be initiated into Isis or Mithras, still the common gods were honored even in the places set aside only for Isis or Mithras. Third, this combining did not lead, in general, to any competition, as adding another god to the pantheon was not religiously problematic. Fourth, the gods just discussed all formed triads of different kinds. Jupiter combined with Mars and Quirinus to form one triad (or with Juno and Minerva). Isis naturally came to Rome with Sarapis and Horus. Mithras mediated between Ahura Mazda and Ahriman. Each of these triads formed a complete unit. Fifth, the Romans had no trouble connecting the new gods to heroes or humans of some sort. Even though Isis was the mother of the pharaohs, this did not stop the Romans from accepting her (though they tended not to use such a title for her), just as Mithras was closely connected to Perseus of Tarsus.

Adherents of these mystery cults were not looking for salvation in eschatological terms nor a life after death experience, instead they wanted help now. Some of the mystery cult members used the cult as a political tool, to make their names known by sponsoring the public events. The focus throughout was on how to help oneself, either by the favor of the god invoked or else by the members with which one would come into contact. Some cults were built around humans who ascended to divine status, such as Heracles or Dionysus. In turn, the idea of humans as gods needs to be investigated.

---

87 Though a common position, see the rebuttal of Finegan's argument for an eschatological focus in Burkert, *Ancient Mystery Cults*, 27–28.

88 Cf. Robert Turcan, "Salut mithriaque et sotriologie noplatoncienne," in *La soteriologia dei culti oriental nell' Impero Romano* (ed. Ugo Bianchi and Maarten J. Vermaseren; Brill, 1982), 173–191.

89 For more information, see Burkert, *Ancient Mystery Cults*, 27. This point cannot be overstressed in this discussion.

2.3 Humans as Gods

The emperor cult was not something invented by the Romans, rather ruler cults were a common phenomena among nations of the world.[90] The Roman Imperial Cult grew quickly outside of Rome itself since it was an outlet for displays of loyalty to or acclamation of the current ruler of Rome.[91] Octavian was worshipped as Augustus by groups from various cities as an appeal for patronage and to cement an alliance.[92] The Imperial Cult was not strictly about magnifying the Emperor as ruler, rather it was about magnifying the Emperor as the one who stands for Rome and the Empire (though this might be disputed in the cases of Nero and Domitian). Octavian, rather than having the cult focus solely on himself, allowed the various groups he conquered to build alters to *Roma et Augustus*, signifying that the ruler was identified directly with the city and Empire.[93] The point is that the Roman Imperial Cult was used as a political tool to bring other peoples into the empire. For this reason, the cult spread through outlying provinces without having a firm foothold in Rome itself. The Imperial Cult originally deified Rome (as the goddess Roma) and the Emperor to the conquered or allied nations by presenting them with altars of Roma and Augustus.

2.3.1 Religious and Historical Foundation

The first person to be deified by the city of Rome, a practice typically performed by a decree from the Senate as in this case, was Julius Caesar.[94] A debate surrounds the timing of this event, especially since the enactment by Rome did not necessarily follow upon the formal ratification of divine honors. In addition, with the making and breaking of alliances by Antony and Octavian, the Senate was unable to carry out much in the way of their own

---

90 See the different precursors listed in Everett Ferguson, *Backgrounds of Early Christianity* (3rd ed.; Eerdmans, 2003), 200–203. For literary backgrounds in Greek and Roman culture, see Andreas Alföldi, *Die monarchische Repräsentation im römischen Kaiserreiche* (Wissenschaftliche Buchgesellschaft, 1970), 9–25.

91 For a sweeping review of literature on and from the Imperial Cult in the first century, see Christian Habicht, "Die augusteische Zeit und das erste Jarhundert nach Christi Geburt," in *Le Culte des Souverains dans l'Empire Romain* (ed. William den Boer; Entretiens sur l'antiquité classique 19; Hardt, 1973), 39–88.

92 For example, the altar where Drusus called together the Gauls.

93 Duncan Fishwick, *The Imperial Cult in the Latin West: Studies in the Ruler Cult of the Western Provinces of the Roman Empire* (3 vols.; Brill, 1987–2002), 1.1:104–105. Fishwick describes how coins portraying the altar had ROM ET AVG stamped on them.

94 This discussion will follow Fishwick, *Imperial Cult*, 1.1:56–72 and Stefan Weinstock, *Divius Julius* (Clarendon, 1971), especially 270–317.

official proclamations.⁹⁵ Julius claimed divinity for himself through Aeneas of Troy, who alleged his own divine status by descent from Venus. The Senate offered him multiple honors for his various victories through 47-44 B.C., and Julius already held the position of pontifex maximus, a position that placed one man between the nation and the gods.⁹⁶ Through these honors, the Senate granted Julius divinity, possibly even during his own lifetime.⁹⁷ People who owed Caesar either favors or money, any sort of debt, made inscriptions calling him god.⁹⁸ Sacrifices were made on Caesar's birthday during his lifetime, an act made official in 42 B.C. An inscription on a statue in the city of Rome labeled him as having divine status, as did many other inscriptions.⁹⁹ Octavian officially deified Julius Caesar after his death and after his murderers were killed. During his lifetime, Julius turned down the title king while not turning down the title of god.¹⁰⁰ This continued the idea of a ruler cult in European politics (obviously something that could not be instituted during the Republic era), a desire of rulers for more political control patterned after Alexander the Great.¹⁰¹ Typically the pattern began with the person who would become a ruler earning great military victories (hence Domitian's striving to earn the name Germanicus), the country prospering, and the emperor dying with witnesses to his spirit ascending to heaven.¹⁰²

This pattern of the deification of the ruler began with divine status in the provinces and conquered nations during the life of the ruler and then in Rome after death (including imperial families in the case of Livia, Augustus' wife, and Trajan deifying his father and sister)¹⁰³ continued during the rules of Nero and Domitian. While there is less direct evidence for Nero, Domitian demanded divine honorifics when holding court. Juventius Celsus and others named him δεσπότης τε καὶ θεός, both in oral and written communication per

---

95 For an overview of the vacillating relationship between the Senate and the emperor, see Alföldi, *Kaiserreiche*, 25–38.

96 With respect to the importance of this position, note that every emperor thereafter took this position to solidify political power with religious trappings.

97 This debate is covered deftly in Fishwick, *Imperial Cult*, 1.1:56–57.

98 Weinstock, *Divius Julius*, 300–301. See 300 n. 7 for details of the use of these titles.

99 Weinstock, *Divius Julius*, 53.

100 Elizabeth Rawson, "Caesar's Heritage: Hellenistick Kings and Their Roman Equals," *JRS* 65 (1975): 148–159.

101 J. P. V. D. Balsdon, "Die 'Göttlichkeit' Alexanders," in *Römischer Kaiserkult* (ed. Antonie Wlosok; Wissenschaftliche Buchgesellschaft, 1978), 254–290. The title "master of the world" was accorded to both Julius Caesar and Octavian, clearly patterned after Alexander. See the discussion about the statue of Julius standing on a depiction of the world, a direct parallel to statues of Alexander, in Fishwick, *Imperial Cult*, 1.1.57.

102 Elias Bickermann, "Die römishce Kaiserapotheose," in *Römischer Kaiserkult* (ed. Antonie Wlosok; Wissenschaftliche Buchgesellschaft, 1978), 82–121.

103 Pliny the Younger, *Panegyricus*, 89.

his instructions.[104] Martial also compared Domitian to Janus and Jupiter, and he described him as Heracles.[105] This last comparison likely is tied to the statue of Heracles bearing Domitian's face. In addition, Martial mentioned how all the gods worship Caesar and how the emperor is to be worshiped by everyone.[106] L. L. Thompson objects that this must be some sort of exaggeration on the part of Cassius and Suetonius, as these terms occur nowhere else together in relation to Domitian in that they never occur on coins or any official documents.[107] D. E. Aune replies to this objection by stating that only official titulature or honors may be used in official documents, "inscriptions, coins, or medallions."[108] At the same time, Thompson makes a good point when he questions the veracity of Suetonius and Dio Cassius. Cassius especially defames Domitian at every opportunity, stating that Domitian reviled his brother.[109] This does not square with the evidence in that Domitian did "more for the cult of Titus, than Titus had done for that of Divus Vespasianus."[110] This does not end the debate, however, for promoting Titus with divine honors necessarily strengthens the rule of the emperor, especially one who had been distanced from his living family (geographically, if not politically) yet sought divine honors for himself. The first step in a living emperor desiring worship would be to ensure the cult was already strong through the worship of past imperators. Rather than a mark of love, the fervency with which Domitian elevated his brother could simply have been politically and religiously expedient (if one can separate the two for Rome), as was the case with the deification of Julius by Octavian.[111] Thompson gives evidence against himself, noting

---

104 See especially Dio Cassius, *Roman History*, 67.5.7 and 67.13.4, and Martial, *Epigrams*, 5.8.1; 7.34.8; 8.2.6; 9.66.3. For other comments using this type of titulature, see Martial (4.67.4; 5.2.6; 5.5.1, 3–4; 6.64.14; 7.5; 7.8.1, 2; 7.12.1; 7.40.2; 7.99.5–8; 8.1.1; 8.31.3; 8.82.1–4; 9.16.3; 9.20.2; 9.23.3; 9.24.6; 9.28.5, 7; 9.65.1–2; 9.101.23–24; 14.76), Statius (1.1.62; 3.3.103, 110; 4.2.6; 5.1.42, 112, 261), and Dio Chrysostom (45:1, 4). All of these references involve the mention of *deus, dominus*, δεσπότης, κυρίος, or θέος in reference to an emperor.

105 Respectively, Martial, *Epigrams*, 7.8.5–6; 9.28.10; 9.101.1.

106 *Epigrams*, 8.4 and 9.64.6.

107 Leonard L. Thompson, *The Book of Revelation: Apocalypse and Empire* (Oxford University Press, 1990), 105. The section on the vocabulary associated with divinity and the emperors covers 104–107.

108 David E. Aune, *Revelation* (3 vols.; WBC 52a–c; Thomas Nelson, 1997–1998), 1:311.

109 67.2.5. Thompson (*Apocalypse and Empire*, 96–104) summarizes well the various problems in the accounts of Cassius and Suetonius, though he does not mention that the latter tends toward a more moderate position, even complimenting Domitian's poetry.

110 Kenneth Scott, *The Imperial Cult Under the Flavians* (Arno, 1975), 62.

111 See Suetonius, *Dom.*, 13.1. With respect to Octavian, he was consumed with being granted his right to bear the name Caesar, knowing how much this name stirred the legions and the people. Note how he agreed to the mediated position of having a Second Triumvirate in order to validate his adoption. With respect to Octavian exalting Julius, and using this for political gain, see Fishwick, *Imperial Cult*, 1/1.75–76.

that the crowds and lower officials used the language of *dominus et deus* and that Martial later had to disavow his use of the same terms for Domitian.[112] Titus minted coins that utilized the title "DIVI F" (divine Flavian or possibly *filius*) for his brother as successor to the throne.[113] In addition, it is clear that Trajan was also called *dominus* (translated by Dio Chrysostom as κυρίος).[114] One should also note that there was a mixture of divine titles used for the emperors throughout the Roman world, with such names as "(1)god, (2)son of god (i.e., *divi filius*, *huiòs theoû*), (3) god made manifest, (4) lord, (5) lord of the whole world, (6) lord's day (*Sebaste* is a pagan, while *Kyriakē* is Christian), (7) savior of the world, (8) epiphany, (9) imperator."[115] Clearly the titles of divinity were used for the emperors not just in the provincial areas of the empire, but even in Rome itself.[116]

The population of Rome also sacrificed to the emperors and their images. As soon as Augustus returned from Actium, the senate ordered that libations be made to him. Some scholars consider this in the light of later developments as being a circumlocution referring to his *genius*,[117] yet nothing in the actual historical documents calls for such speculation.[118] Fishwick seems to side with those who argue for the *genius* to be the one receiving the sacrifice, yet he also notes that for Dio and other authors, "the distinction between a man and his *genius* may not always have been safe,"[119] a tacit admission to a lack of evidence and a telling remark regarding the fine distinction between *genius* and person. What happened in the Greek lands became common in that existing groups (often called *koinon*) adopted the current emperor as their cause or patron, devoting time and money to worshipping their person of choice. Thus, Octavian only needed to agree to the request of the groups in Asia and Bithynia in order to begin a cult there.[120] The establishment of the cult under Octavian resulted from a passive acquiescence, not an active policy. This allowed the cult to gain power for the emperor without the emperor

---

112 Thompson, *Apocalypse and Empire*, 106.
113 Thompson, *Apocalypse and Empire*, 223 n. 19.
114 Thompson, *Apocalypse and Empire*, 104. See Dio Chrysostom, *Or.*, 45.4.
115 David E. Aune, "The Influence of Roman Imperial Court Ceremonial on the Apocalypse of John," *BR* 28 (1983): 5–26, here 20. Aune examines the relevant texts to make his case.
116 For a brief overview of some of the more crucial references, see Alföldi, *Kaiserreiche*, 49–53.
117 In Roman mythology, *genius* refers to the divine spark in each person. It functions like a guardian angel, as the *genius* is external in source but internal in position. They were linked to the male portion of the family line, much as how ancestors function in some Eastern religions. The female line had *iuno* (or *juno*) as their guide. In this case, then, the speculation is that the family spirit of male headship in the line of Augustus was being worshiped.
118 Fishwick, *Imperial Cult*, 2.1.375–376 n. 2.
119 Fishwick, *Imperial Cult*, 2.1.375–376.
120 G. W. Bowersock, *Augustus and the Greek World* (Clarendon, 1965), 116.

being seen as grasping for political strength, and therefore the Senate accepted this since it gave more control to Rome especially in light of Octavian's typical request of altars to Rome and himself.[121] Octavian had no need to press his divine status, as others thrust the honors upon him of their own wills.[122] Various emperors, including Gaius Caligula and Nero, built statues and temples in their own honor, with Caligula building a temple in Rome itself.[123] Both of these rulers used Jupiter/Helios imagery (a sun crowning the head) for themselves, making an explicit claim. The Senate even prostrated themselves at the empty throne of Gaius when he was gone, a clear sign of worship.[124] They went so far as to waste a full day praying for Gaius while he was absent from Rome.[125] In addition, Tiriadates I prostrated himself before Nero in AD 66.[126]

2.3.2 Emperors as Gods Outside of Rome

While most of the early emperors refused divine titles or worship within Rome itself, many of them allowed for or even encouraged the promulgation of the cult outside of Rome. Various cities and provinces vied for the opportunity and authorization to build a temple to the current emperor. Pergamum held a temple to Augustus and Rome, a temple that tied Octavian's power directly to the people, as per his description of himself as *"per consensum universorum potitus rerum omnium."*[127] Tiberius refused divine honors when given to him while living, yet that did not stop them from occurring.[128] He rejected statues and other forms of honor typically reserved for either Augustus or dead emperors.[129] This did not, however, keep the populous from doing as they wished. Contrary to Tiberius' stated desires, the title *DIVUS* appeared on coins with his face and there is a written record of him being called son of the god.[130] Smyrna won the right to build a temple for Tiberius from among eleven candidates.[131] Other cities built temples associated with the living em-

---

121 See especially Suetonus, *Aug.*, 52 and Tacitus, *Ann.*, 4.37.
122 Andreas Alföldi, "Die zwei Lorbeerbäume des Augustus," in *Römischer Kaiserkult* (ed. Antonie Wlosok; Wissenschtliche Buchgesellschaft, 1978), 403–422.
123 Dio Cassius, *Roman History*, 59.11.12 and 28.1–2. Cf. Donald L. Jones, "Roman Imperial Cult," *ABD* 5:806–809, here 806.
124 Dio Cassius, *Roman History*, 59.24.3–4.
125 Dio Cassius, *Roman History*, 59.24.5.
126 Dio Cassius, *Roman History*, 62.2.
127 *Res Gestae Divi Augusti*, 34.
128 For example, Tacitus, *Ann.*, 4.37–38.
129 For certain titles being used only for Augustus, see Tacitus, *Ann.*, 4.37–38. For the rejection of divine titles for himself, see Suetonius, *Tib.*, 26.1.
130 See Jones, "Roman Imperial Cult," 806.
131 Tacitus, *Ann.*, 4.55–56.

peror, as Pompeii constructed a temple of Fortuna Augusta, which consisted of white marble that extended into the street, displaying the importance of the temple.[132] The temple even had niches prepared in order to hold statues of the Imperial family. The temple stood north of the forum, directly opposite the baths, a very prominent place for a temple. Claudius disallowed a cult of himself as well, yet according to a letter he sent to a prefect, he still permitted statues of himself and his family to be erected in Alexandria.[133] The introduction to this letter, written by a local prefect, named him "our god Caesar," and the significant portion reads "I have deemed it necessary to display the letter publicly in order that reading it one by one you may admire the majesty of our god Caesar and feel gratitude for his good will towards the city."[134] Even though Claudius rejected divine accolades everywhere, a temple was erected in his honor in Britain.[135] Vespasian, the ruler after Nero, also refused divine honors during his life. However, upon his death bed he reportedly declared "I am becoming a god."[136] Titus, successor to his father Vespasian, consecrated both his father and his sister Domitilla, building a temple for the former in Rome.[137] Trajan, the last emperor during the first century, deified Domitian.[138] He also verbally rejected divine honors, yet he had a temple built for himself in Pergamum. He was considered to be an aspect of Jupiter by the people. With respect to the persecution of Christians under Pliny the Younger, he used the litmus test of offering incense, wine, and worship to the image of Trajan, a practice which Trajan endorsed.[139] These emperors (the so-called sane ones, when compared to Nero, Gaius Caligula, and Domitian) offered lip service to denying deification during their lives, but they let statues be built in their image, offerings of incense and wine be given, temples be erected in foreign locals, and various titles to appear in public all of which point toward an informal form of deification. At the very least, the people offered them worship as gods even if they in life denied the honors themselves. While no formal evidence for deification of these emperors occurs within Rome during their lives, those who lived within the Roman empire outside of the city

---

132 Paul Zanker, *Pompeii: Public and Private Life* (Harvard University Press, 1998), 82.

133 C. K. Barrett, ed., *The New Testament Background: Selected Documents* (rev. ed.; Harper & Row, 1989), 47–50. Cf. Jones, "Roman Imperial Cult," 806–807.

134 Barrett, *Selected Documents*, 47.

135 Tacitus, *Ann.*, 14.31.

136 Suetonius, *Vesp.*, 23.4. Jones ("Roman Imperial Cult," 807) takes this to be a joke, yet this seems an unlikely interpretation of the event, especially when those who heard him took him seriously, as Suetonius describes the event.

137 Scott, *Imperial Cult*, 45–48.

138 Jones, "Roman Imperial Cult," 807. The following information about Trajan derives from the article by Jones.

139 Jones, "Roman Imperial Cult," 807. Cf. Pliny the Younger, *Epistulae*, 10.96.

hailed these rulers as gods, and therefore those in Rome knew of the divine status afforded them.

2.3.3 Emperors as Gods in Rome: Caligula, Nero, and Domitian as Case Studies

In contrast to these emperors, Caligula, Nero, and Domitian demanded divine honors while living. Caligula had a troubled childhood, often being shuttled from one parent figure to the next, spending time with his great-grandmother Livia and his grandmother Antonia.[140] He enacted popular legislation and cleared many prominent citizens of wrong doing when he first ascended the throne, albeit in an illegal manner since he ignored the legal will of Tiberius.[141] After this, however, Caligula changed dramatically. He pushed for the deification of Tiberius, something that the Senate rejected. He moved from asking for the formal approval of his grand-uncle's divinity to asserting his own.[142] He caused temples to be erected in his own honor in Miletus and, more importantly, in Rome herself.[143] He deified his favorite sister upon her death, going so far as to push a senator under oath to state that he had witnessed her apotheosis.[144] Drusilla is understood as his favorite because some of his other sisters had likely been involved in plots against him with Lepidus, their lover.[145] As his rule grew more authoritarian, so did Caligula encourage the establishment of his cult as a private practice (as opposed to the public, state sponsored cult of dead emperors), though the Senate did give him honors with respect to temples, a priesthood, and linking him with Castor and Pollux.[146] This makes his assassination more likely to be linked to his poor rule, overwhelming arrogance, and poor sense of humor.[147] The importance occurs in that the reason the leaders of Rome began to dislike Caligula was based more on his personality and vicious politics than on his desire to be deified, as is commonly argued.[148] Even Seneca's attribute of divinity to Caligula raises the point in that Seneca's description of sacrifices (clearly an ironic

---

140 Tacitus, *Ann.*, 6.20.1 and Suetonius, *Gaius*, 10.1; 23.2.
141 Suetonius, *Gaius*, 13–16; Philo, *Leg.*, 8–13; Dio Cassius, *Roman History*, 59.2–3.
142 Note the use of different titles mentioned in Manfred Clauss, *Kaiser und Gott: Herrscherkult im römischen Reich* (Teubner, 1999), 90.
143 Dio Cassius, *Roman History*, 59.11–12; 28.1–2.
144 Dio Cassius, *Roman History*, 59.11.3.
145 Anthony A. Barrett, *Caligula: The Corruption of Power* (Yale University Press, 1989), 104–112.
146 Clauss, *Kaiser und Gott*, 92–93.
147 Ittai Gradel, *Emperor Worship and Roman Religion* (Oxford Classical Monographs; Clarendon, 2004), 155–159. The poor sense of humor relates to the immediate cause of his murder, as he was humiliating a guard who then killed him.
148 Gradel, *Emperor Worship*, 159.

reflection on the context of the execution of Caligula's enemies) is ironic in terms of the sacrificial content, not the act of sacrifice.[149] In terms of titles, Caligula readily received divine recognition from the eastern portion of the empire, as the culture there included worship of whoever ruled.[150] He did not stop with accepting honors, but extended his policy to force the spread of his cult by such rash acts as planning a temple in Miletus (of his own accord) and attempting to raise a statue of himself as Zeus Epiphanes in the Temple in Israel.[151] He was worshipped as Jupiter Latiaris in Rome.[152] Gaius Caligula gathered unto himself the worship due the gods and the titles bestowed upon them, until such point as commoner and high ranking officials alike both granted him divine honor.[153]

Nero tended toward the more aggressive pursuit of divinity during his lifetime as well. The early part of Nero's reign remained a quiet affair, as his mother and two counselors governed in his stead since he was so young and deferred to them. As he lived his life publicly, often spending his leisure time in theaters, he also performed politics publicly. He entertained Tiridates, king of Armenia, who made public obeisance to him twice.[154] He performed music before the crowds, and people called for his "divine voice" (*caelestem vocem*).[155] He sang or performed often in the guise of a hero or god.[156] He left Rome for Greece, where he competed in sundry games. After leaving Greece, he entered Rome as though he were Augustus himself by using one of Augustus' chariots, wearing a purple robe trimmed with gold stars, sporting an Olympic crown, and holding the Pythian.[157] Suetonius reports of anecdotal evidence where people compared Nero to Apollo in terms of music, the Sun in terms of chariot driving, and that Nero wanted to follow in the footsteps of Heracles as well.[158] Athens bestowed upon him the name "new Apollo," and Cos called him "Asclepius Caesar," both of which display connections to prominent gods who had well established cults of their own.[159] Nero held the East, and partic-

---

149 Seneca, *Tranq.*, 14.9. For a discussion of the irony of the scene, see Gradel, *Emperor Worship*, 157–158.

150 A. A. Barrett, *Caligula*, 142–143. For the references to Caligula's divinity from the east, see 143 n. 15.

151 Josephus, *Antiq.*, 18.8. Cf. Barrett, *Caligula*, 143.

152 Suetonius, *Gaius*, 22.2 and Dio Cassius, *Roman History*, 59.28.5.

153 Gradel, *Emperor Worship*, 155–156. Gradel pins this conclusion onto Dio Cassius. Cf. Caligula calling himself "*optimus maximus Caesar*" in Suetonius, *Gaius*, 22.1.

154 Suetonius, *Nero*, 13.

155 Suetonius, *Nero*, 21.1.

156 Suetonius, *Nero*, 21.2.

157 Suetonius, *Nero*, 25.2.

158 Suetonius, *Nero*, 53.

159 Michael Grant, *Nero: Emperor in Revolt* (American Heritage, 1970), 83–107. Cf. Elias Bickermann, "Consecratio," in *Le Culte des souvrains dans l'Empire Romain* (ed. William den

ularly Greece, in high regard due to their culture and due to the worship they gave to rulers.¹⁶⁰ He promulgated worship of his *genius* throughout Rome, something that essentially equated worshipping the emperor, especially as *genius* worship was slowly disappearing.¹⁶¹ The latter portion of Nero's reign rocked the Roman Empire with its turbulence and Nero's disregard for anything but himself.¹⁶² When Nero died, many thought he was still alive since some reports said he was and some people believed he was alive because the way he died differed in the various reports.¹⁶³ The belief that he still lived was active enough twenty years after he died that false Nero figures appeared and gained support of various factions.¹⁶⁴ Writings even call him the ἀγαθὸς δαίμων δὲ τῆς οὐκουμένης ("the good *genius* of the world").¹⁶⁵ Nero claimed divine status as one of the gods, though not as seriously as Caligula did.¹⁶⁶

The last of the emperors in this case study is Domitian, about whom much has already been said. Domitian began his reign by advocating the cult of his brother, Titus.¹⁶⁷ This was not done incidentally, rather Domitian planned on using this for his own gain. With both his father and brother declared divine and with his brother already having minted coins acceding divine titles to him,¹⁶⁸ Domitian took the next logical step. He never forced the issue in formal or legal documents, staying within the bounds of the titles that the Senate had voted him, but he did insist on those words in person.¹⁶⁹ He asked to be called lord and god, and spoke of his divine perch.¹⁷⁰ Within Rome, Domitian raised statues of himself made in gold and various other metals

---

Boer; Entretiens sur l'antiquité classique 19; Hardt, 1973), 9.

160 Michael Grant, *The Roman Emperors: A Biographical Guide to the Rulers of Imperial Rome 31 BC–AD 476* (Charles Scirbner's Sons, 1985), 39.

161 Gradel, *Emperor Worship*, 188–189. Gradel also points out how the iconography worked, the same picture moving from depicting the Roman *genius* to depicting that of the emperor.

162 Miriam T. Griffin, *Nero: The End of a Dynasty* (Yale University Press, 1984), 100–118.

163 Tacitus, *Hist.*, 2.8.1.

164 See the discussion of false Neros in Hans–Josef Klauck, "Do They Never Come Back? Nero Redvivus and the Apocalypse of John," in *Religion und Gesellschaft im frühen Christentum* (WUNT 152; Mohr Siebeck, 2003), 269–273. Klauck gives a full description of the various pretenders.

165 POxy 7, 1021.

166 For more information on Nero and his will to be a god, see Clauss, *Kaiser und Gott*, 98–111.

167 Michael Grant, *The Roman Emperors*, 61. Grant states that "whatever their personal relations had been, it was still necessary to exalt the Flavian house."

168 Thompson, *Imperial Cult*, 223 n. 19.

169 See above. Note especially Dio Cassius, *Roman History*, 67.5.7 and 67.13.4.

170 Suetonius, *Dom.*, 13.1–2. For a strong discussion of Domitian's use of "lord and god," see Clauss, *Kaiser und Gott*, 120–121.

and put them in prominent places.¹⁷¹ He placed so many of them around the city and they were so expensive that some graffiti read ἀρκεῖ (meaning "it is enough," and also a pun on the word arch, since that is where the statues were placed).¹⁷² He wore a purple robe to the quinquennial contest he held in honor of Jupiter Capitolinus, at which he wore a crown with the images of Jupiter, Juno, and Minerva while the priests seated with him wore the same with the addition of his own image.¹⁷³ He named himself *censor perpetuus* in A.D. 85, a political power play that resulted in Rome understanding he had taken absolute control of the Empire.¹⁷⁴ He reinstituted the *genius* of the emperor within two weeks of taking the office, a practice which Vespasian had halted since it harkened unto the Julio-Claudian family instead of the Flavians.¹⁷⁵ However, with Domitian encouraging the cults of Titus and Vespasian, the use of the *genius* promoted Domitian even more since his family (including his dead son) were all deified.¹⁷⁶ He also propagated his cult outside of Rome herself, erecting temples in his own honor.¹⁷⁷ Domitian required the titles and sacrifices of a god, persecuting those who did not bow to his whims. He was wise enough to keep his demands from reflecting in official documents or inscriptions in order to not anger the Senate by using names he had not earned or been granted, yet he still felt as if it were his right. The people of Rome did not object to his usurping divinity; they objected to his cruelty. His assassination was a political issue and not a theological one.

2.3.4 Summary

With respect to the position of the emperor, the Imperial Cult had become a political tool used to smooth the subjugation of people by connecting the emperor with the pagan gods. This is an understated conclusion, however, as the importance of sacrifices, titles such as "god" and "savior," the construction of temples, and other uses of divine honors demonstrate. The emperors in

---

171   While it was normal for the client nations to place a statue of the current emperor or the emperor who conquered them inside their major temple, it was considered unseemly for this to be done in a prominent place inside of a Roman temple, especially a temple dedicated to one of the greater gods. See Fishwick, *Imperial Cult*, 2.1.547. Domitian and Gaius both placed statues of themselves next to the temple statue, a clear claim to equivalence with a god.

172   Suetonius, *Dom.*, 13.3.

173   Suetonius, *Dom.*, 4.4.

174   Michael Grant, *The Roman Emperors*, 65.

175   Gradel, *Emperor Worship*, 190–191.

176   Robert A. G. Carson, *Coins of the Roman Empire* (Routledge, 1990), 32–33. Coins appeared with a child entitled as "DIVVS CAESAR IMP DOMITIANI F." Later, Domitilla was named Diva on a coin as well.

177   See Fishwick, *Imperial Cult*, 2.1.486 n. 68.

general may have declined certain names or edifices, yet Caligula brought the matter to its logical conclusion when he declared himself a god. His youth helped him to ignore the political obfuscation of denying divinity to himself while still accepting all of the privileges, something that the "sane" emperors tended to do only outside of Rome. The various emperors would deify their predecessors and families in order to heighten their own power, linking themselves directly to divinity. The citizens of the Empire, both inside the city and everywhere outside her walls, comprehended the importance of what it meant to offer sacrifices to statues of whoever currently reigned.[178] The emperors of Rome may not have always held the name of god, yet they accepted the titles, worship, and authority inherent in such a position. Roman citizens understood what these various honors meant, and they did not hold back in offering worship and sacrifices to those men, departed or living, who had ruled them.[179] Divinity was conferred formally by the Senate, but the population often conferred it through private practices. Being born a human was not an insurmountable barrier to godhood within the mindset of first-century Rome.

2.4 Conclusion

The disparate threads of Jupiter, the mystery cults, and the Imperial Cult all point toward one conclusion: the concept of θεός (and deus) had a large semantic domain in first-century Rome. Jupiter was the one god above all other gods, especially when linked with Greek mythology as Zeus. At the same time, Zeus could be controlled by fate or he could wrestle with fate, there was no set understanding. Zeus ruled the Greek pantheon with an iron fist, yet those same gods who quaked in his presence worked to ignore his commands. Jupiter did not compete with his fellow gods for worshippers as he remained a focal point of being Roman, though some people would gravitate toward a particular god. Participation in the cult of Jupiter did not bring about a future salvific state, rather participation in the cult was part of being a citizen of Rome. In addition, Jupiter was not the only god of Rome, in fact he was not even the only main god of Rome. Whereas Athens would hold to Athena and Ephesus to Artemis, Rome itself held to a triad of gods.

This idea of a triad links closely with the mystery cults mentioned. Isis occurred in a divine triad as well, having her husband Osiris/Sarapis and son Horus be part of her worship. Horus became the father of the pharaohs, and

---

178 Gradel, *Emperor Worship*, 228.
179 On the significance of sacrificial offerings to emperors living and dead, along with the combined cults of emperors and gods, see S. R. F. Price, *Rituals and Power: The Roman Imperial Cult in Asia Minor* (Cambridge University Press, 1984), 216–220.

thus through him the Egyptian rulers could be gods, but this was not a formal part of the Roman version of the cult. Although some aspects of the Isis cult looked for a future salvation, the research has found this to be the exception rather than the norm, as most adherents of the cult looked for benefits in this life. Isis did not compete with other gods, as their statues appeared in the midst of her temples. The cult of Isis did not replace public worship,rather it added a private dimension to the religious life of the adherent.

In the same way, the Mithras cult was a private cult that did not disrupt from public rites. Those who were initiates in the cult also worshipped the major Roman gods. Mithras also had a triad, as he mediated between Ahriman and Ahura Mazda. The idea of a life after death was not a central focus of Mithraism, and the Roman version in particular displayed virtually no signs of an afterlife salvation. Mithras was closely related to Perseus through various drawings and inscriptions, such that some of the same characteristics appeared in depictions of both.

The Imperial Cult of Rome deified some Roman emperors upon death and some attestation of apotheosis. Ascending upon death was not enough for some of them who wanted to be declared gods or treated like gods while alive. While these typically were the "mad" emperors, they were not censured for their desire but for other reasons. The Imperial Cult was a state cult such that participation was seen as an act of reaffirming citizenship rather than replacing or superseding normal observances to the pantheon. In fact, honoring the emperors honored the gods since the emperors were descended from them. The Imperial Cult was a form of politics and had nothing to do with next-world orientation.

Combining these various aspects together, one begins to see the picture of what θεός meant to a Roman citizen. First, there was no theological barrier between divinity and humanity, as certain humans (emperors or heroes) could aspire to be or become gods. Gods becoming human was not a problem either, though this was done simply for the amusement of the god. Roman citizens would not object to human beings of special lineage claiming to be gods or having others advocate divine status them.

Second, religion in Rome was focused more on the state than on the afterlife of the individual, so the concept of god meant appealing for help now rather than an eschatological hope. The typical resident of Rome worried more about money and food than about tomorrow. The state was a powerful entity that controlled what occurred in the life of each Roman, thus the state religion focused on the state. Politics and religion were combined through both the Imperial Cult as well as the regular cults (both mystery and normal) since the festivals and memberships were used to gain political power by gaining votes through public religious service to the city. Life for the typical citizen focused on this life and this city, not other places or times.

Third, the gods occasionally occurred in a triad, such that the main deity being worshipped fit in a group with two other gods, all closely associated with one functionally above the others, even if it was not the god typically venerated (e.g. Osiris ruled over Isis even though the cult was of Isis). When gods had overlapping functions, the greater of the two would absorb the other and be renamed. The citizens of Rome had no problem with new gods being added or old ones absorbed, what mattered to them was that the function continued and some sort of unity prevailed. Thus θεός (and deus) is a loose term, allowing much flexibility while stressing power and accomplishment. ing arrogance, and poor sense of humor.[180]

---

[180] Ittai Gradel, *Emperor Worship and Roman Religion* (Oxford Classical Monographs; Clarendon, 2004), 155–159. The poor sense of humor relates to the immediate cause of his murder, as he was humiliating a guard who then killed him.

Chapter 3

God and Mankind

This chapter seeks to introduce Paul's theology of God as expressed in Romans 8. In order to set the context of Romans 8 within the epistle, this chapter will discuss how Romans 8 connects to the rest of the book before concentrating on the connections between Romans 5, 7, and 8 in particular. After that, the chapter will focus on God in relation to creation, recreation, and finally salvation. Paul argues for a gospel for all people. This line of thought can be traced from the opening greeting (1:1, 4, 5) through the closing remarks (16:17, 25).[1] The epistle also reveals who God is and how he operates in response to the problem of sin.

3.1 The Context of Romans 8: God's Gospel

After the initial greeting of 1:1–7 and the prayer of 1:8-15, Paul states the thesis of the letter in 1:16–17.[2] In 1:18–3:20 he delineates the problem of sin,[3] whereas in 3:21–4:25 he discusses God's response to sin universally and his historical response to sin for the person Abraham and consequently to those in his

---

1 James C. Miller, *The Obedience of Faith, the Eschatological People of God, and the Purpose of Romans* (SBLDS 177; SBL, 2000), 128. Miller summarizes Romans by saying, "This theme, a gospel equally available to all, sounds the key note for the argument of the letter." This is more likely a theme in Romans, not the only theme.

2 E.g. Ben Witherington III with Darlene Hyatt, *Paul's Letter to the Romans: A Socio-Rhetorical Commentary* (Eerdmans, 2004), 47–48. They call 1:16–17 the *propositio*, and he relates each part of the thesis to the rest of the book, a standard understanding in scholarship, though he does not include Romans 16. Cf. Robert Jewett, *Romans: A Commentary* (Hermeneia; Fortress Press, 2007), vii.

3 Contra Douglas Moo, *The Epistle to the Romans* (NICNT; Eerdmans, 1996), 90–91. He views 1:18–4:25 as concerning justification. While in some sense he is correct, it is hard to call this the major theme of the entire section when it only comes to the fore in 3:21-4:25. A better understanding would categorize only the latter part as being about justification.

line.[4] Romans 5:1–11 details how reconciliation through Christ is now available whereas 5:12–21 discusses the problem of sin and death as seen in light of Adam. Paul then asks how one should react in light of God's grace instantiated in the person of Jesus Christ, and his response spans Romans 6–8. Each section centers on how God acts, how God responds, and who God sends. The center of Romans, then, is God and his response to sin, specifically in the person of Jesus Christ. Though Paul describes the problem of sin in detail, the focus in the end remains on God, as Paul describes how God has dealt with sin, is dealing with sin, and will deal with sin. The epistle to the Romans is intimately concerned with God's interaction with humanity (and all creation) in the past, present, and future.[5]

How does Romans 8 fit within the letter? Stanley Porter argues for a literary unity within Romans 1–8, especially 1:16–8:39, since 1:1–15 is the introduction to the letter.[6] Porter argues for unity by noting the literary features of the various chapters. He begins by agreeing with the scholarly consensus that 1:16–17 delineates the major themes of Romans, or at least 1–8.[7] This is followed by the major section of 1:18–4:25, which serves the function of raising the tension or building the argument in terms of complexity and nuance, especially 1:18 as it introduces the section.[8] The climax is reached in Romans 5, when Paul uses Adam to emphasize the concept of reconciliation, and this chapter connects the arguments of Romans 1–4 with 6–8.[9] Romans 6–7 detail the lull before and after the storm, as these chapters contain the action between the climax and the resolution.[10] J.-N. Aletti has argued in numerous places for the unity of Romans 5–8, such that it comprises a complete subunit of the *probatio* that extends from Rom 1:18–11:36.[11] What makes this analysis

---

4   See the helpful outline of Romans in Thomas R. Schreiner, *Romans* (BECNT 6; Baker Books, 1998), vii.

5   Brendan Byrne, "How Can We Interpret Romans Theologically Today?" *ABR* 47 (1999): 29–42. Byrne stresses God's grace.

6   Stanley Porter, "A Newer Perspective on Paul: Romans 1–8 Through the Eyes of Literary Analysis," in *The Bible in Human Society: Essays in Honor of John Rogerson* (ed. M. Daniel Carroll R., David J. A. Clines, and Philip R. Davies; JSOTSup 200; Sheffield Academic Press, 1995), 366–392.

7   Porter, "A Newer Perspective," 374. E.g. C. E. B. Cranfield, *Romans* (2 vols.; ICC; T&T Clark, 1975, Repr., T&T Clark, 2003) 1:87 and Joseph A. Fitzmyer, *Romans: A New Translation with Introduction and Commentary* (AB 33; Doubleday, 1993), 253–255.

8   Porter, "A Newer Perspective," 377; Schreiner, *Romans*, 78–79; Urlich Wilckens, *Der Brief an die Römer* (3 vols.; EKKNT 6.1–6.3.; Neukirchener Verlag, 1978-1982), 1:98.

9   James D. G. Dunn, *Romans* (2 vols.; WBC 38a-b; Word, 1988), 1:242–244; Porter, "A Newer Perspective," 382–383. Dunn calls Romans 5 a bridge between 1–4 and 6–8.

10 Porter, "A Newer Perspective," 383.

11 Jean-Noël Aletti, "La présence d'un modèle rhétorique en Romains," *Biblica* 71 (1990): 1-24; "La *dispositio* rhétorique dans les épîtres pauliniennes," New Testament Studies 38 (1992): 385-401; and "The Rhetoric of Romans 5–8," in *The Rhetorical Analysis of Scripture: Essays from*

helpful is how Porter rightly ties together every element rhetorically without minimizing any.[12] He is careful to note each section's contribution to the whole,[13] and that if any piece of Romans 1–8 were missing the whole would be incomplete.[14] Porter summarizes this portion of Romans (citing 5:3–5 as the climactic highpoint) by saying, "it spans the distance from the dire human condition (1.18–3.20) through to glorification (8.18–30)."[15] Romans 8, however, provides the resolution to this plot concerning the gospel.[16] C. Myers usefully notes how Paul often reverses direction in his arguments, he states that his work,

> suggests, however, that Paul's argument in Romans 3–8 does not move in only one direction. While Paul at times advances his thought by arguing in a forward-moving, linear logical fashion, particularly in chaps. 3 and 8, Paul also reverses direction in his argumentation other times in this epistle.[17]

C. Talbert approaches the problem of following Paul's arguments through the lens of Greco-Roman rhetorical technique.[18] He links all of 5:12–8:39 together as a unit, and then also links 6–8 as one unit (though he does not give a reason why he ignores 5:12–21).[19] He notes that questions occur in 6:1 and 15, with Paul laying out the answers in 6:1–14 and 6:15–7:6. He breaks 7:7–8:39 into small sections based on diatribe markers (7:7–12 and 7:13–20) and the statement of a problem and its solution (7:21–8:17 and 8:18–39). The most helpful portion of Talbert's analysis is the way he unifies Romans 6–8 based upon the question and answer format. Paul opens one long line of discussion in 1:18, the problem of mankind's fallen nature, which carries the main thread

---

the *1995 London Conference* (ed. Stanley E. Porter and Thomas H. Olbricht; JSNTSup 146; Sheffield Academic Press, 1997), 294–308.

12 Cf. Wilickens, *Römer*, 1:286–287.

13 Contra Changwon Song, *Reading Romans as a Diatribe* (Studies in Biblical Literature 59; Peter Lang, 2004), 101. Song turns Romans 8 into a footnote on ethics and ignores 9:1–5 completely.

14 Cf. Cranfield, *Romans*, 1:254; Moo, *Romans*, 290–291. Moo stresses the theological continuity rather than the literary, which Porter discusses. Cranfield looks at the flow of the argument in general.

15 Porter, "A Newer Perspective," 389.

16 Porter, "A Newer Perspective," 385.

17 Charles D. Myers, Jr., "Chiastic Inversion in the Argument of Romans 3–8," *NovT* 35 (1993): 30–47, here 47.

18 Charles H. Talbert, *Romans* (Smyth & Helwys Bible Commentary; Smyth & Helwys, 2002) and "Tracing Paul's Train of Thought in Romans 6–8," *RevExp* 100 (2003): 53–63.

19 Talbert, "Paul's Train of Thought," 54.

of the letter until Romans 8.[20] Romans 5 functions as a sort of crux in that the problem deepens yet Christ appears as the resolution.[21] Once the problem of sin finds its solution in Christ, the question of the law remains. Paul utilizes Adam as a symbol, and he stands for unregenerate mankind who are unable to be saved by the law. This creates an extended argument, one in which Romans 5 builds toward 6–7 before being answered in 8.[22] The structure of Romans 5–8 displays a reflexive construction.[23]

Aletti posits three different *probatio* sections in Romans, consisting of Rom 1:18–4:25; 5–8; and 9–11.[24] The link relies on rhetorical ties, especially between Romans 5 and the middle of 8.[25] Aletti explains that the beginning of Romans 8 is linked to Romans 7 due to the question of Romans 7 being answered in Romans 8, and the end of Romans 8 (8:31–39) serves as the *peroratio* for the whole of Romans 5–8.[26] B. Byrne, among others, has noted the rhetorical and lexical links between the two chapters as well.[27] He also notes how some of the major themes in Romans 5 occur again in Romans 8, for example life and death.[28]

The connections between Romans 5 and 8 will help the analysis of Paul's arguments in chapter 8.[29] Romans 7 recasts the problem of sin in terms of its relationship to the law. Romans 8 closely follows Romans 5 in terms of lexical and theological connections and answers the problem of sin and death raised in Romans 5. If Paul answers the issues raised in Romans 5 with 8, then why does chapter 8 follow 7 instead of following 5?

To answer this question, one needs to discern if there is a connection between Romans 7 and 8. Most scholars focus on Romans 7 connecting only

---

20 Moo, *Romans*, 291. Moo speaks of the contrast "between sin and justification" covering 1–4 and the contrast "between life and death" covering 5–8.

21 Moo, *Romans*, 290–292.

22 Miller, *Purpose of Romans*, 130.

23 June E. Lewers, "The Relationship of Suffering and Hope in Romans 5 and 8" (M.A. thesis; Trinity Evangelical Divinity School, 1984).

24 See especially Aletti, "Romans 5–8," 295.

25 See Nils Alstrup Dahl, "Two Notes on Romans 5," *ST* 5 (1951): 37–48.

26 See the argument, with slight modifications, in Jean– Noël Aletti, *Israël et la Loi dans la latter aux Romains* (Lectio Divina 173; Les Éditions du Cerf, 1998), 15–33.

27 Brendan Byrne, '*Sons of God*'–'*Seeds of Abraham*': *A Study of the Idea of the Sonship of God of All Christians in Paul Against the Jewish Background* (AnBib 93; Biblical Institute, 1979), 85–86. For lexical links, see also Philippe Roland, "L'antithèse de Rm 5–8," *Biblica* 69 (1988): 396–400.

28 Byrne, '*Sons of God*', 88.

29 See Richard N. Longenecker, *The Epistle to the Romans: A Commentary on the Greek Text* (NIGTC; Eerdmans, 2016), 683–684. He makes the connection partially by the use of κατάκριμα in 8:1 to the same word in 5:16 and 5:18 concerning Adam, so in essence making 8 a response to 5, especially 5:12-21.

to the beginning of 8.³⁰ For example, R. Weber pushes for 7:7–8:4 being one unit.³¹ Romans 7 centers on the problem of the law for the person in Adam, the before Christ state, whereas Romans 8 gives the answer.³² Romans 8 balances θάνατος with ζωή.³³ Paul builds on this contrast by adding πνεύματος to ζωή, and ἁμαρτίας to θάνατος in 8:2.³⁴ Weber argues that Paul does not center his argument on either salvation-history or individualistic anthropology, instead Paul focuses on God as the creator of both the law and the Christian, which in turn points to a Christological solution. After stating how Romans fits the structure of an ancient letter (linking 6:1–8:30 together as the *probatio*), C. Grappe limits his discussion to 7:24 and 8:2, connecting them based on two things: (1) an allusion to 4 Esdras 3:4–5 that makes an explicit Adamic claim³⁵ and (2) the use of Adamic language in Romans 5-8, which is referenced in 7:24 and 8:2.³⁶

B. Morrison and J. Woodhouse describe the connection as including Romans 7:1-8:17.³⁷ The grammatical structure of the passage connects 7:6, 25 to 8:1, as the ἄρα νῦν ("so then now") in 8:1 picks up the νυνὶ δέ ("but now") in 7:6³⁸ and the ἄρα οὖν ("therefore then") in 7:25.³⁹ The point lies in correctly seeing both strands of the connection in that Romans 8:1 not only resumes Paul's ex-

---

30 E.g. Cranfield (*Romans*, 1:372), who connects Rom 8:1–11 with 7:6 and Wilckens (*Römer*, 2:121), who connects 7:6, 25a with 8:1. Pace Moo (*Romans*, 469), who denies any strong connection between Romans 7 and 8 at all, linking Romans 5 and 8, yet admits slight links between 7:7–24 and 8:2–4.

31 Reinhard Weber, "Die Geschichte des Gesetzes und des Ich in Römer 7,7–8,4: Einige Überlegungen zum Zusammenhang von Heilgeschichte und Anthropologie im Blick auf die theologische Grundstellung des paulinischen Denkens," *Neue Zeitschrift für systematische Theologie und Religionsphilosophie* 29 (1987): 147–179.

32 Herman Lichtenberger, *Das Ich Adam und das Ich der Menschheit: Studien zum Menschenbild in Römer 7* (WUNT I/164; Mohr Siebeck, 2004), 266–269; Weber, "Die Geschichte des Gesetzes," 157, 159.

33 Dunn, *Romans*, 1:426; Weber, "Die Geschichte und des Gesetzes," 158.

34 Weber, "Die Geschichte und des Gesetzes," 165. Moo (*Romans*, 468) takes "life" (in addition to "Spirit") to be the key word for Rom 8:1–13.

35 Christian Grappe, "Qui me délivrera de ce corps de mort? L'Esprit de vie! Romains 7,24 et 8,2 comme éléments de typologie adamique." *Biblica* 83 (2002): 472-92, here 473. Cf. Henning Paulsen, *Überlieferung und Auslegung in Römer 8* (Wissenschaftliche Monographien zum Alten und Neuen Testament 43; Neukirchener Verlag, 1974), 111–127; Peter von der Osten–Sacken, *Römer 8 als Beispiel paulinischer Soteriologie* (Vandenhoeck & Ruprecht, 1975), 78-101.

36 Grappe, "Qui me délivrera," 480. Cf. Dunn, *Romans*, 1:419; Moo, *Romans*, 469-70.

37 Bruce Morrison and John Woodhouse, "The Coherence of Romans 7:1–8:8," *RTR* 47 (1988): 8–16.

38 Cranfield, *Romans*, 1:373; Morrison and Woodhouse, "Coherence," 9.

39 Dunn, *Romans*, 1:415; Morrison and Woodhouse, "Coherence," 12. Käsemann (*Romans*, 214–215) links 7:25 with 8:1 but considers 8:1 a likely gloss. For how Bultmann and Müller take 8:1 and a response to both, see Longenecker, *Romans*, 683.

planation of 7:6, but it also answers the problem of 7:14-25.[40] They conclude that, "There is one argument from 7:1 to 8:17, and if we lose the continuity of the argument we cannot understand Paul as he speaks about either the law in Romans 7 or about the Spirit in Romans 8."[41] Romans 7 connects to Romans 8 both in terms of the negative argument in 7:6 (no longer under the law) but also the positive argument in response to 7:14-25 (death is overcome by God).

In order to understand the function of Romans 8 in Paul's argument, one must first analyze Romans 7. This will be a brief overview of the chapter, as this work will not offer a solution to the difficulties of understanding the "I" of Romans 7. To this point in the letter, Paul has dealt with the problem of sin and the resolution found in Christ Jesus. Romans 7 introduces further complexity by reiterating the problem of the law in terms of how it relates to sin.[42] The chapter includes some kind of allusion to Adam, though many dispute the extent.[43] R. Jewett, after noting numerous weaknesses in other theories, contends that Paul speaks in character as his pre-conversion self, a figure that would be known by his Roman audience and thus rhetorically persuasive.[44] M. Seifrid describes the chapter as referring to the state of early Judaism, based upon the subject matter of the law and the use of penitential language.[45] One may also discern this through Paul's language in 7:1 (γινώσκουσιν γὰρ νόμον λαλῶ, "for I speak of those who know the law"). However, Paul does not leave off addressing his readers directly, as he then calls them καὶ ὑμεῖς ἐθανατώθητε τῷ νόμῳ διὰ τοῦ σώματος τοῦ Χριστοῦ ("even you who died to the law through the body of Christ") in 7:4. These Christians then know the law, but they have died to it. The passive ἐθανατώθητε displays action by God, the so-called divine passive.[46] Through this death, no longer do they belong to sin (7:5) but to Christ (7:6). This death leaves behind the old and brings in a new relationship, one found in union with Christ (and through baptism, e.g. 6:3–4).[47] The problem

---

40   Morrison and Woodhouse, "Coherence," 12. They say, "In 7:25b Paul summarizes his argument of 7:14–25 and uses it as a starting point for the second half of his argument in 8:1ff." Contra Moo, *Romans*, 469; Schreiner, *Romans*, 398.

41   Morrison and Woodhouse, "Coherence," 15.

42   One need only notice the title of Daniel Napier's article, "Paul's Analysis of Sin and Torah in Romans 7:7–25" (*ResQ* 44 [2002]: 13–32).

43   Reinhard von Bendemann, "Die kritische Diastase von Wissen, Wollen und Handeln: Traditionsgeschichtliche Spurensuche eines hellenistischen Topos in Römer 7," *ZNW* 95 (2004): 35–63, here 37–38; Dunn, *Romans*, 1:377; Wilckens, *Römer*, 2:102–104.

44   Jewett, *Romans*, 441–445.

45   Mark Seifrid, "The Subject of Rom 7:14-25," *NovT* 34 (1992): 313-33.

46   So Cranfield, *Romans*, 1:336; Dunn, *Romans*, 1:361; Fitzmyer, *Romans*, 458.

47   Ernst Käsemann, *Commentary on Romans* (trans. Geoffrey W. Bromiley; Eerdmans, 1980), 188; Jan Lambrecht, *The Wretched "I" and Its Liberation: Paul in Romans 7 and 8* (Louvain Theological and Pastoral Monographs 16; Eerdmans, 1992), 21–22.

then becomes more pointed as Paul turns to address the function and power of the law.

Sin, the overarching problem to this point in the rhetoric of Romans, and the law are related in that the law enables one to have a better knowledge of sin (7:7).[48] From 7:7–25 Paul answers the question posed in 7:5.[49] The answer, though, focuses purely on the human aspect and not on the divine, as evidenced by the lack of Spirit language.[50] Other than the brief doxological interjection of 7:25a, Paul only mentions God in terms of the source of the law (7:22, 25b, νόμος [τοῦ] θεοῦ) in contrasting God's law with a different law (7:21, εὑρίσκω ἄρα τὸν νόμον, τῷ θέλοντι ἐμοὶ ποιεῖν τὸ καλόν, ὅτι ἐμοὶ τὸ κακὸν παράκειται, "so I find the law, when I want to do the good, that the evil is at hand").[51] For Paul's argument, it is important to recognize that the law does not cause death; sin does.[52] Sin remains the main problem and the law only a secondary one. Paul has already named the law as a means to increase sin, both in terms of sinning and in terms of identifying it (3:20; 4:15; 5:13, 20; 7:7, 13).[53] Romans 7 only clarifies the relationship between sin and the law, but it does not offer support for the solution of 7:6.[54]

Paul has two problems left to discuss in Romans 8 (with another problem dominating Romans 9–11) after describing the extent to which sin controls people and the law seems to enable it. The first problem arises in terms of a Christian living with sin and the law still being active. The second problem deals with the effects of sin still present in the world. The answer to both of these concerns is the subject of Romans 8.[55] Romans 7 sharpens the issues opened in Romans 3 and 5, and thus Romans 8 follows 7 instead of 5, though it responds to both.

---

48 E. P. Sanders, *Paul, the Law, and the Jewish People* (Fortress, 1983), 71.
49 Lambrecht, *Wretched "I"*, 33. He argues that 7:6 and 8:2 form an inclusio that brackets and finalizes this section. Contra Käsemann (*Romans*, 215) and Moo (*Romans*, 469) who connect 7:25a to 8:2 upon the basis of style, though for vastly different reasons.
50 Napier, "Sin and Torah," 18.
51 Cranfield, *Romans*, 1:363.
52 Napier, "Sin and Torah," 23.
53 Ibid., 25. He sees four separate functions for the law ("increase of transgression...the identification...and quantifying of sin...and the coming of wrath"), but his distinctions are too fine and not necessarily helpful.
54 Bendemann, "Distase," 45; Käsemann, *Romans*, 199; Moo, *Romans*, 469-70.
55 John Pester, "The Organic Law in Romans 8," *Affirmation and Critique* 2 (1997): 44-49. Pester respects the separate nature of the two questions, yet he answers them with the concept of "organic law," a type of law that combines the "objective condemnation" inherent in the interplay between law and sin along with the "organic level" of sin that stems from "the consequences of the fall" (45).

3.2 God and Creation

Paul explicitly calls God the creator in Rom 1:25: οἵτινες μετήλλαξαν τὴν ἀλήθειαν τοῦ θεοῦ ἐν τῷ ψεύδει καὶ ἐλάτρευσαν τῇ κτίσει παρὰ τὸν κτίσαντα ("these who exchanged the truth about God for a lie and worshipped the creation above the creator," cf. Col 3:10).[56] In Roman religion, only the creation of the Roman state held significance (e.g. Romulus as Quirinus).[57] Part of the reason for this is that Jupiter was not a creator god, nor were any of the other great gods of the Capitoline hill. Even Isis, the great mother, was known for fertility and giving birth to the rulers of men, but not for any act of creation.[58] This topic, then, already moves beyond the scope of typical religious conversation for a Roman. However, the assumption of God as creator plays a pivotal role in Paul's argument in Romans 8.[59] Paul contends that the curse, which comes from sin, derives from God's authority as creator.[60]

The sons of God serve as the focus of Rom 8:19–23.[61] At the same time, κτίσις ("creation")[62] functions as the subject of most of the verbs throughout these verses (ἀπεκδέχεται [the logical subject, not the grammatical], ὑπετάγη, ἐλευθερωθήσεται, συστενάζεται, and συνωδίνει).[63] Paul stresses the anguish of creation as it exists in its fallen and cursed state, as seen in the usage of ματαιότητι ("futility"), δουλείας τῆς φθορᾶς ("slaves to destruction"), συστενάζεται, and συνωδίνει. What then fits within the scope of κτίσις[64] in this passage? Commentators have come to different conclusions as to the significance of the word κτίσις throughout this section of Romans 8. While many options have been offered for what κτίσις might signify in Rom 8:19, they essentially reduce to three: (1) mankind,[65] (2) a portion of mankind (e.g. the un-

---

56 It is one of the assumptions in Paul's argument in Romans 1, per Longenecker, *Romans*, 216.

57 On the status of Quirinius in Rome, see Gros, *Aurea templa*, 116–117.

58 Le Corsu, *Isis*, 7–13.

59 Cranfield, *Romans*, 1:410. Cranfield notes the importance of understanding God as the creator of both Christians and non-Christians for Paul's line of reasoning (411).

60 Moo, *Romans*, 516. Moo declares that only God has "the right and power to condemn all of creation." Cf. Dunn, *Romans*, 1:488; Robert H. Mounce, *Romans* (NAC 27; Broadman & Holman, 1995), 184–185.

61 Schreiner, *Romans*, 437–438. Cf. Fitzmyer, *Romans*, 507.

62 See also below 3.3.1.

63 Schreiner, *Romans*, 437. Respectively, the verbs mean eagerly await, be subject to, be set free, groan together, and suffer together.

64 Note the broad scope of the word in Werner Foerster, "κτίζω, κτλ.," *TDNT* 3:1000–1035.

65 Cf. Adolf Schlatter, *Romans: The Righteousness of God* (trans. Siegfried S. Schatzmann; Hendrickson, 1995), 184.

saved),⁶⁶ (3) the "cosmic totality."⁶⁷ For a point of reference, κτίσις in 8:38–39 stands out as an example of an unbounded use, such that anything could fit within the sphere of meaning.⁶⁸ The inclusion of all mankind but no "subhuman" elements finds little defense in the text.⁶⁹ Throughout this subsection of Romans, Paul has discussed only the sons of God and no other creatures. Thus, if one takes κτίσις as referring to mankind, one must choose either the saved or unsaved since Paul has been specific up to this point. The only mediating possibility were if Paul had included a modifier that clarified his use of the word. In terms of the second option, Paul's use of αὐτοί in 8:23 in contradistinction to κτίσις in 8:22 displays the differentiation of the referent of these two words.⁷⁰ N. Walter opts for the understanding that κτίσις refers to the unsaved based upon its usage in other areas of the canon.⁷¹ He notes that contextually there is a differentiation between creation and the children of God, God is working in mankind throughout Romans (with special reference to Adam), it rarely does not include humanity within its scope, that it means only mankind within the NT occasionally, and it fits the meaning of the reference to the fall.⁷² Of these five points, only the second and the fifth are cases specifically for fallen mankind being in view, as the first point fits κτίσις as a reference to non–human creation and the third and fourth points only show the possibility of such an interpretation, not the necessity of it. Walter's contention that Paul's argument in this portion of Romans is specifically anthropological contradicts the ending of the chapter, as 8:38–39 does not list anthropological concerns.⁷³ The last argument, and the only one specifically focused on Rom 8:19-22, goes against Paul's mention of the curse from Gen 3:17-19, where because of Adam the curse also falls on the non-human creation. With respect to the personification of creation, an objection Walter does not raise, Moo rightly points to the poetic personifications in the OT as something that would influence Paul in giving human qualities to non-hu-

---

66 For support of the notion of the unsaved as the referent, see Nikolaus Walter, "Gottes Zorn und das 'Harren der Kreatur': Zur Korrespondenz zwischen Römer 1,18–32 und 8,19–22," in *Christus Bezeugen: Festschrift für Wolfgang Trilling zum 65. Geburtstag* (ed. Karl Kertelege et al.; Erfurter theologische Studien 59; St. Benno-Verlag, 1989), 218–226. Cf. Käsemann, *Romans*, 232–233. Käsemann does not hold this position but he does give a brief defense of it.

67 John G. Gibbs, *Creation and Redemption: A Study in Pauline Theology* (NovTSup; Brill, 1971), 39–40. Gibbs reduces to a man/everything dichotomy, but this oversimplifies the issue.

68 The term functions as a catch–all word, covering anything the list in 8:38–39 might lack. See the discussion below.

69 Käsemann, *Romans*, 233. Cf. Cranfield, *Romans*, 1:411; Frederic Louis Godet, *Commentary on Romans* (Kregel, 1977), 313; Schreiner, *Romans*, 435.

70 So Moo, *Romans*, 514; Schlatter, *Romans*, 186–187. Cf. Godet, *Romans*, 313–314.

71 Walter, "Gottes Zorn," 218–226. His canonical argument tends to be overly selective.

72 Ibid., 221–223.

73 See below.

man creation.⁷⁴ Wilckens asserts that κτίσις includes both mankind and everything else, and thus is a synonym for everything that is not God.⁷⁵ He does so based upon 8:22 with the unqualified πᾶσα in front of κτίσις. The problem with Wilckens understanding lies in 8:23, with the differentiation between αὐτοί and κτίσις, such that Paul places himself and his readers beyond the scope of κτίσις, since Paul distinguishes between the two (οὐ μόνον δέ, ἀλλὰ καὶ αὐτοί, "yet not only, but even these"). Thus, κτίσις most likely refers to the non-human portions of creation.⁷⁶ Why does Paul bring creation into the equation at all? The answer is that creation bears a portion of the punishment for sin, as detailed in Gen 3:17-19.

The Genesis account of creation and the fall looms large in the background of Rom 8:19-23.⁷⁷ Due to the nature of Paul's usage, this is one of the few OT texts with which this book will interact. Paul makes the logic of the section easy to follow. First, he states that creation is waiting. This raises two issues: why is it waiting and for what is it waiting (for whom is already answered in 8:19). Creation is waiting because it was made subject (ὑπετάγη) to futility (ματαιότητι). The passive form raises the question of who subjected creation, and the only explicit answer Paul gives is ὑποτάξαντα, the one who subjected it. This answer gives rise to three possibilities: Adam, Satan, and God. Adam, because it was through his sin that all of creation became cursed.⁷⁸ Satan, because he tempted Adam into falling and thus corrupted creation. God, because He cursed creation in response to Satan's temptation and Adam's subsequent sin.⁷⁹ Adam cannot be in view due to the authority wielded in subjecting creation: Adam simply sinned. Schreiner rightly notes that Adam lost authority over the world by sinning, he did not gain any.⁸⁰ The διά + accusative carries the idea of agency, not cause.⁸¹ Satan is a poor choice for the same reasons, though no recent scholar has seriously argued for this option. The answer must be God. In addition to the previous evidence, there

---

74   Moo, *Romans*, 514. Cf. Schreiner (*Romans*, 435) who points to non-canonical literature.

75   Wilckens, *Römer*, 2:152–153. This is also the stance of Sylvia Keesmaat, *Paul and His Story: (Re)Interpreting the Exodus Tradition* (JSNTSup 181; Sheffield Academic Press, 1999), 102–123.

76   So, e.g., Cranfield, *Romans*, 1:411–412; Dunn, *Romans*, 1:469; Jewett, *Romans*, 511; Longenecker, *Romans*, 719–722; Moo, *Romans*, 514; Schreiner, *Romans*, 435. Longenecker gives the best defense of this understanding, following and expanding the arguments of Cranfield.

77   Cranfield, *Romans*, 1:410. Cf. Otto Michel, *Der Brief an die Römer* (KEK; 4th ed.; Vandenhoeck & Ruprecht, 1966), 202–203; Schreiner, *Romans*, 436; Wilckens, *Römer*, 2:154–155.

78   The most recent proponent of this position is Brendan Byrne, *Romans* (Sacra Pagina 6; Liturgical Press, 1996), 260–261.

79   So the majority of commentators, but see especially Dunn, *Romans*, 1:470–471; Moo, *Romans*, 515–516; Schreiner, *Romans*, 435; and Wilckens, *Römer*, 2:154.

80   Schreiner, *Romans*, 435.

81   So Wilckens, *Römer*, 2:154. Contra Byrne, *Romans*, 260-1, who argues for cause.

remains the connection between the two forms of ὑποτάσσω in this sentence, with the first clearly referring to God through the use of the divine passive (a passive with no agent listed, referring to God alone due to the type of act involved).[82] Schreiner adds a convincing point in recognizing that all of the uses of ὑποτάσσω by Paul have or imply God (or Christ) as their subject (1 Cor 15:27-28; Eph 1:22; Phil 3:21).[83] Dunn notes the possible allusion to LXX Ps 8:7, with God subjecting (ὑπέταξας, second person because the Psalm addresses God directly) all of creation to man.[84] Thus Adam is the cause, but God is the agent. The topic of creation being subjected to some sort of vanity or futility (not absurdity)[85] in terms of not fulfilling its purpose,[86] with God as the one who does the actual subjection, can only point to one place: God cursing the earth due to Adam's sin.

Does this futility of creation refer only to the curse? Exegeting the passage in Genesis is the clearest way to decide, both by considering the MT and the LXX. The description of the curse is found in Gen 3:17b–19. Since the sin of Adam was literally eating the wrong thing (though it was a form of disobedience), the response to his sin makes eating a thematic issue, as God mentions eating five times within 3:17–19.[87] Therefore, in order to punish Adam according to his sin, God makes eating, or getting the food in order to eat, more difficult by cursing the ground. The results of the curse are twofold: thorns and thistles will fight against man (וקוץ ודרדר תצמיח) and obtaining sustenance from the ground will be hard work (בזעת אפיך). The main idea of the curse is found in 3:17, with the actual curse upon the ground in that man will only eat in pain or by painful toil (בעצבון), the same term used for the kind of childbirth women will have (cf. Rom 8:22).[88] God curses the earth, which is the source (man created from dust) and destiny of man (to dust he will go), as part of the man.[89] The text of the LXX does not offer any parallel words or phrases with the text of Rom 8:19–22, yet no other narrative has the thematic or theological connections to fit within the context of Paul's discussion, nor

---

82 Cranfield, *Romans*, 1:413. Wilckens, *Römer*, 2:154; John Ziesler, *Paul's Letter to the Romans* (TPINTC; Trinity Press International, 1989), 220.
83 Schreiner, *Romans*, 435.
84 Dunn, *Romans*, 1:471.
85 O. Bauernfeind, "μάταιος, κτλ.," *TDNT* 4:519–524.
86 Cf. Cranfield, *Romans*, 1:413; Schreiner, *Romans*, 436. Schreiner notes the significance of the Genesis allusion in terms of interpreting the terms in the verse. Contra C. K. Barrett, *The Epistle to the Romans* (HNTC; Harper and Row, 1957), 165–166, who sees this as angelic or spiritual forces.
87 Victor P. Hamilton, *The Book of Genesis* (2 vols.; NICOT; Eerdmans, 1990–1995), 1:202.
88 Bruce K. Waltke with Cathi J. Fredricks, *Genesis: A Commentary* (Zondervan, 2001), 95.
89 Gerhard von Rad, *Genesis: A Commentary* (OTL; Westminster, 1972), 94.

have scholars offered other suggestions.[90] Thus, Gen 3:17–19 is the background for Paul's reference to the subjugation of creation, and God is the one who subjects it to futility.[91]

Paul acknowledges God's place as a position above that of creation. This is evident in Rom 8:19–22, as God subjects creation to his will and under his wrath.[92] At the same time, this also becomes clear in Rom 8:38–39, as creation is unable to hinder God.[93] Paul gives a list of hindrances that are unable to stop God's love in those verses.[94] Each of the pairs in 8:38–39 encompass a different aspect of creation. First, Paul notes that neither θάνατος nor ζωὴ can limit God.[95] This in fact encapsulates the theme of the chapter in many respects, by picking up two of the key terms throughout this longer portion of Romans (5:1–8:39).[96] Paul has linked death to sin (5:12, 14, 17, 21; 6:16, 21, 23; 7:5, 13; 8:1), the law (7:10, 13; 8:2), to Jesus' payment for sin (5:10; 6:3–5, 9, 10), and to life (6:13). Paul has linked life to Jesus (5:10, 17–18, 21; 6:4, 10, 23), to a new life in the Spirit (6:22; 7:6; 8:1, 6, 10–11), to death (6:13), and to the law (7:10). Death and life are the counterpoints throughout this section of Romans, with death coming strictly from sin (and indirectly from the law due to sin) and life coming from both the Son and the Holy Spirit. Some scholars postulate that Paul might be referring to spiritual beings who are the personifications of these forces.[97] Due to the thematic connection to the rest of Romans, it is unlikely that these terms refer to spiritual beings of any kind, and instead renew some of the themes from Romans 5–8.[98] The next pair, ἄγγελοι and ἀρχαί, refer

---

90   Longenecker (*Romans*, 722) says that, "while not stated explicitly, there can be little doubt" that the curse of Genesis 3 is in mind.

91   So, e.g., Cranfield, *Romans*, 1:413; Dunn, *Romans*, 1:471; Moo, *Romans*, 515–516; Schreiner, *Romans*, 435–436; Wilckens, *Römer*, 2:154.

92   Walter, "Gottes Zorn," 218–226.

93   Wilckens (*Römer*, 2:152–193) links 8:19–22 with 8:39, not just due to lexical concerns (κτίσις) but also to thematic ones.

94   Dunn, *Romans*, 1:508. Cf. Schreiner, *Romans*, 463.

95   Jewett's puzzlement (*Romans*, 551) as to Paul's usage here seems strange, as he assumes a negative view of life with life as a barrier instead of realizing Paul is using different words to show the boundaries around humanity. Besides, he makes a good point in noting that someone else's life could infringe on another's life.

96   Only Robert Jewett (*Romans*, 550), Grant Osborne (*Romans* [IVPNTCS 6; InterVarsity, 2004], 230), and James Dunn (*Romans*, 1:506–507) of the major commentators notes the connection, and Osborne considers death alone. Byrne ('*Sons of God*', 88) notes the words only in the context of Romans 5 and 8. Jewett makes the further point that life and death are reversed from their typical order due to context.

97   Cf. Matthew Black, *Romans*, (NCBC; Eerdmans, 1981), 127. Black posits this as an idea only, not his conclusion.

98   Moo, *Romans*, 544–545. Contra C. H. Dodd, *The Epistle of Paul to the Romans* (MNTC; Harper & Row, 1932), 146.

unambiguously to spiritual powers.[99] The third pair, ἐνεστῶκα and μέλλοντα, most likely are temporal references (i.e. present and future), since they occur as a pair with such a meaning in 1 Cor 3:22.[100]

After the three pairs, δυνάμεις stands alone. It can have two possible meanings here, either as a reference to spiritual powers or as a reference to miracles. The majority of commentators takes the first option, trying to explain the placement after temporal considerations as a summary of "celestial beings."[101] The problem with such an understanding, however, is the unlikely parallel it creates. If indeed δυνάμεις refers to spiritual beings and summarizes the preceding list, then Paul placed it in apposition to the coming list, which would be physical beings. Throughout Paul, the plural form only refers to the occurrence of miracles (Rom 15:19; 1 Cor 12:10, 28-29; 2 Cor 12:12; Gal 3:5, an exhaustive list not including Rom 8:38), and the singular refers to God's or his agent's power (Rom 1:4, 16, 20; 9:17; 15:13; 1 Cor 1:18; 2:5, 4:20; 5:4; 6:14; 2 Cor 4:7; 6:7; 12:9; 13:4; Eph 1:19; 3:7, 16, 20; Phil 3:10; Col 1:11, 29; 1 Thess 1:5; 2 Thess 1:11; 2 Tim 1:7–8), some power on earth (1 Cor 15:56; Paul's own strength in 2 Cor 1:8; monetary in 2 Cor 8:3; political power in Eph 1:21[102]), or an indeterminate or euphemistic use of power (1 Cor 2:4, likely God's power in Paul; 1 Cor 4:19, contrasting the power of the arrogant with God's power; 1 Cor 14:11, referring to the ability to understand speech; 1 Cor 15:43, Paul speaking of how the resurrection body is raised) with two notable exceptions: 1 Cor 15:24 and 2 Thess 2:9. The passage in 1 Cor 15:24 is ambiguous due to the context of God's kingdom (which likely has some political element to it[103]), yet the metaphorical nature of the passage (Christ as first fruits and death personified as an enemy) makes the understanding of a spiritual power possible. A. Thiselton notes the ambiguity and concludes with others that the condition of earthly subjugation does not negate the possibility of supernatural subjugation.[104] The second passage, 2 Thess 2:9, stands out due to its negative nature. The

---

99 The question of the nature of the angels (are they good or evil) is irrelevant to this discussion. See Dunn, *Romans*, 1:506 for a balanced summary. Contra Jewett, *Romans*, 552. Jewett argues that this refers to earthly powers since, in Paul, it often does.

100 So Byrne, *Romans*, 280; Cranfield, *Romans*, 1:443; Dunn, *Romans*, 1:507. Cf. Gordon Fee, *The First Epistle to the Corinthians* (NICNT; Eerdmans, 1987), 154. Contra Wilckens, *Römer*, 2:177.

101 Osborne, *Romans*, 230. Cf. Käsemann, *Romans*, 251–252.

102 The context of this verse, listing words for authority, makes this sense more likely, though this is disputed. See Harold W. Hoehner, *Ephesians: An Exegetical Commentary* (Baker, 2002), 277–278. Hoehner ably argues against his own position, noting that all of the other words refer to earthly power and only this one might not.

103 E.g. Scott McKnight, *A New Vision for Israel: The Teachings of Jesus in a National Context* (Studying the Historical Jesus; Eerdmans, 1999), especially 85–88 and 103–115.

104 Anthony C. Thiselton, *The First Epistle to the Corinthians: A Commentary on the Greek Text* (NIGTC; Eerdmans, 2000), 1232–1233.

power here is not that of God or Christ, nor does it refer to an extant entity or earthly authority. Rather the power in question belongs to the "lawless one" who comes according to the design of Satan. This power comes from Satan, for he empowers the enemies of God.[105] In fact, these false signs (such as seeing the future) accompanied the Imperial Cult as well.[106] All of this points toward the use of δυνάμεις as a sign or wonder, likely one to distract the believer,[107] instead of a supernatural being.[108] This is also how the first readers would understand the word, as there is no evidence to the contrary and the Imperial cult would have come to mind.

The last pair leading into the concluding term also causes controversy. Some commentators see ὕψωμα and βάθος as referring to the spiritual beings inhabiting the heavens or the astronomical representations of them.[109] The former interpretation, however, requires all of the items in the list to be spiritual powers of some sort, otherwise the sense of spiritual beings does not logically follow.[110] The latter interpretation does not fit the context of the argument unless Paul uses the terms metaphorically. In this case, the two words capture everything above to below, a likely merismus.[111]

The ultimate term in the list is κτίσις, which Paul uses to sum up everything that came before and to cover anything that did not fit within the preceding descriptions. What makes this last item difficult to interpret is the use of the adjective ἑτέρα, which typically connotes different as of another kind instead of different but of the same kind, or it can mean an item that is different from the rest of the list.[112] Does this then negate the possibility that κτίσις functions as a summary term? No, since the word functions as a safety net for all that were previously mentioned. In other words, Paul utilizes κτίσις to summarize

---

105 Gene L. Green, *The Letters to the Thessalonians* (PNTC; Eerdmans, 2002), 321; Charles A. Wanamaker, *The Epistles to the Thessalonians* (NIGTC; Eerdmans, 1990), 259.

106 Suetonius, *Aug.*, 96. Cf. *Aug.*, 94; Tacitus, *Ann.*, 4.81; Stephen J. Scherrer, "Signs and Wonders in the Imperial Cult: Rev 13:13–15," *JBL* 103 (1984): 599–610.

107 Cf. Moo, *Romans*, 545–546, who lists deceptive signs as a possible understanding, though he holds to spiritual beings himself.

108 Contra Jewett, *Romans*, 552. He also thinks that understanding ἀρχαί as an earthly political force keeps δυνάμεις from being redundant, as he sees it as a spiritual being, even though it comes after two more terms. His argument that this power ties into the gospel message is unconvincing.

109 Fitzmyer, *Romans*, 535; Godet, *Romans*, 334–335; Jewett, *Romans*, 554; Käsemann, *Romans*, 251.

110 See Cranfield, *Romans*, 1:443. He notes, "The assumption of many that all the items of this list must refer to spiritual powers of one sort or another must be challenged...such an interpretation is far from being natural."

111 Cranfield, *Romans*, 1:443–444. Longenecker (*Romans*, 759) defines the entire list as functioning rhetorically as *polysyndeton*.

112 BDAG, 399, which lists Romans 8:39 as an example of the latter.

the list by not allowing anything to be outside of the list.¹¹³ The demonstration of God's power over all creation was the point of examining 8:38–39. Both Rom 8:19–22 and 8:38–39 display the control God has over his creation.

Paul focuses on God as creator in Romans 8 for three reasons. First, he overturns the Roman idea that the emperor as the son of a god controls this world. Paul argues for God's control, mentioning his cursing of the world, something that links directly to the understanding of God as creator. Paul continues to elaborate on God's power by listing what cannot overcome God, which is everything. Paul highlights this especially in 8:38–39. Second, Paul connects God and creation to the fall, giving a reason as to why the world needs renewal. If there was no fall, then there would be no need for salvation. Paul mentions the fall in order to reinforce the need for salvation, since the typical concept of salvation for a Roman was based in this world, such as a longer life instead of eternal life.¹¹⁴ Third, Paul stresses God's absolute control over creation. Not only was God the one who created, but he cursed the earth when Adam sinned and is able to overcome any obstacle that humanity or the world could put in his way.

For the Roman Christians, this encourages faith and hope, helping them to focus upon God by overcoming any objections they would have to Paul's words. It also causes them to focus on God instead of any previous religious experience they knew, since only God solved the problem of sin as the Roman religions and cults were not interested in sin, only in benefits.¹¹⁵ A pagan in Rome concentrated on this life and looked for salvation in the present or else immediate future,¹¹⁶ yet Paul does not fulfill this expectation. Instead, Paul wants his readers to look past this world and toward the future. Therefore, Paul speaks of not only the fall of creation, he also points toward its renewal.

3.3 God and Recreation

God does not leave creation under a curse with no way for the curse to be lifted. Instead, God provides a way for creation to be renewed, indeed for a recreation to occur. Paul describes this recreation as occurring through two different

---

113   See especially Moo, *Romans*, 546–547. Cranfield (*Romans*, 1:443–444) argues from κτίσις to the previous phrases, saying that Paul adds it "in order to make the list completely comprehensive" (1:444).

114   Mary Beard, John North, and Simon Price, *Religions of Rome* (2 vols.; Cambridge University Press, 1998), 1:290.

115   Walter Burkert, *Greek Religion* (Harvard University Press, 1985), 27; Robert Turcan, "Salut mithriaque et sotériologie noplatoncienne," in *La soteriologia dei culti oriental nell' Impero Romano* (ed. Ugo Bianchi and Maarten J. Vermaseren; Brill, 1982), 173–191, here 173.

116   Walter Burkert, *Ancient Mystery Cults* (Harvard University Press, 1987), 27–28.

acts of God: first, through God adopting sons, and second, through creation being freed (ἐλευθερωθήσεται) by God. In order to make these points, Paul discusses the method of adoption in Rom 8:9–11, the signs of adoption in 8:13–17, and the purpose of adoption in 8:19, 23. Paul also discusses how God frees creation from its bondage by the glorification of the newly adopted children.

3.3.1 God and Adoption

Roman adoption had very specific nuances.[117] First, the son had the right to inherit, not anyone else unless no son existed.[118] Second, one could become a son through adoption. The most common reason for adoption was the lack of an heir, or at least the lack of a competent one. This adoption eliminated all previous ties, including links to family and to any debt.[119] This occurred since the previous family no longer existed, as the possessions and family of the one adopted came under the command of the one adopting. Adoption also immediately gave the one adopted the right to inherit.[120] Inheritance in Roman law was a reality during life and not only after the death of the *paterfamilias* (the father, specifically functioning as the head of the household and family in a legal sense), as the heir was a legal extension of the head of the family (except in testamentary adoption). In this case, the *paterfamilias* became responsible for the conduct of the heir and of any debts or assets the heir acquired even when the heir had previously been *homo sui iuris* (the state of being legally free from one's *paterfamilias*).

Paul utilizes the language of adoption to explain the new status people receive when joining the family of God. Paul uses explicit terminology in Rom 8:15, 23 (υἱοθεσία, a particularly Pauline term within the NT, also found in Rom 9:4; Gal 4:5; Eph 1:5) and in Rom 8:17 (κληρόνομοι).[121] The background of Paul's

---

117 The following section follows Craig S. Wansink, "Roman Law and Legal System," *DNTB* (ed. Craig Evans and Stanley Porter; InterVarsity, 2000), 984–991, specifically 990–991; James M. Scott, *Adoption as Sons of God* (WUNT II/48; Mohr-Siebeck, 1992), 3–14, 44–57; Francis Lyall, "Roman Law in the Writings of Paul—Adoption," *JBL* 88 (1969): 458–466 and *Slaves, Citizens, Sons: Legal Metaphors in the Epistles* (Zondervan, 1984), 67–118.

118 Then typically inheritance went to the closest male relative, often posthumously adopted in Greek culture and occasionally in Roman. See Scott, *Adoption*, 5.

119 One had to be free of debt to the city in Greek adoption before one could be adopted. This was not the case for Roman adoption. See Scott, *Adoption*, 5, 10. Cf. Lyall, *Slaves, Citizens, Sons*, 83.

120 This is debated in the case of Roman testamentary adoption, which occurs when one is adopted according to someone's legal will (Scott, *Adoption*, 10). However, if the will also gives all property to the one now named heir, the distinction is moot. Cf. Lysall, *Slaves, Citizens, Sons*, 69–70.

121 On υἱοθεσία, see Osborne, *Romans*, 205; Schreiner, *Romans*, 425. For the patron–client usage, note the phrase "Christians were indebted to God," in N. T. Wright, "The Letter to the Romans," in *The New Interpreter's Bible* (12 vols.; Abingdon, 2002), 594.

metaphor of adoption is often disputed. Cranfield lays out the three possible options that scholars pursue.[122] First, the background could be that of Judaic practice or linguistic usage.[123] Second, the background could be that of OT textual evidence without the explicit formulation of adoption.[124] Third, the background could be Greco-Roman practice, or more strictly speaking Roman practice since Roman law was in effect and not Greek.[125] The first is unlikely due to the lack of evidence, as there is no mention of inheritance rights when a child was raised by a different family or set of parents (if within the family) nor is there an established practice of adoption as a formal institution in the Old Testament.[126] The second case is stronger, as different texts (Gen 15:2-4; 48:5; Exod 2:10; 2 Sam 7:14; 1 Chr 28:6; Ps 2:7) seem to support such a background.[127] The strength of this position lies in the phrase אֲנִי אֶהְיֶה־לּוֹ לְאָב וְהוּא יִהְיֶה־לִּי לְבֵן ("I will be a father to him and he will be my son"), found in 2 Sam 7:14.[128] While this could form part of the basis for Paul's metaphor,[129] the Roman culture remains more likely to be the context. The Roman context fits because the letter was written to Rome, adoption was a common practice in the Roman community for advancing one's status, adoption was not a typical Jewish concept, and Paul utilized the technical term for it.[130] Thus, the majority of commentators hold to either mostly or exclusively the Roman background.[131] Within the discussion of Romans, this background makes the most sense.[132]

While the background of adoption is Roman, the question remains as to how Paul describes the role of God in the metaphor. In Roman adoption,

---

122 Cranfield, *Romans*, 1:397–398 Cf. Jewett, *Romans*, 498. Jewett notes the possible Roman, Greek, and Jewish backgrounds, and sees the concept as widespread and thus not needing further clarification.

123 Seemingly Schreiner, *Romans*, 425.

124 Scott, *Adoption*, 115–117.

125 Lyall, "Roman Law," 466.

126 See Fitzmyer, *Romans*, 500.

127 This is the conclusion of Byrne, *Romans*, 250. See also his '*Sons of God*', 97–103.

128 Scott (*Adoption*, 61–117) posits this text as the beginning or anchor of the tradition of adoption in Judaism, as evidenced by documents throughout Jewish history including the early Second Temple period.

129 Cranfield, *Romans*, 397–398; Moo, *Romans*, 501; Osborne, *Romans*, 205–206. Only Moo holds the OT background as a stronger influence than the Roman concept of adoption.

130 For the other terms Paul could have used (e.g. εἰσποιεῖν, ἐκποιεῖν, ποιεῖσθαι, υἱοποιεῖσθαι, τίθεσθαι), see Scott, *Adoption*, 14–44.

131 For the position that this exclusively refers to the Roman background and not the Jewish, see Dunn, *Romans*, 1:452; Fitzmyer, *Romans*, 500; Witherington, *Romans*, 217. Dunn misreads Cranfield at this point, stating that Cranfield believes adoption is not a Jewish practice. Cranfield, as noted above, believes the OT does shed some light on Paul's usage, albeit scant light.

132 Kyu Seop Kim, "Another Look at Adoption in Romans 8:15 in Light of Roman Social Practices and Legal Rules," *Biblical Theology Bulletin* 44 (2014): 133–143, here 134–137. Cf. Lyall, "Adoption," 459–465.

the *paterfamilias* legally takes into the family the person being adopted. In this case, the patron-client relationship gives a deeper sense to what was involved.[133] In such a relationship, the client praised the patron and tried to arouse others to feel the same way or to vote for the patron, if an election was the goal. The patron, on the other hand, would protect and finance the client, such that both profited from the relationship. This basic structure is how adoption worked in the world of first-century Rome.[134] The father would extend the opportunity to become a son to a client (typically though not always a family member). The client would agree to the adoption in order to ascend socially, politically, and almost always financially (since adoption eliminated previous debt due to the break with the previous family).[135] The reason for adoption from the father's point of view was to continue the family cult and to keep the line of succession intact.[136] God, in Romans 8, fulfills the role of the father in this Pauline metaphor. He is the patron who extends adoption into his family to those who are in a lower position or are in debt. This is most clearly seen in Rom 8:13–17, as it stands in contrast to Romans 7. In order to appreciate the place of God in Paul's metaphor, one must first understand the argument as Paul built it in the chapter with respect to adoption.[137] Romans 7 contrasted life in Christ with life according to or under the law.[138] Paul gives a solution to this problem of sin, namely life in Christ (or in the Spirit, cf. Rom 7:6).[139] This life occurs only for those who are in fact sons of God.[140] Paul's solution to the problem posed in Romans 7 requires adoption, for those who are not God's children must become sons of God, and adoption is the only way for this to occur. Adoption brings the Spirit (8:14–16), and the Spirit brings life (8:6, 10–11), and life cancels out the problem of the law, for the law ends in death.[141] Paul's argument continues, but this covers the usage of adoption.

Those who put their faith in God (or in Christ) become sons of God. This transformation of status occurs due to God's activity through the Spirit. Paul employs a circumlocution for the "divine passive" (ἐλάβετε without an indica-

---

[133] Cf. Scott, *Adoption*, 7–10. Scott notes the importance of the patron–client model before the act of adoption.
[134] Scott, *Adoption*, 9.
[135] Scott, *Adoption*, 9.
[136] Lyall, *Slaves, Citizens, Sons*, 83–86.
[137] On the disputed connection to Rom 1:3–4, see Scott, *Adoption*, 227–244.
[138] See 3.1 above.
[139] For the "in Christ" language at the beginning of Romans 8, see 4.2.1 below. Cf. Johann Tibbe, *Geist und Leben* (Biblische Studien 44; Neukirchener Verlag, 1965), 12.
[140] The reason for Paul changing between υἱοί (e.g. 8:14) and τέκνα (e.g. 8:16) will be discussed below.
[141] For a fuller exposition of this issue, including the relationship between law and sin, see 4.1 below.

tion of who gave) in order to describe the Spirit the believers received (8:15). If believers have received the Spirit, then someone has given the Spirit, and this can only be God the Father, or one could postulate that the Spirit can give himself, as Paul provides no other candidates.[142]

This leads to another question, then. Based on the question of agency, does the Spirit give adoption or does the Spirit merely confirm the adoption granted by God? Paul gives three reasons why God adopts and the Spirit confirms the adoption. First, the Spirit functions as the agent of God throughout the chapter.[143] God utilizes the Spirit as a means of enabling humans to please him and defeat sin (8:7-9). Paul describes how the law and flesh keep people from pleasing God. Moo states that the flesh "does not, and cannot, submit to God's law."[144] The importance of the law being from God (genitive of source) stands out in 8:7, again placing the emphasis on God.[145] The quandary of 8:9 lies in the problematic assignation of the antecedent of αὐτοῦ in the phrase οὐκ ἔστιν αὐτοῦ. The majority of commentators see this as referring to Christ, likely due to the proximity of the title (εἰ δέ τις πνεῦμα Χριστοῦ οὐκ ἔστιν αὐτοῦ).[146] The problem with this interpretation, however, lies in the misdirection of Paul's argument. Paul has not made the concept of "in Christ" (ἐν Χριστῷ or just Χριστῷ) prevalent in this section (the only close occurrences are in 8:1-2). He does not explain that Christians belong to the Messiah,[147] rather Paul focuses on the Holy Spirit as the seal of sonship (cf. 8:14).[148] In fact, relationship with God remains the major theme in this section, both in positive terms and negative. Paul emphasizes how one relates to God by speaking of being in enmity (ἔχθρα) with God (8:7), the inability to please (ἀρέσαι οὐ δύναται) God (8:8),[149] the three circumlocutions in 8:11,[150] and finally the cli-

---

142 As noted by Moo, Romans, 501–502.

143 Cf. Gordon Fee, God's Empowering Presence: The Holy Spirit in the Letters of Paul (Hendrickson, 1992), 516; though the name of Fee's book also gives this impression. Witherington (Romans, 216) explicitly calls the Holy Spirit the agent of God.

144 Moo, Romans, 488. Cf. Fitzmyer, Romans, 489.

145 Dunn (Romans, 1:427) notes the positive nature of the law here, in that it remains a standard by which God judges humanity. Cf. Fitzmyer, Romans, 489.

146 Byrne, Romans, 245; Dunn, Romans, 1:429; Fee, God's Empowering Presence, 548; Fitzmyer, Romans, 490; Moo, Romans, 471; Osborne, Romans, 200.

147 N. T. Wright ("Romans," 583–584) stresses that the variance in Paul's language for the titles of Jesus in Romans 8 is meant to stress different aspects of Jesus' functions and person.

148 Byrne, 'Sons of God', 97–98. Cf. Fitzmyer, Romans, 490.

149 Likely both phrases drawing upon the covenant curses from Leviticus 26 and Deuteronomy 28. Cf. Frank Thielman, "The Story of Israel and the Theology of Romans 5–8," in Pauline Theology Volume III: Romans (ed. By David M. Hay and E. Elizabeth Johnson; SBL, 2002), 169–195, here 182–183.

150 Cranfield (Romans, 1:390–391) notes the penchant for speaking of God according to his acts rather than by my name or title.

max of the passage in declaring God the father of believers (8:15–17). The only contextual problem lies in 8:10, which explicitly brings to the fore the relationship with Jesus. Dunn, however, points out that Paul's use of Christ functions synonymously with the Spirit in this verse.[151] Therefore, if those who believe are to belong to anyone, it would be God rather than Christ or the Spirit. The grammar allows such an interpretation, with αὐτοῦ agreeing in gender and number (case agreement is irrelevant for pronouns) with θέος, Χριστός, or even πνεῦμα, all of which occur within the immediate context. The claim of belonging to Christ does not fit the line of thought Paul is developing in Rom 8:9–11, thus αὐτοῦ more likely refers to God and not Christ. This in turn reflects that both the Spirit and Christ function as agents of God.[152]

In addition, the Spirit enables believers to call God father. The Abba portion of the exclamation often takes the focus from two different issues. On the one hand, the Spirit gifts believers with the ability to even call God their father. Moo notes that this cry cements the status of believers as rightful children of God.[153] On the other hand, the call demonstrates the relationship between God and believers, namely that of adoptive father. The Spirit who enables the crying out is the same one whom Paul labels the Spirit of adoption. Thus, Paul directly links adoption with the ability of believers to call on God as father. The use of Abba connects the believer with Jesus since he employed the same form of address toward God (Mark 14:36). Though originally a Semitic word, Abba was used in churches throughout the Roman empire as a form of address to God, as Paul evinces by assuming the liturgical function of the word in the churches at Rome (which he had not yet visited) and Galatia.[154] Regardless as to whether one considers Abba as a form of baby–talk[155] or typical address to a father,[156] the word carries the significance of an intimate vocative.[157] The Spirit allows such address for the believer through his action as an agent of God.

Second, and closely tied to the previous point, God is the father of Jesus. The trueborn heir, just like the adopted son, lives within the legal parameters

---

151 Dunn, *Romans*, 1:430. One should not infer, though, that Christ and the Spirit are the same. Chapter 4 will delve into these issues.

152 Dunn, *Romans*, 1:455. He contends the inheritance language of 8:17 carries the same idea.

153 Moo, *Romans*, 503. Cf. Karl Barth, *The Epistle to the Romans* (6th ed.; trans. Sir Edwyn Hoskins; Oxford University Press, 1968), 297–298; Fitzmyer, *Romans*, 501.

154 Cf. Fee, *God's Empowering Presence*, 410.

155 Joachim Jeremias, *The Prayers of Jesus* (trans. John Bowden; SCM, 1967), 11–65.

156 James Barr, "'Abba' Isn't 'Daddy'" *JTS* 39 (1988): 28–47 and "'Abba, Father' and the Familiarity of Jesus' Speech," *Theology* 91 (1988): 173–179.

157 Fee, *God's Empowering Presence*, 411. For a more comprehensive bibliography on the significance of Abba, see 401 n. 150.

of the father such that the father is responsible for the actions of the heir and thus the heir is a legal extension of the father. The title of heir does not obtain upon the death of the father, rather it exists as a legitimate status throughout life.[158] Paul names Jesus as the son of God three times in Romans 8 (vv. 3, 29, 30). Paul does not describe him as adopted anywhere in the chapter (or in any other writing). Thus, Jesus functions as the trueborn son of God, the natural heir. This is why Paul names those who are adopted as συγκληρονόμοι ("co-heirs") with Christ, since Christ already had and maintained his status as heir. Being a coheir with Christ is implied in the status of being God's heir in the first place.[159] The appositional character of the word κληρονόμοι with the phrases κληρονόμοι μὲν θεοῦ and συγκληρονόμοι δὲ Χριστοῦ proves the point, as the two explain one another.[160] The best understanding of the genitive in the former phrase is as one of source rather than objective, such that the inheritance comes from God and does not consist of God.[161] Murray argues for a genitive of source based upon Jesus' glorification ending in his inheriting God.[162] This depends upon an exclusive OT understanding of inheritance (based upon Ps 73:25–26; Lam 3:24)[163] and misreads Paul's glorification motif, whereby glorification is synonymous with the physical redemption of bodies (cf. 8:23).[164] Cranfield also hints in this direction, but he relies more strongly on the inheritance language than on naming God the content of the inheritance.[165] An OT background would take the inheritance as a reference to the land, yet Paul has not mentioned land within this context, nor even hinted in such a direction. Moo rightly notes that the focus on the land in earlier Judaism gave way to a focus on "eschatological life" as seen in such passages as Pss. Sol. 14:10; 1 En. 40:9; and 4 Macc 18:3.[166] At the same time, one must remember that the readers are Romans, not necessarily Jews or god-fearers, so one should not overemphasize the non–canonical literature, or even the implicit ideas in the OT.[167] The Roman pagan mindset would not necessarily

---

158 Wansink, "Romans Law," 991.

159 Byrne, 'Sons of God', 102; John Murray, *The Epistle to the Romans* (Eerdmans, 1997), 299. Cf. Schreiner, *Romans*, 428, though he states the reverse, that believers are heirs of God because of being coheirs with Christ.

160 Murray, *Romans*, 299. Cf. Cranfield, *Romans*, 1:406–407.

161 Moo, *Romans*, 505. Cf. Cranfield, *Romans*, 1:407. Contra Murray, *Romans*, 298 and Schreiner, *Romans*, 427.

162 Murray, *Romans*, 298–299.

163 Ibid., 298.

164 See section 3.3.2. Glorification ends in the redemption of bodies but is not synonymous with it.

165 Cranfield, *Romans*, 1:406–407. Contra Moo, *Romans*, 505 n. 47, in which he lists Cranfield and Murray as holding the same view.

166 Moo, *Romans*, 505. Cf. Byrne, 'Sons of God', 68–69; Schreiner, *Romans*, 427–428.

167 See 1.3 above.

recognize any non–Roman understanding of adoption other than Greek, especially when technical legal language appears. The idea of Jesus as the son of God would fit the Roman model of the emperors as sons of gods.[168] The emperors claimed divinity based upon descent or kinship with those who were gods (Julius Caesar with Venus via Aeneas) or other emperors who were proclaimed gods (Domitian and his father Vespasian and brother Titus).

Third, God becomes the father of believers, or, conversely, believers become[169] the children of God. Paul heavily uses this terminology throughout Rom 8:14–23[170] in order to make several points (e.g. the adoption status of believers, the special status of Jesus, the result of inheritance), only one of which intersects this discussion. The adoption motif dominates the earlier portion of this section, including the use of υἱοθεσία.[171] The significance of the Abba exclamation also carries weight in this discussion in that believer can call on God as father.

A question arises as to the alternation between υἱοί and τέκνα for those God adopts. The former occurs in 8:14 (and 15, implicitly), 19 when referring to Christians and the latter in 8:16–17, 21. One wonders as to why Paul vacillates between the two terms in his explanation of adoption. Sanday and Headlam argue for a differentiation between the two words based upon τέκνον being a relational term and υἱός being a legal title and status.[172] Most commentators, however, agree with Käsemann in eliminating any major difference between the two words.[173] He likely goes too far, though, in pushing for total equality between the two terms, since Dunn notes that Paul in his extant letters never uses τέκνον for Jesus, with υἱός as a regular title for him.[174] Paul does not take this distinction to the same extent that John does in using the latter only for Christ and the former only for Christians.[175] The majority of commentators see little difference between the two terms.[176] Moo claims that the flow of Paul's argument does not allow for any significant distinction between the

---

168 E.g., Donald L. Jones, "Roman Imperial Cult," *ABD* 5:806–809, here 806; Wayne E. Mills, "Sons of God: The Roman View," *BI* 10/1 (1983): 37–39.

169 See below for a discussion on the problem of the timing of "becoming" a son of God.

170 There are 7 occurrences in this section of either sons (υἱός) or children (τέκνον).

171 The term appears only in Paul and only in Rom 8:15, 23; 9:4; Gal 4:5; and Eph 1:5. Longenecker, *Romans*, 703–704, notes that it does not appear in the LXX, a cognate in the Hebrew MT, or any Second Temple literature, making it a unique theological contribution of Paul.

172 William Sanday and Arthur C. Headlam, *The Epistle to the Romans* (ICC; 5th ed.; T&T Clark, 1980), 202. Cf. Godet, *Romans*, 311.

173 Käsemann, *Romans*, 229.

174 Dunn, *Romans*, 1:454–455.

175 See the comment by Byrne, '*Sons of God*', 160 n. 83.

176 Most following Cranfield, *Romans*, 1:396 n. 1. Cranfield overrides the position of Sanday and Headlam without making an argument, only pointing to verses. Cf. Käsemann, *Romans*, 229; Moo, *Romans*, 504 n. 41; Schreiner, *Romans*, 423.

two names.¹⁷⁷ Τέκνα occurs in the setting that "we" are heirs of God and co-heirs with Christ based upon the testimony of the Spirit. It is then linked to the act of recreation. Υἱοί occurs in defining adoption and in the future revelation that brings about recreation.¹⁷⁸ The only possible contextual variation within the argument of Paul relies on the timing implicit within the argument, namely that "we" are now children of God yet creation waits for the revelation of the sons of God.¹⁷⁹ The only possible differentiation between the two terms lies in the eschatological cast of υἱοί, and the lack of such a shading in τέκνα. The latter clearly belongs to this world in 8:16–17 with the use of ἐσμέν (present active). Rom 8:21 does not give a clear indication to the time of when one is a child of God, as the future tense refers to when God will free creation, not to when there are extent children of God. With respect to the υἱός, Rom 8:19 dominates as an explicit link to the future rather than the present based upon the sense of ἀπεκδέχεται (since whatever one waits for is in the future from the moment of waiting).¹⁸⁰ Though the waiting is for the revelation of the sons of God, the revelation is future oriented and the status may or may not be. The difficulty in this interpretation lies in the understanding of 8:14. Dunn understands the verse to push towards an "enthusiastic, even ecstatic behavior," though he does not think this is the point of the language.¹⁸¹ This builds on the work of Käsemann, who rightly notes the power of the Spirit evident here occurs in conjunction with the human will, such that during this life one cannot be completely "driven" by the Holy Spirit: this only comes to fruition at the eschaton.¹⁸² Thus, Paul uses τέκνον for believers as a term that draws on Roman legal understandings with respect to inheritance and other adoptive issues, whereas he employs υἱός to draw in an additional eschatological understanding.

That daughters were included in the Roman system of inheritance (and very rarely adopted) only strengthens the claim of a Roman background for the inheritance and adoption motifs.¹⁸³ In turn, this clarifies why the word

---

177 Moo, *Romans*, 504 n. 41.
178 It should be noted here that "sons" refers to both male and females within the Christian sphere, such that Paul is not using the plural as gender specific, as can be seen by the lack of contrast with "children," such that both include all people.
179 Cranfield (*Romans*, 1:412–413) states that the present sonship is "veiled" and "impenetrable except to faith" based upon the future revelation.
180 The type of waiting is irrelevant for this discussion since any waiting points toward some sort of expectation, whether good or bad, regardless if one follows either Georg Bertram ("Ἀποκαραδοκία," *ZNW* 49 [1958]: 264–270) or D. R. Denton ("Ἀποκαραδοκία," *ZNW* 73 [1982]: 138–140) with respect to the significance of ἀποκαραδοκία.
181 Dunn, *Romans*, 1:450.
182 Käsemann, *Romans*, 250–251.
183 See John K. Evans, *War, Women, and Children in Ancient Rome* (Routledge, 1991), 71.

τέκνον can be closely associated with inheritance since it fits both male and female,[184] yet not necessarily with the eschaton. In addition, the contents of the cry of the believer holds the lynchpin of the argument, as the Spirit enables believers to call God by the same address that Jesus uses, "Abba, father." This does not convey a name for God,[185] rather it carries a verbal idea of intimacy. McCasland's case is built by making one dubious exegetical decision after another, finally arriving at the sense of "God our father" based upon the article having the ability to be possessive or function as a possessive pronoun and non-Aramaic speakers never asking about the original meaning of Abba and therefore assuming it functions as a name for God. The later assertion remains pure conjecture as McCasland offers very limited textual evidence and relies on anecdotal evidence (about how people often address the head of a monastery as "Father Abbot" in ignorance) instead.[186] Paul considers God the father of believers within the metaphor of adoption, yet also in a way that transcends purely metaphoric grounds based upon what he expects believers to call God.

With God as the one who adopts, though not the agent of adoption, that places God in the role of the *paterfamilias*. Jesus maintains his status as the firstborn son of God, yet siblings are added into the family.[187] The method of adoption is through the firstborn son and the Spirit, with God as father. The signs of adoption also come through the agents of God. The purpose of adoption, though, comes about according to God's own design.

God has adopted those who believe into his family as sons and heirs, but the typical reason for adoption does not fit here. In Greco-Roman culture, one could adopt a son as heir in order to continue one's family line and to honor one's family god(s).[188] Paul does not contemplate the death of God, and thus the idea of an inheritance based upon death cannot be in view.[189] What reason is there for adopting sons other than to perpetuate a family line? Scott lists three other possibilities in Roman society: social movement, political maneuvering, or *patria potestas*,[190] while Lyall adds another, which is continuing devotion to the family gods.[191] God certainly does not need any social

---

184 Nigel Watson, "'And If Children, Then Heirs' (Rom 8:17)–Why Not Sons?" *ABR*, 49 (2001): 53–56.

185 Contra S. Vernon McCasland, "'Abba, Father,'" *JBL* 72 (1953): 79–91.

186 McCasland, "'Abba, Father,'" 90.

187 For the relationship between Jesus and the children of God, see chapter 4.

188 Scott, *Adoption*, 4–5, 9. This is true for both the Greek and Roman background.

189 The difficulty of following the argument of Hebrews 9 is outside the bounds of this study.

190 Scott, *Adoption*, 9.

191 Lyall, *Slaves, Citizens, Sons*, 84. Continuing the family cult was as important as continuing the state cult.

or political gain as he is the creator of the world. This leaves only the last two options. *Patria potestas* is the technical term for the type of control the *paterfamilias* had over his blood relations. As a Roman father, he would be able to control the associations, income, and relationships in which the other members of the family took part. Since everything revolved around his honor, he would have the power to limit his children in terms of where they went and what they did. In the mystery cults, when one joined one became a member of a new group, yet this did not constitute a break with any previous group.[192] Being adopted by God, however, would be a complete shift in status, since adoption went beyond adding an allegiance into changing allegiance. Does God really need to expand his influence of family relationships? This also does not fit the pattern of argument which Paul is making in Romans 8. God is not running out of worshippers, so the last reason must be rejected as well.

The idea of God (or a god) adopting a human would not fit within a typical Roman mindset. While emperors often adopted an heir (e.g. Julius Caesar with Octavian), gods did not adopt. God taking believers as his children and heirs would be a unique concept for the Roman audience, and the only filter to understand it would be through the Roman laws of adoption. Since there would be no standard legal or theological reason for this adoption, the readers would have to follow Paul's argument in Romans. The only textual reason one can find for adoption appears in the result: the renewal of creation, which signifies freeing it from the curse.[193]

3.3.2 God and Glory

In Rom 8:19, Paul states that κτίσις waits for τὴν ἀποκάλυψιν τῶν υἱῶν τοῦ θεοῦ ("the revelation of the sons of God"). On a straightforward reading, ἀποκαραδοκία is the subject of ἀπεκδέχεται, yet the sense of the Greek remains even when translating the Greek subject as an adjective and the modifying genitive as the subject.[194] Paul's point lies in the act of creation waiting in hope, ἐλπίς, which is a key word throughout this section of Romans 8 (and a link to Romans 5).[195] With the contextual tie to ἐλπίς, ἀποκαραδοκία likely carries positive connotations rather than negative ones, signifying hoping for

---

192 Gary Lease, "Mithraism and Christianity," *ANRW* 28.2:1302–1332, here 1322; Burkert, *Ancient Mystery Cults*, 14.

193 Byrne (*'Sons of God'*, 104–105) also sees glorification as a result, but Paul's argument has glorification as the means by which God renews creation. See below.

194 Moo (*Romans*, 513) says, "'eager expectation,' the grammatical subject, is put in the place of the real subject, 'creation.'"

195 Cf. 3.1.

rather than dreading the future occurrence.¹⁹⁶ As Paul writes to a Roman audience, the word usage in Aquila's Old Greek version of the OT (offered as a possible background to Paul's word choice)¹⁹⁷ would carry little relevance for the recipients of the letter to the Romans in terms of understanding this passage, as they were unable to have had a copy of Aquila's version since he finished it in the early second century.¹⁹⁸ If Paul was using Aquila, his audience would not have been likely to follow him. Thus creation has a positive expectation for the future.

Creation has a positive expectation based upon the hope it has.¹⁹⁹ The content of this hope seems unclear in the passage, as Paul alludes to four different issues. First, he connects the hope with the revelation of the sons of God. Second, this hope stands in contrast to the curse creation lies under. Third, creation seeks freedom. Fourth, creation will be freed εἰς τὴν ἐλευθερίαν τῆς δόξης τῶν τέκνων τοῦ θεοῦ ("for the freedom from the glory of the children of God").²⁰⁰

Why does creation look forward to the revelation of the sons of God? The title υἱοὶ θεοῦ carries eschatological force, as previously argued. The expectation, then, relies on the future (i.e. eschatological) force of the title, especially since those holding the title have not been unveiled. There exists a tension between the "already" and the "not yet" with respect to the sons of God and the culmination of adoption.²⁰¹ The "already" consists of the aspect of being children of God, those who already hold the status of heir (as seen in the Roman background). The "not yet" pertains to the final revelation of those adopted and the reception of their inheritance, that to be shared with Christ.²⁰² The future orientation focuses on the act of revelation, such that those who are children have not yet been recognized as adopted sons.²⁰³ This tension also appears with the Spirit being τὴν ἀπαρχὴν ("the first fruit"), which requires a future or ongoing harvest to complete the metaphor. Creation looks

---

196 See D. R. Denton, "Ἀποκαραδοκία"; contra Bertram "Ἀποκαραδοκία."

197 Cf. the study of Hae-Kyung Chang ("[ἀπο] καραδοκία bei Paulus und Aquila," *ZNW* 93 [2002]: 268–278), who does not help solve the problem of the meaning of the word here, though he decides on the positive aspect of the word.

198 Karen Jobes and Moisés Silva, *Invitation to the Septuagint* (Baker, 2000), 38–39.

199 Longenecker, *Romans*, 722.

200 For the particulars of this translation, see the discussion below.

201 This line of thought flows from the structure of Paul's argument, as noted in Susan Eastman, "Whose Apocalypse? The Identity of the Sons of God in Romans 8:19," *JBL* 121 (2002): 263–277. Cf. Moo, *Romans*, 515. Moo speaks of the future revelation while explaining that the status of heir is already held by believers.

202 Eastman, "Whose Apocalypse?," 265; Moo, *Romans*, 504; Schreiner, *Romans*, 423.

203 Trevor J. Burke, "Adoption and the Spirit in Romans 8," *EvQ* 70 (1998): 311–324, especially 317.

forward simply because it is a future revelation. Paul's apocalyptic vision does not contain the coming of Christ as the culmination as far as creation is concerned, rather the climax resides elsewhere.[204] The sons of God are the content of the revelation, but that does not speak to the significance or climax of the revelation.

The hope of creation stands in direct contrast to its present state of cursedness. Longenecker notes that Vergil prophesied that a future golden age would come, and that many connected that to Augustus.[205] The negative of this world would have a reprieve through some future savior. God subjected creation, and he gave hope for the change in the status of creation. The agency matters here, for creation has an expectation, but God subjected it. Syntactically, ἐφ' ἐλπίδι ("in hope") stands next to ὑποτάξαντα, likely modifying this participle.[206] Even if one were to argue that the prepositional phrase connects to ὑπετάγη (a popular position[207]), God remains the "logical subject" due to the divine passive.[208] Creation does not activate hope, God does as the only actant in the section.[209] The reason for this hope likely lies in the *protoevangelium* of Genesis 3:15 in light of the curse this hope is to overcome.[210] Hope must be understood as the opposite of what creation undergoes. While creation lies under the curse, everything experiences futility. Only the lifting of the curse can bring about any change. Creation waits for this change, but the hope itself derives from God alone.

The specific content of the hope carries both a negative and a positive portion. The negative precedes the positive logically in Paul's line of thought. Creation being set free ἀπὸ τῆς δουλείας τῆς φθορᾶς carries a negative aspect, meaning that Paul relates how creation will no longer be shackled by slavery. The genitive phrase, δουλείας τῆς φθορᾶς, allows for a few different understandings of the relationship between the words. The preposition ἀπό denotes the state from which creation obtains freedom. Δουλεία, is in the genitive since it is the object of ἀπό. The problem lies in τῆς φθορᾶς, as one can construe it in numerous ways. First, the genitive could be qualitative, describ-

---

204 Walther Bindemann, *Die Hoffnung der Schöpfung: Römer 8,18-27 und die Frage einer Theologie der Befreiung von Mensch und Natur* (Neukirchener Verlag, 1983), 92.
205 Longenecker, *Romans*, 724; and more briefly Jewett, *Romans*, 512. Longenecker's entire discussion is interesting, catching the historical significance and noting how the lower classes did not hold to this view necessarily.
206 Fitzmyer, *Romans*, 508.
207 E.g. Cranfield, *Romans*, 1:414; Moo, *Romans*, 516; Schreiner, *Romans*, 436.
208 Fitzmyer, *Romans*, 508. Cranfield (*Romans*, 1:414) leans in this direction, as he notes that this hope is for or about creation, not creation's hope.
209 Fitzmyer, *Romans*, 508.
210 Cranfield, *Romans*, 1:414; Moo, *Romans*, 516. Contra Fitzmyer, *Romans*, 508.

ing the kind of slavery. Second, it could be possessive or source, delineating to what one is in slavery. Third, it could function subjectively, such that the decay enslaves. Fourth, it could carry an epexegetical tone such that slavery actually is decay (or vice versa). Finally, the genitive could be understood objectively, such that the slavery moves toward decay. The first understanding sees φθορᾶς as describing the kind of slavery,[211] yet Paul does not speak of slavery as the entity here, he speaks of a contrast between slavery and freedom that parallels the contrast between decay and glory, such that the antithesis of the former pair encompasses or helps define the antithesis of the latter. The second position carries a strong contrast between creation existing under a slavery that finds its source in decay, and thus eventual death.[212] The genitive is unlikely to be subjective,[213] as decay cannot functionally do anything. The epexegetical option, favored by Wilckens, Schreiner, and Murray, though the latter calls it appositional,[214] holds little value since the parallel construction (ἐλευθερίαν τῆς δόξης) cannot be epexegetical, as freedom cannot be equated with glory.[215] In fact, this is unlikely due to the preposition, as the object of a preposition is rarely in an epexegetical or appositional relationship. The final position, that favored by Moo and others,[216] understands the genitive as the object of the implied verbal idea of slavery, such that one is enslaved for the goal of decay. The most likely options tend to be the genitive of source (slavery that comes from decay)[217] or objective (slavery that leads to decay). Dunn observes that "an inescapable feature of the natural order is decay," a comment that fits both interpretations.[218] In order to make a decision, one must understand the rest of the verse.

In contrast to the negative portion of the content of hope, Paul speaks of εἰς τὴν ἐλευθερίαν τῆς δόξης τῶν τέκνων τοῦ θεοῦ. Paul does not add a positive concept only to balance the negative, rather this phrase delineates the goal toward which God will free creation.[219] Paul indicates this goal or end by us-

---

[211] This is the position of Leon Morris, *The Epistle to the Romans* (PNTC; Eerdmans, 1988), 322.

[212] Contra Moo (*Romans*, 517 n. 47) and Schreiner (*Romans*, 436), this is the position taken by Cranfield, *Romans*, 1:415–416. Both link Cranfield with the subjective understanding, but Cranfield says it is, "the condition of being the slaves of death and decay."

[213] Though Osborne (*Romans*, 212) does take this position. He says, "the enslaving force is *decay*" (emphasis original).

[214] Murray, *Romans*, 304 n. 30; Schreiner, *Romans*, 436; Wilckens, *Römer*, 2:155 n. 676. Schreiner favors it because "it adds the least meaning it to the text."

[215] Contra Murray, *Romans*, 304 n. 30. See below.

[216] Byrne, *Romans*, 261; Fitzmyer, *Romans*, 509; Moo, *Romans*, 517 n. 47; Sanday and Headlam, *Romans*, 208.

[217] Cf. Käsemann, *Romans*, 230.

[218] Dunn, *Romans*, 1:472.

[219] Byrne, 'Sons of God', 107.

ing an εἰς phrase,²²⁰ a typical construction for denoting purpose.²²¹ The difficulty arises in assessing the import of the phrase εἰς τὴν ἐλευθερίαν τῆς δόξης τῶν τέκνων. God gives the glory to his children, so he is the source of it, and likely that means the children are the possessors of the glory.²²² The difficulty lies in relating ἐλευθερίαν and δόξης. Three options come to the fore in this discussion. First, and least likely, some commentators defend the qualitative relationship between the two.²²³ The point of Paul's line of thought is not the "glorious freedom" creation will experience, rather the focus lies on the relationship between creation and the children of God.²²⁴ The second option for this relationship is possessive. Thus, the freedom belongs to glory, though this is understood loosely as the possessive rendering might be better labeled a genitive of sphere.²²⁵ The final option is one of source, that the freedom comes from glory. Cranfield paraphrases this understanding as "liberty– resulting–from–glory."²²⁶ In this instance, there exists just a shade of difference in meaning, such that the decision between source and possessive does not affect the significance of this phrase. However, source and objective were the only options left for the phrase ἀπὸ τῆς δουλείας τῆς φθορᾶς. The two phrases (ἀπὸ τῆς δουλείας τῆς φθορᾶς and εἰς τὴν ἐλευθερίαν τῆς δόξης τῶν τέκνων τοῦ θεοῦ) both speak to the content of the hope (hence being introduced by ὅτι, an indirect discourse marker).²²⁷ Therefore, the option of source for both sets of words makes the most sense.

The two phrases give parallel ideas in terms of what creation waits for: it waits for God to reveal the sons of God so as to free creation from slavery

---

220 Moo, *Romans*, 517 n. 49. Cf. Gibbs, *Creation and Redemption*, 37.
221 Nigel Turner, *Syntax* (A Grammar of the Greek New Testament 3; T & T Clark, 1963), 266–267; Daniel B. Wallace, *Greek Grammar Beyond the Basics* (Zondervan, 1996), 369.
222 Cf. Cranfield, *Romans*, 1:416 n. 1; Moo, *Romans*, 517 n. 48. Contra Schreiner (*Romans*, 437), who mistakenly asserts that, "δόξης...modifies not ἐλευθερίαν...but τέκνων," as "glory received by the children of God." The true relationship is exactly the opposite, as genitive words (including their attendant articles) almost always modify the word preceding them, unless context makes it crystal clear. Thus, in Rom 8:21, θεοῦ modifies τέκνων (God's children), τέκνων modifies δόξης (children's glory), and so on.
223 Fitzmyer, *Romans*, 509.
224 Gibbs, *Creation and Redemption*, 37; Morris, *Romans*, 322.
225 Byrne, '*Sons of God*', 107; Moo, *Romans*, 517 n. 48. Byrne paraphrases the Greek as "freedom associated with the glory," which communicates a genitive of sphere.
226 Cranfield, *Romans*, 1:416.
227 Ibid., 414–415. The text critical problem (διότι or ὅτι) does not change the meaning. The internal problems (dropping the δι based on the end of ἐλπίδι or adding it for the same reason) balance each other, but the manuscript evidence weighs on the side of ὅτι (P46 A B C D2 Ψ 0289 33 1739 1881 for and a D* F G 945 pc against) Thus, ὅτι is more likely to be the original, even if, per Cranfield, διότι is the more difficult reading (which is less relevant due to the internal issues). Cf. Bruce Metzger, *A Textual Commentary on the Greek New Testament* (2nd ed.; German Bible Societies, 1994), 456.

which comes from decay and to free it for the freedom which comes from the glory of God's children. There remain two questions in understanding this portion of the hope. First, to what does φθορᾶς refer? Second, what does Paul mean by ἐλευθερίαν τῆς δόξης? The first question comes down to two positions, namely a moral sense or a physical sense. The term can refer to an ethical concept (Col 2:22),[228] yet the context of Rom 8:21 points in a different direction. Just as Rom 8:20 refers to the curse in Genesis 3, so does 8:21 draw on the same image. The result of sin for Adam was not just moral decay, rather God cursed mankind with death exactly as he promised.[229] Byrne goes so far as to state, "the δουλείας τῆς φθορᾶς appears to define the ματαιότητι...ὑπετάγη of the previous verse."[230] In addition, the sons of God attain redemption for their σῶμα (Rom 8:23),[231] a purely physical connection. Thus, this φθορά, alludes to physical decay, which is death.[232] If Romans were written to a strictly Greek audience instead of a Roman one, the Platonic connection would be to understand Paul as arguing against the goodness of the physical.[233] Since this was intended for those in Rome, however, the same mindset does not apply, and therefore Paul does not argue for or have to argue for the positive nature of the physical. Romans wanted to live longer, and this was part of their religious sacrifices and requests from their gods and a reason for participating in mystery cults.[234] Either way, Paul upholds the positive aspect of physicality in 8:23 (see below).

The second question, regarding the significance of ἐλευθερίαν τῆς δόξης, follows the same line of thought. Freedom for creation would not be destruction/annihilation, for that would stretch the concept of freedom beyond what one would reasonably expect as its significance. Moo rightly argues for a transformational understanding of this freedom, a freedom from physical problems.[235] He believes the NT points in this direction in general (cf. Rev 21:1–22:7). This freedom retains a future orientation, as does the redemption of the bodies of the sons of God (8:23).[236] Paul does not focus on the freedom (even though he repeats the verb with a noun), rather the focus returns to glo-

---

228 Morris (*Romans*, 322) notes this connection before disagreeing with it. Cf. Günther Harder, "φθείρω, κτλ.," *TDNT* 9:93–106.

229 Gordon Wenham (*Genesis* [WBC 1–2; Word, 1987–1994], 1:82–83) notes that even though the lexeme for death is not used in the curse, it is assumed in both 3:17 (days of your life) and 3:19 (to dust you will return).

230 Byrne, '*Sons of God*', 107. Cf. Schreiner, *Romans*, 436.

231 Dunn, *Romans*, 1:472.

232 E.g. Cranfield, *Romans*, 1:415; Schreiner, *Romans*, 436. Pace Dunn, *Romans*, 1:472.

233 Cf. Dunn, *Romans*, 1:472.

234 Beard et. al., *Religions of Rome*, 290. Cf. Burkert, *Ancient Mystery Cults*, 27.

235 Moo, *Romans*, 517.

236 Fitzmyer, *Romans*, 509; Gibbs, *Creation and Redemption*, 37; Moo, *Romans*, 517.

ry (cf. 8:17–18).[237] The glory of creation derives from the glory of the children of God. Glory comes from God and to his children, and in this glory, creation finds its freedom. Freedom is experiencing the glory which comes from God, both for creation and for mankind.[238]

For the inhabitant of Rome, glory would be tied to victory, not to freedom. The conquering generals of Roman history typically had a special entrance into Rome surrounded by the cheering masses celebrating the victory on behalf of the Roman state.[239] Glory was found in one's own accomplishment, not the accomplishment of others or even one's family (note Domitian manufacturing a victory to give himself the title "Germanicus" to have a military honor equivalent to those that his brother and father had earned[240]). Paul, however, is not speaking of this kind of glory.

What glory does God give his children? The glory will be a future occurrence for creation, but is the attainment of glory completely future? Romans 8:17–18 begins the discussion concerning the glory God gives to his heirs. Paul gives one condition for receiving glory, namely that εἴπερ συμπάσχομεν. Dunn links this suffering directly with sonship based upon the Jewish background (citing Prov 3:12; Tob 13:4–5; Wis 3–5; among others).[241] Paul does not connect suffering and sonship per se, Paul puts together suffering and inheritance. The heir does not suffer alone, however, as made manifest by the συν-prefix.[242] While no pronoun is present in the text in order to provide a clear indication with whom the heir suffers, Χριστοῦ modifies the previous συν–word (συγκληρονόμοι), so it makes sense that an elided αὐτῷ would point to him.[243] How does the εἴπερ function here? Cranfield believes it introduces an ongoing condition currently being experienced by believers that is directly related to being followers of Christ in this world, suffering is an intrinsic part of faithfulness.[244] Paul's argument, however, does not allow for εἴπερ to introduce a

---

237 Cranfield, *Romans*, 1:416; Moo, *Romans*, 517, Schreiner, *Romans*, 437.

238 Dunn, *Romans*, 1:472; Jewett, *Romans*, 515. Jewett argues that true freedom for humanity includes a new creation within which humans would function as intended at creation, such that Eden is restored. Cf. Moo, *Romans*, 517.

239 Cf. the cynical comments in Suetonius, *Nero*, 25.2, when Nero enters in this way after participating in the Greek games.

240 Suetonius, *Dom.*, 13.3.

241 Dunn, *Romans*, 1:456.

242 Morris (*Romans*, 318 n. 75) states that Paul "is not talking about a religion of solitude" due to the proliferation of the prefix throughout these few verses.

243 See the argument in Arland J. Hultgren, "Suffering Together with Christ: A Study of Romans 8:17," in *God, Evil, and Suffering: Essays in Honor of Paul R. Sponheim* (ed. Terence E. Fretheim and Curtis L. Thompson; Word and World Supplement Series 4; Luther Seminary, 2000), 120–126.

244 Cranfield, *Romans*, 1:407–408; Peter Siber, *Mit Christus leben. Eine Studie zur paulinischen Auferstehungshoffnung* (ATANT 61; Theologischer Verlag, 1971), 139–140.

present state, the entire concept is focused on a specific result per the ἵνα clause.²⁴⁵ The result is glorification, the entire aim of becoming sons of God. Glorification does not arise through a past experience of suffering. The participation does not refer to baptism, as this subject does not naturally arise in Paul's comments here since he does not utilize the imagery of death with Christ.²⁴⁶ In addition, God will conform believers to the image of Christ (8:29), and God will use suffering as an agent for this.²⁴⁷ Dunn summarizes Paul's thoughts by connecting the beginning of the new era with the death and resurrection of Christ, an era wherein believers are free from sin but still suffer in the body until the time of redemption (cf. 8:23).²⁴⁸ The verb (συμπάσχομεν) gives the condition to be met before glorification can occur.²⁴⁹ Glorification is not conditional itself, rather anyone who will be glorified will also suffer in some sense. This last part (from the εἴπερ on) is hortatory, directed toward the Roman recipients.²⁵⁰ The use of ἵνα plus the subjunctive (συνδοξασθῶμεν) lends itself toward a future concept here (even though the verb is aorist tense, signifying perfective aspect), such that God glorifies believers strictly in the future. Once again, Paul overturns the expectations of his readers in rejecting a life of glory now and embracing suffering whereas Roman religion pointed in the exact opposite direction.

Paul continues the connection between glory and suffering in the next verse (8:18).²⁵¹ Paul explicitly states that suffering happens now, in the present, for his readers. The phrase τοῦ νῦν καιροῦ has occurred previously in Romans, appearing prominently in 3:26.²⁵² The words arise within a prepositional phrase in 3:26 and 11:5, ἐν τῷ νῦν καιρῷ. Cranfield describes the phrase as giving a specific, limited time period in which certain theological events occur.²⁵³ The age lasts from the resurrection (or ascension) until the return of Christ. Cranfield believes that 3:26 refers to the beginning of the period, 11:5 to events in the midst of the period, and 8:18 to the end of the period of time.²⁵⁴ In other

---

245 Moo, *Romans*, 506; Schreiner, *Romans*, 428. Contra Cranfield, *Romans*, 1:407–408; Siber, *Mit Christus leben*, 140–141.
246 Dunn, *Romans*, 1:456; Moo, *Romans*, 505–506.
247 See the discussion below in 3.4.
248 Dunn, *Romans*, 1:456. Cf. Moo, *Romans*, 505; Schreiner, *Romans*, 428.
249 Dunn, *Romans*, 1:456, where he states, "suffering with Christ is not an optional extra… Without it future glory would not be attained."
250 Käsemann, *Romans*, 229; Schreiner, *Romans*, 428.
251 See Longenecker, *Romans*, 717–718. He sees 8:18 as starting a new section and as the thesis statement of 8:18–30, yet also notes the postpositive indicates a "continuation of thought" from 8:17 (718).
252 Dunn, *Romans*, 468. Moo (*Romans*, 512 n. 18) points to Rom 11:5; 1 Cor 7:29; 2 Cor 6:2.
253 Cranfield, *Romans*, 1:212–213 n. 2. Cf. Moo, *Romans*, 512 n. 18.
254 Dunn (*Romans*, 1:468) considers the time period about the same, but he does not place 8:18 in any specific spot during the era.

words, the suffering refers not to the exact moment the recipients receive the letter, rather Paul draws in the "sufferings characteristic of this age."[255] Glory does not come because of suffering, rather through suffering one is able to be glorified. The concepts of glorification and suffering are tied very closely together, yet unlike John, Paul does not equate suffering with glorification.[256] While some argue that Paul consoles his readers by letting them know how present suffering does not remove or replace future glory,[257] this would not be how Paul's audience understood this passage. Based upon the Greco-Roman theological understanding of salvation being a present expectation rather than a future one,[258] Paul lets his readers know that the present should not be the goal, rather the future is. By utilizing adoption as a metaphor, including inheritance language, and downplaying present suffering, Paul informs his readers that God will not remove suffering based upon how they live, instead God will give future glory based upon their perseverance in the midst of their suffering.[259] The glory here must be entirely future, as Paul calls it μέλλουσαν and ἀποκαλυφθῆναι, both pointing toward the future.

This builds toward an understanding that the glory Paul speaks of lays only in the future. The problem with such an understanding, however, occurs with Paul calling the Spirit ἀπαρχήν in 8:23.[260] The term can hardly mean anything beyond first fruits with respect to harvest and sacrifice imagery, especially considering the use in the LXX.[261] Murray believes that πνεύματος functions as a partitive genitive in relation to ἀπαρχήν, such that God bestows part of the Spirit as a first fruit to the believer.[262] Some commentators object to such an understanding based upon the idea that having only a portion of the Holy Spirit seems or feels objectionable.[263] The problem should be resolved by context, as Paul has stated previously that believers are ἐν πνεύματι and

---

255 Morris, *Romans*, 319. Cf. Charles B. Cousar, "Continuity and Discontinuity in Romans 5–8 (In Conversation with Frank Thielman)," in *Pauline Theology Volume III: Romans* (ed. David M. Hay and E. Elizabeth Johnson; SBL, 2002), 196–210, here 201. He says Christians are "in a vulnerable spot, subject to the hostility of an unredeemed world."
256 E.g., D. A. Carson, *The Gospel According to John* (PNTC; Eerdmans, 1991), 96. Carson says, "the Son of Man is 'lifted up' in death, glorified through death."
257 Andrzej Gieniusz, *Romans 8:18-30: "Suffering Does Not Thwart the Future Glory"* (ISFCJ; Scholars Press, 1999), especially 130.
258 E.g. Turcan, "Salut mithriaque et sotériologie noplatoncienne," 173–174.
259 Crandfield, *Romans*, 1:410; Moo, *Romans*, 511; Schreiner, *Romans*, 434.
260 Contra Murray, *Romans*, 306–307.
261 E.g. Lev 23:10; Num 15:20–21; 18:30, 32; Neh 10:37. Cf. Gerhard Delling, "ἀπαρχήν," *TDNT* 1:484–486; C. Spicq, "ἀπαρχήν," *TLNT* 1:145–152.
262 Murray, *Romans*, 307 n. 38; Sanday and Headlam, *Romans*, 209. Cf. Delling, *TDNT* 1:486.
263 E.g. Käsemann, *Romans*, 237.

the Spirit should οἰκεῖ ἐν ὑμῖν ("dwell in you," 8:9).[264] Believers do not receive a portion of the Spirit, for in some sense this also makes the Spirit measurable, rather the first fruits are the Spirit, understanding the genitive as epexegetical.[265] First fruits, by the very name, refers to the first portion given, often in expectation of more to come (though not necessarily more given, especially in sacrificial contexts). The question the text raises points toward the context of the first fruits. The Spirit is the content, but of what does the later fruit consist? In context, the only logical answer is glory. Paul argues from inheritance/being an heir to glory (8:17). He then contrasts the worth of suffering and glory, pointing toward suffering as temporally limited and glory as a future reality (8:18). He next discusses how creation itself awaits the fullness of the glory of God's sons (8:19–23). The fullness occurs through the redemption of the sons' bodies (8:23). Glory, therefore, has a future aspect due to the redemption of the physical, yet the mention of first fruits gives a present aspect, an aspect fulfilled by the Spirit.[266] Glorification has a present activity in believers through the Spirit. One of God's goals for adoption is the recreation of creation (including humanity),[267] and God uses the inheritance of glory as the means by which recreation occurs.

Creation was not an emphasis in Roman religion, rather the focus was upon the state and how the individual fit within the state and the state religion.[268] Life and death mattered, but the creation of everything was not significant. At the same time, family connections and inheritance were very important matters.[269] Paul would not have aroused interest in creation by speaking of the act of creation, instead he alludes only to the curse in Genesis 3 and draws out the importance of the implications. This would impress Roman readers since Roman religion was about avoiding the wrath (or curse) of the gods,[270] and so Paul spoke of how to do so. Paul used the metaphor of adoption, one which would be readily recognizable to the recipients of the epistle. While Roman adoption was about continuity (whether a family line, political power, or worshipping family gods), Paul posits adoption by God as

---

264 Dunn (*Romans*, 1:473) also points to 8:11, 15.
265 For the best explanation, see Moo, *Romans*, 520. Cf. Cranfield, *Romans*, 1:418; Käsemann, *Romans*, 237; Schreiner, *Romans*, 438.
266 For how the Spirit achieves this, see 4.3 below.
267 See 3.4, 4.3, and 4.4.
268 John Ferguson (*The Religions of the Roman Empire* [Aspects of Greek and Roman Life; Thames and Hudson, 1970], 13) notes the concentration of early Italy in the period before Rome rose to prominence on fertility and the female divine. The only creation that mattered to them was birth.
269 Cf. Scott, *Adoption*, 5–7.
270 Ferguson, *Religions*, 156–157.

a new thing, leading to the redemption of bodies. In Romans 8, this belongs within the realm of how God saves.

3.4 GOD AND SALVATION

The two main descriptions for salvation within Romans 8 are adoption and recreation. Salvation in the Greco–Roman world focuses on the physical realm. The Romans did not think of their souls in terms of needing salvation, rather they thought of their lives. Salvation was not an other–worldly issue, it was a temporal and constant need. When Paul wrote to the Romans, he held this in mind as he crafted the discrepancy between suffering and glory. Salvation for a Roman was to escape suffering,[271] but Paul declared that the only way to salvation is through suffering. Thus, Paul has to explain salvation as something other than freedom from pain, and so he first writes concerning from what believers are saved.

Romans 8 begins with a well-known phrase, οὐδὲν ἄρα νῦν. This resumes the line of thought Paul left in 7:6 in order to clarify the problem in 7:7–25.[272] The resumption can be seen by Paul's use of νῦν, picking up on the word in 7:6.[273] Paul gives the solution offered in 7:6 fuller exposition in 8:2–8.[274] The ἄρα draws on the previous statements of 7:1–6.[275] Condemnation (κατάκριμα) alludes to the discussion of being under the law (7:7–25) and a sinner like Adam (5:13, 16, 18). Condemnation and death are tied together closely due to both coming from sin.[276] At the same time, sin and death border on synonymy due to their usage in 8:2 (νόμου τῆς ἁμαρτίας καὶ τοῦ θανάτου).[277] If condemnation is tied together with death, and Paul connects death with sin directly in Rom 8:2, then by extension Paul relates condemnation directly to sin in Romans 8.[278] How can Paul state that condemnation no longer holds for τοῖς ἐν Χριστῷ Ἰησοῦ? Lowe narrows the options down to two, the "substitutionary atonement of Christ" or else "the death and resurrection of sinners in union

---

271 E.g. Burkert, *Ancient Mystery Cults*, 27.
272 See 3.1. Cf. Bendemann, "Diatase," 45.
273 See 3.1. This does not mean there is no connection to the immediate context, only that Paul resumes the argument of 7:6 while also taking 7:24–25 into consideration as well. Cf. Wilckens, *Römer*, 118–119.
274 Lambrecht, *The Wretched 'I'*, 33–34. Lambrecht considers 8:1 part of 7:7–25, though he offers no reason other than saying Paul does not pick up 7:6 in full until 8:2.
275 Cranfield, *Romans*, 1:373; Schreiner, *Romans*, 398; Wilckens, *Römer*, 2:118.
276 Chuck Lowe, "'There Is No Condemnation' (Romans 8:1): But Why Not?" *JETS* 42 (1999): 231–250; Moo, *Romans*, 473.
277 Cranfield, *Romans*, 1:376; Moo, *Romans*, 476. Cranfield states, "the ultimate end of sin's lordship is over us in death."
278 Lowe, "But Why Not?" 234–235.

with Christ."²⁷⁹ The use of "substitutionary," however, does not fit the context (though "atonement" does), as Paul does not speak of Christ's death in place of others, rather Paul argues that there is no longer condemnation based upon the sending of Christ to his death and the gift of the Spirit.

The death of Christ is not highlighted in this chapter by Paul, yet much of his discussion of sin and the law depends upon his understanding of it. Earliest Christianity certainly understood the impact of Jesus' death theologically, as it became the central focus for understanding God's plan for the fledgling faith.²⁸⁰ Paul in turn places the death of Christ near the center of the theology of Romans,²⁸¹ most notably in 3:21–26 and chapter 5 (explicitly in 6, 8–10, implicitly throughout), explaining that his death opens the way for reconciliation after the sin of Adam. Romans 5–8 assumes the efficacious nature of Jesus' death in that Paul builds upon this while explicating why his death enables salvation.²⁸² The blood of Christ (e.g. Rom 3:25) points directly to the nature of Jesus' death, namely a sacrificial death.²⁸³ Christ died to save those who were apart from God (5:6, 8, 15). For Paul in Romans, this death opens the way for the work of the Holy Spirit and the final declaration of the vindicated as sons of God (see 3.3.1 and 4.2.1). Thus, in Romans 8, Jesus' death is an understood and unstated (though cf. 8:34) part of the argument.

How does God overcome the condemnation set for humanity? He does so by instead condemning sin itself. Paul elaborates on this by saying how sin was condemned: ὁ θεὸς τὸν ἑαυτοῦ υἱὸν πέμψας ἐν ὁμοιώματι σαρκὸς ἁμαρτίας ("the God who sent his own son in the likeness of sinful flesh"). Paul does not say the actual sending accomplished this, rather the contents of Rom 8:3–4 as a whole does, per the explanatory γάρ.²⁸⁴ The law could not accomplish a lack of condemnation on its own, since it in fact highlights sin (7:7).²⁸⁵ Though

---

279 Lowe, "But Why Not?" 236. Lowe here follows Murray, *Romans*, 274–277. Cf. Longenecker's discussion of "in Christ" (*Romans*, 686–694).

280 Cf. Joel B. Green, *The Death of Jesus: Tradition and Interpretation in the Passion Narrative* (WUNT II/33; Mohr–Siebeck, 1988), 321–322.

281 Cf. Thomas Söding, "Sühne durch Stellvertretung: Zur zentralen Deutung des Todes Jesu im Römerbrief," in *Deutungen des Todes Jesu im Neuen Testament* (ed. Jörg Frey and Jens Schröter; WUNT I/181; Mohr Siebeck, 2005), 375–396. Söding's main contention is to show the centrality of Jesus' death for Paul's theology in Romans, not necessarily Paul's arguments.

282 Kenneth Grayston, *Dying, We Live: A New Inquiry into the Death of Christ in the New Testament* (Oxford University Press, 1990), 98.

283 Dunn, *Romans*, 1:170; Haacker, *Römer*, 92. For the type and significance of the sacrifice, see Dunn, *Romans*, 1:170–172.

284 Schreiner, *Romans*, 401.

285 Dunn, *Romans*, 1:419–420; Moo, *Romans*, 477; Schreiner, *Romans*, 401. N. T. Wright (*The Climax of the Covenant* [Fortress, 1993], 202) wants to turn this around by saying that the problem with the law was that it could not give life. While true, Paul goes beyond such a statement.

the phrase τὸ γὰρ ἀδύνατον τοῦ νόμου ἐν ᾧ ἠσθένει διὰ τῆς σαρκός remains notoriously difficult to translate,[286] the significance lies in the interplay of the law's[287] inability to solve the problem of sin due to the flesh.[288] In sending his son, God enacts a plan different from the law in order to condemn sin.

What is significant about this sending?[289] Though the sending motif arises in many different contexts throughout the NT, the consideration of Paul utilizing traditional material rather than his own does not help to clarify why Paul spoke of God sending Jesus.[290] In coming, Jesus then is κατέκρινεν τὴν ἁμαρτίαν ἐν τῇ σαρκί ("condemning sin in the flesh"). Though within the context of Paul utilizing the noun κατάκριμα earlier, not all commentators believe he wants to indicate the same nuance with the verbal form throughout the sentence. Moo believes Paul indicates that the law was unable to break the power of the flesh as it was not designed to condemn sin.[291] However, this would break the contrast Paul builds between the work of God in sending Christ and the inability of the law. Schreiner rightly notes that one should not remove the forensic sense of κατέκρινεν in understanding the import of God sending his son.[292] Does this mean the incarnation or only a sacrificial aspect is in view when Paul employs πέμψας? In a partial answer to the question, at least some aspect of sacrificial language is in view due to the cultic tones of the rest of the passage.[293] The law occurs in both 8:3 and 8:4, while the phrase περὶ ἁμαρτίας carries cultic overtones by itself. F. F. Bruce notes that the LXX uses περὶ ἁμαρτίας for translating "sin offering" throughout the OT.[294] In fact the phrase is used 17 times in Leviticus and 32 in Numbers for the sin offering (among other books within the OT).[295] Though some have offered other interpretations, nothing in the context militates against a sacrificial understand-

---

286 Cf. J. F. Bayes, "The Translation of Romans 8:3," *ExpTim* 111 (1999): 14–16. My best attempt would be "for the law by itself weakened through the flesh was unable."

287 Though disputed, this most likely refers to the OT law. See Brice L. Martin, *Christ and the Law in Paul* (NovTSup 62; Brill, 1989), 29–30 and 4.1 below.

288 Dunn, *Romans*, 1:419–420, 437; Moo, *Romans*, 477–478; Schreiner, *Romans*, 401.

289 Longenecker's contention (*Romans*, 695) that this comes from an early Christian confession has little contextual explanatory power and remains unconvincing.

290 Cf. Eduard Schweizer, "Zum religionsgeshichtlichen Hintergrund der 'Sendungsformel' Gal 4,4f. Rm 8,3f. Joh 3,16f. I Joh 4,9," *ZNW* 57 (1966): 199–210. In turn, this idea has been defended by Käsemann, *Romans*, 216–218; M. Dwaine Greene, "A Note on Romans 8:3," *BZ* 35 (1991): 103–106; and Jewett, *Romans*, 483. See below as 4.2.2 will discuss the significance of sending and what it implies with respect to Jesus.

291 Moo, *Romans*, 478.

292 Schreiner, *Romans*, 402.

293 Moo, *Romans*, 478–479.

294 F. F. Bruce, *Romans* (rev. ed.; TNTC 6; Eerdmans, 1985), 152. Cf. Käsemann, *Romans*, 216; Schreiner, *Romans*, 403; Wilckens, *Römer*, 2:127.

295 The phrase occurs in the following verses, all referring to sin offerings: Lev 5:6–7, 11; 7:37; 9:2–3; 12:6, 8; 14:13, 22, 31; 15:15, 30; 16:3, 5, 9; 23:19; Num 6:11, 16; 7:16, 22, 28, 34, 40, 46, 52, 58,

ing. How does this display the condemnation of sin in the flesh? Some look to the defeat of sin through the incarnation alone, some see it as part of Jesus' sinless life,[296] but the most likely response ties into the sacrificial overtones of the passage.[297] Jesus' death appears later in the passage (8:11), so Paul does have it in mind, especially in relation to life. The incarnation, however, does come into view when Paul states Jesus came ἐν ὁμοιώματι σαρκὸς ἁμαρτίας. What Paul signifies by describing Jesus being in this flesh is irrelevant for this discussion,[298] what matters is Jesus had to be in the flesh in order for God to condemn sin.

In sending Jesus, God provided a sin offering (περὶ ἁμαρτίας) so that the Spirit would be able to fulfill the law (8:4). Paul argues that God sent the son and handed him over for the sake of the believers (8:32). Jesus is mentioned as God's son only three times in this passage (8:3, 29, 32). Each time the title is used in relation to salvation. With 8:3, Paul begins describing how God condemned sin in the flesh by sending Jesus. In 8:29, the focus remains on God as he conforms believers to the image of Christ, a part of the process of salvation. In 8:32, Paul draws on the imagery of Gen 22:12, the binding of Isaac, as an image for the God's sacrifice in sending his only son. Paul stresses whose son Jesus is through emphatic pronouns in both 8:3 (ἑαυτοῦ) and 8:32 (ἰδίου).[299] The difference between the two modifiers likely comes from the positioning of the two statements in relation to Paul's overall argument. The first pronoun would be the expected one, as Paul stresses whose son this is.[300] However, in 8:32, there are two other considerations at work. First, as seen in Figure 3.1, Paul draws on the story of Isaac by making a strong verbal allusion to Gen 22:12 (22:16 uses the same wording):

Genesis 22:12 (LXX)	Romans 8:32
καὶ εἶπεν μὴ ἐπιβάλῃς τὴν χεῖρά σου ἐπὶ τὸ <u>παιδάριον</u> μηδὲ ποιήσῃς αὐτῷ μηδέν νῦν γὰρ ἔγνων ὅτι φοβῇ τὸν θεὸν σὺ καὶ οὐκ <u>ἐφείσω</u> τοῦ <u>υἱοῦ</u> σου τοῦ <u>ἀγαπητοῦ</u> δι'ἐμέ	ὅς γε τοῦ <u>ἰδίου υἱοῦ</u> οὐκ <u>ἐφείσατο</u> ἀλλὰ ὑπὲρ ἡμῶν πάντων παρέδωκεν αὐτόν, πῶς οὐχὶ καὶ σὺν αὐτῷ τὰ πάντα ἡμῖν χαρίσεται;

Figure 3.1: Verbal Allusions between Genesis 22:12 LXX and Romans 8:32. Various types of underline indicate corresponding lexemes or concepts.

64, 70, 76, 82, 87; 8:8, 12; 15:24, 27; 28:15, 22, 30; 29:5, 11, 16, 19, 22, 25, 28, 31, 34, 38; 2 Kgs 12:16; 2 Chr 29:21, 23-24; Ezra 6:17; 8:35; Neh 10:33; Job 1:5; Ps 40:6; Isa 53:10; Ezek 42:13; 43:19, 21.

    296 Godet, *Romans*, 300.
    297 Moo, *Romans*, 480–481.
    298 See 4.3.2.
    299 Moo (*Romans*, 479 n. 41) and Cranfield (*Romans*, 1:379) point out the connection but do nothing with it.
    300 Cranfield (*Romans*, 1:379) calls the usage "emphatic." Cf. Dunn, *Romans*, 1:420–421.

Some form of ἐφείσω (from θείδομαι, "I spare") occurs in both along with υἱοῦ σου τοῦ ἀγαπητοῦ (Gen 22:12) or τοῦ ἰδίου υἱοῦ (Rom 8:32). Paul likely changes the ἀγαπητοῦ to ἰδίου for 8:32 due to his argument earlier depending upon God's many sons. Thus, Paul highlights in Rom 8:32 not the son God loves, since he loves all of them (cf. 8:39), rather he highlights God's unique son.[301] In both 8:3 and in 8:32 God acts through or by means of the son. In 8:3, God sends the son, whereas in 8:32, God hands over (παραδέδωμι) his son. Acting through the son begins the process (8:33–34 details how God justifies through the death of his son), but condemnation does not disappear yet. Only through the Spirit can condemnation be set aside.[302] Life in the Spirit gives the believer the ability to meet the righteous requirement of the law.

Through the sacrificial sending of the son (8:3 linked with 8:32), God gave the Spirit to believers. The believers are described in Rom 8:4 as τοῖς μὴ κατὰ σάρκα περιπατοῦσιν ἀλλὰ κατὰ πνεῦμα ("those who do not walk according to the flesh but according to the Spirit"). Typically, forms of περιπατέω function as euphemisms for conduct in living, and so it functions here.[303] Thus, believers live according to the Spirit as opposed to according to the flesh. The entire phrase modifies or further describes ἐν ἡμῖν, as the τοῖς agrees in number and case. The function of ἵνα is certainly purpose,[304] but to what should it be attached? Moo condones the position that ἵνα explains the purpose of God condemning sin in the flesh.[305] Cranfield believes it describes the purpose both for the condemnation of sin and for which God set believers free.[306] Dunn and Schreiner both connect the ἵνα clause with the sending of Jesus based upon Paul's line of thought.[307] While there is close proximity between ἵνα and κατέκρινεν, Paul's argument does not develop such that the gift of the Spirit comes about because of the condemnation of sin, or even that the purpose of the condemnation of sin was life in the Spirit as an end in itself,[308] rather Paul argues the opposite. Dunn rightly notes that the fulfillment of the law and life in the Spirit function as nominal synonyms here, such that Paul connects Jesus' coming with how the law is fulfilled (due to his death being in

---

301 Cf. Nils Alstrup Dahl "The Atonement-An Adequate Reward for the Aqedah? (Ro 8:32)" in *Neotestamentica et Semitica: Studies in Honor of Matthew Black* (ed. E. Earle Ellis and Max Wilcox; T&T Clark, 1969), 15–29, here 17.

302 Fee, *God's Empowering Presence*, 530; Käsemann, *Romans*, 216; Schreiner, *Romans*, 407.

303 Cranfield, *Romans*, 1:385; Fitzmyer, *Romans*, 488; Schreiner, *Romans*, 405–406.

304 The position of many scholars, e.g. Cranfield, *Romans*, 1:383; Dunn, *Romans*, 1:423; Schreiner, *Romans*, 404.

305 Moo, *Romans*, 481.

306 Cranfield, *Romans*, 1:383.

307 Dunn, *Romans*, 1:423; Schreiner, *Romans*, 404.

308 Wilckens, *Römer*, 2:128.

view in his coming in 8:2), not the condemnation of sin with the fulfillment of the law.[309] Thus, ἵνα connects to God sending his son, and the purpose of the sending is to enable believers to have the law fulfilled by God[310] through the Spirit (cf. 7:6).

The Spirit also consummates the adoption of the children of God, which in turn enables the renewal of creation, both subhuman and human. God gives the Spirit to those who are his children. The Spirit in turn leads those who are God's children (8:14). Godet's assertion that this leading (ἄγονται) must refer to some sort of force against the human will by the Holy Spirit[311] is exegetically unsupportable.[312] Rather, God's Spirit gives guidance to those who are children of God, thus giving evidence for their status.[313] The Spirit enables them to decree their status through their speech, calling upon God as father.[314] In turn, this status leads to glorification, and part of glorification lies in the redemption of their material bodies, all a result of the work of the Spirit.[315] Creation itself takes part in the renewal, as God recreates to overthrow the curse. The recreation and the redemption of the bodies of the sons of God are tied closely together both to the work of Christ and to the work of the Spirit.[316] All of this, God sending Jesus and utilizing the Spirit, are aimed at defeating sin in the flesh.

God overcomes the condemnation of all creation, human and subhuman, through a twofold action. First, he sent his son. Second, he gives the Spirit to his children. These two actions have lasting effects, both for believers and for creation. In terms of believers, it opens the way for adoption, such that God becomes their father in the adoptive process. In being adopted children of God, and one day attaining the title sons of God, they enjoy the rights of inheritance with Christ. This balances a present status with a future reality.[317] Glory represents a portion of the future for believers, and it also contains a portion of the present reality as well. Salvation constitutes both a present status as children of God along with the eschatological title of sons of God and

---

309 Dunn, *Romans*, 1:423.

310 The passive πληρωθῇ is a divine passive. Cf. Byrne, *Romans*, 237; Fitzmyer, *Romans*, 487; Schreiner, *Romans*, 405.

311 Godet, *Romans*, 309. Cf. Käsemann, *Romans*, 226; Dunn, *Romans*, 1:450. The idea of "driving" is not present in the verb nor is there any support for such an understanding in Greek literature. Dunn's position is untenable.

312 Fee, *God's Empowering Presence*, 563. Cf. Schreiner, *Romans*, 422.

313 Byrne, *Romans*, 249–250; Moo, *Romans*, 499; Schreiner, *Romans*, 422–423.

314 See 3.3.1.

315 Fee, *God's Empowering Presence*, 573–574.

316 Gibbs, *Creation and Redemption*, 37. Gibbs' argument continues into other portions of Romans as well.

317 Wilckens, *Römer*, 2:139–142.

final justification (note that in 8:33 θεὸς ὁ δικαιῶν is in response to ἐγκαλέσει, a future tense verb). Paul demonstrates God's activity throughout by displaying God working by means of his two agents: Jesus and the Holy Spirit. The Roman recipients of the letter would have understood God acting through proxies just as Jupiter often used others for his will to be carried out, such as Mercury, the Roman legions, or even circumstances in life.

3.5 SUMMARY

After discussing the context of Romans 8 with respect to the literary, lexical, rhetorical, and theological connections to the rest of the book, this chapter focused on God and his relationship with humanity. The first section discussed how God relates to and connects with creation. As the Roman mind did not consider the creation of the world to be a matter of import, Paul's discussion focused briefly on the distinction between creator and creation, and then he pivoted to how humans fit within and relate to the creatd order. Since sin mars all of creation, Paul also speaks of how creation can be relieved of the pain it is in due to this curse. It is only through God as *paterfamilias* adopting sons and revealing them in glory that creation can be renewed and recreated. Adoption and the revelation of this glory come about through the future aspect of salvation, something which runs opposite normal Roman religious tendencies. Time and again Paul uses Roman practices, both religious and political, to make his argument clear. The discussion will now turn to focus on God's two agents: Jesus and the Holy Spirit.

Chapter 4

God and the Son and the Spirit

Paul focuses on God the Father[1] as the one who determines the actions in Romans 8, yet God acts through his agents in giving salvation. His agents are Jesus his Son[2] and the Holy Spirit. The Son and Spirit both accomplish many different functions for God in Romans 8, most linked with salvation. This chapter will describe how the Son and Spirit interact with sin, recreation, salvation, each other, and God. First, this chapter will discuss the role of the Son and Spirit in dealing with sin, including their relationship to the law (cf. 8:1-4).[3] Second, the topic of recreation will come to the fore.[4] Third, and as a summary of the previous two sections, the relationship of the Son and Spirit to salvation will be explained as it is presented in Romans 8.[5] Fourth, this chapter will analyze the overlapping functions of the Son and Spirit.[6] Finally, this chapter will draw together the relationship between the Son and Spirit and God. This chapter incorporates the exegesis in Chapter 3 and will integrate the conclusions of Chapter 2. The focus will be on the actions of God through the Son and Spirit with respect to how the Roman pagan mindset would have understood them, and thus Jewish parallels (whether in the OT or from other literature) will not be fully investigated.

---

1 "Father" here is titular due to the special role Paul gives to God as father of both his own son and of his adopted sons.
2 As established above in 3.4, Jesus is God's only "natural" (non-adopted) son, and therefore "Son" becomes a significant title for him in Romans 8.
3 Brice L. Martin, *Christ and the Law in Paul* (NovTSup 62; Brill, 1989), 29.
4 Cf. John G. Gibbs, *Creation and Redemption: A Study in Pauline Theology* (NovTSup; Brill, 1971), 47.
5 Gibbs, *Creation and Redemption*, 47.
6 E.g. Paul's use of ἐντυγχάνω for both.

4.1 Son, Spirit, and Sin

Romans 7 and 8 are linked by the problem of sin, specifically how the law relates to sin (see 3.2). Bendemann summarizes Romans 7 as "Sünde, Gesetz und 'Ich' treten in eine *dramatische Interaktion*" ("sin, law, and 'I' combine in a *dramatic interaction*," emphasis original).[7] The link between Romans 7 and 8 lies in Paul's review of the problem of sin and the law along with his preview of the solution contained in Rom 7:6.[8] Sin encompasses a larger significance than just failure to keep the law, yet the law remains a central focus in this section of Romans. Rom 7:6 refers to both the Son (ἀποθανόντες, "having died," as related to ἐθανατώθητε τῷ νόμῳ διὰ τοῦ σώματος τοῦ Χριστοῦ in 7:4) and the Spirit (ἐν καινότητι πνεύματος, "in the new way of the Spirit") in regards to a solution.[9] The lack of condemnation that begins the chapter sets the tone for the conclusion concerning the law in 8:1–11 and the link with sin and flesh.[10] The mention of the law of sin and death (8:2, τοῦ νόμου τῆς ἁμαρτίας καὶ τοῦ θανάτου) brings the problem Paul sees to a point. Mankind always finds death, and the law leads directly to death by way of sin, a pattern reversed in the "solution" summarized by Paul in 7:4–6,[11] which in turn sets the stage for Romans 8.[12] The Son is sent and the Spirit is given, both by God, in order to combat the problem of sin. Paul connects the problem of sin and its solution to the law.

4.1.1 The Law

The New Perspective on Paul has brought about radical ways of rethinking the approach Paul takes to the law. Contemporary scholarship has spilled

---

7 Reinhard von Bendemann, "Die kritische Diastase von Wissen, Wollen und Handeln: Traditionsgeschichtliche Spurensuche eines hellenistischen Topos in Römer 7," *ZNW* 95 (2004): 35–63, here 47.

8 Ernst Käsemann, *Commentary on Romans* (trans. Geoffrey W. Bromiley; Eerdmans, 1980), 190–191. He goes too far in calling this a "baptismal exhortation" but rightly notes that 7:6 (or 7:4–6, he is not clear on this point) "presents something like a summary of the main theme of chs. 7–8" (190). Cf. Richard N. Longenecker, *The Epistle to the Romans: A Commentary on the Greek Text* (NIGTC; Eerdmans, 2016), 637. Longenecker connects the work of the Spirit to the eschatological now, a clear connection to 8 (though he does not make that reference explicit).

9 Romans 7:6 also brings 2:29 to mind. See Ira J. Jolivet Jr., "An Argument from the Letter and Intent of the Law as the Primary Argumentative Strategy in Romans," in *The Rhetorical Analysis of Scripture: Essays from the 1995 London Conference* (ed. Stanley Porter and Thomas H. Olbricht; JSNTSup 146; Sheffield University Press, 1997), 309–335, here 312.

10 Chuck Lowe, "'There Is No Condemnation' (Romans 8:1): But Why Not?," *JETS* 42 (1999): 231–250, here 241–242.

11 Lowe, "But Why Not?," 240.

12 Bruce Morrison and John Woodhouse, "The Coherence of Romans 7:1–8:8," *RTR* 47 (1988): 8–16, here 14–15.

much ink on the subject.[13] The New Perspective essentially sees the law as a boundary marker for religious–ethnic identity or keeping it as a sign of covenantal status.[14] With respect to Romans 8, the key question is concerned with what Paul actually means by the five occurrences of the term νόμος (8:2 [two times], 3, 4, 7). Each usage will be examined in order to discover to what Paul is referring before synthesizing the result and comparing it to the current debate.

The first two uses come together in a parallel construction in 8:2, with Paul having written ὁ γὰρ νόμος τοῦ πνεύματος τῆς ζωῆς ἐν Χριστῷ Ἰησοῦ ἠλευθέρωσέν σε ἀπο τοῦ νόμου τῆς ἁμαρτίας καὶ τοῦ θανάτου ("for the law of the Spirit of life in Christ Jesus sets you free from the law of sin and death"). The νόμος τοῦ πνεύματος τῆς ζωῆς is grammatically balanced by the νόμου τῆς ἁμαρτίας καὶ τοῦ θανάτου, such that one can tell Paul intended an antithesis as evidenced by the genitive modifiers. Life and death are key words throughout Romans,[15] and here Paul emphasizes them in order to make a point. His point, reminiscent of Galatians 3, follows the trajectory of Rom 7:10 in describing the law as a force for death (albeit inadvertently since sin perverts the law). Do both occurrences of νόμος in 8:2 refer to the OT law? Some argue that the first usage must be a metaphor, not referring to the literal law.[16] However, following on the heels of Romans 7 and Paul's discussion of the law, this understanding would contradict the force of Paul's arguments.[17] Paul has already stated

---

13 For the best brief summary that includes the major players in the debate on all sides, see Stephen Westerholm, "The 'New Perspective' at Twenty-Five," in *Justification and Variegated Nomism: Volume 2-The Paradoxes of Paul* (Baker, 2004), 1-38.

14 Admittedly, there are different camps within this view, but this is the definition of "covenantal nomism." Cf. John A. Bertone, *"The Law of the Spirit": Experience of the Spirit and Displacement of the Law in Romans 8:1–16* (Studies in Biblical Literature 86; Peter Lang, 2005), 5–17, 209–69.

15 Outside of Romans 8, see Rom 2:7; 4:17; 5:10, 12, 14, 17–18, 21; 6:3–5, 9–10, 13, 16, 21–23; 7:5–6, 10, 13, 24; 11:3, 15; 16:4. Cf. Brendan Byrne, *'Sons of God'–'Seeds of Abraham': A Study of the Idea of the Sonship of God of All Christians in Paul Against the Jewish Background* (AnBib 93; Biblical Institute, 1979), 88.

16 E.g. Brendan Byrne, *Romans* (Sacra Pagina 6; Liturgical Press, 1996), 242; C. E. B. Cranfield, *Romans* (2 vols.; ICC; T&T Clark, 1975, repr., T&T Clark, 2003) 1:375–376; Joseph A. Fitzmyer, *Romans: A New Translation with Introduction and Commentary* (AB 33; Doubleday, 1993), 483; Gordon Fee, *God's Empowering Presence: The Holy Spirit in the Letters of Paul* (Hendrickson, 1992), 522; Longenecker, *Romans*, 685; Frank Thielman, *Paul and the Law: A Contextual Approach* (InterVarsity, 1994), 201; John Zeisler, *Paul's Letter to the Romans* (TPI New Testament Commentaries; Trinity Press International, 1989), 202.

17 Thomas R. Schreiner, *Romans* (BECNT 6; Baker Books, 1998), 400. Contra Longenecker, *Romans*, 685. He pushes for the idea that these are general principles and not specifically the law, yet he makes no case other than to say it cannot be a contrast between the law of Jesus against the law of Moses. However, Paul's argument is not black and white: he specifically notes that the law has both a positive side and a negative side, as sin brings out the bad and only through Christ is the good of the law seen.

that the law places one under condemnation not due to itself, but due to sin. Sin is linked directly with death (τῆς ἁμαρτίας καὶ τοῦ θανάτου). Thus, the law of sin and death could only refer to the OT law, as no other understanding fits the context, so the second occurrence is uncontroversial. In turn, Paul does not have a purely negative understanding of the law, though, as it also allows life by agency of the Spirit.[18] The first occurrence of νόμος in Rom 8:2 refers to the OT law as well.[19] Paul had already unambiguously linked law and life previously in Romans (e.g. 7:10, 14).[20] In fact, Paul brings together the key roots from those two passages into a succinct phrase (ἐντολὴ ἡ εἰς ζωήν + νόμος πνευματικός ἐστιν = νόμος τοῦ πνεύματος τῆς ζωῆς).[21] The next supporting argument for this position comes from the context of the verse, as 8:4 states that τὸ δικαίωμα τοῦ νόμου πληρωθῇ...κατὰ πνεῦμα, which points toward a positive understanding of the law only in light of the Spirit.[22] Käsemann's contention that this refers only to some pre–Pauline tradition which Paul uses to speak of doing the will of God carries little weight as Käsemann states the pre–Pauline tradition did refer to the law but Paul changes the referent here.[23] In other words, Käsemann identifies not only an alleged tradition that Paul uses, but he speculates that it is a tradition Paul even misuses. Due to all of these considerations, both mentions of the law in Romans 8:2 refer to the Mosaic law.[24]

Paul, then, directly relates the Spirit to the law, but how does he express the function of Christ? This question centers on the syntax of the verse and on what the prepositional phrase ἐν Χριστῷ Ἰησοῦ modifies. It can either modify τῆς ζωῆς or the verb ἠλευθέρωσεν. Cranfield does mention two other options: the phrase could modify either τοῦ πνεύματος τῆς ζωῆς or νόμος. He re-

---

18 See Eduard Lohse, "ὁ νόμος τοῦ πνεύματος τῆς ζωῆς Exegetische Anmerkungen zu Rom. 8.2," in *Neues Testament und christliche Existenz: Festschrift für Herbert Braun zum 70* (ed. Hans Dieter Betz and Luise Schottroff; Mohr, 1973), 101–117.

19 E.g. Byrne, *'Sons of God'*, 92; James D. G. Dunn, *Romans* (2 vols.; WBC 38a-b; Word, 1988), 1:416–417; Robert Jewett, *Romans: A Commentary* (Hermeneia; Fortress Press, 2007), 480–481; Eckhard Schnabel, *Law and Wisdom from Ben Sira to Paul: A Tradition Historical Enquiry into the Relationship of Law, Wisdom, and Ethics* (WUNT II/16; Mohr-Siebeck, 1985), 288-9; Schreiner, *Romans*, 400; Urlich Wilckens, *Der Brief an die Römer* (3 vols.; EKK 6.1–6.3.; Neukirchener Verlag, 1978-1982), 2:122–123.

20 Dunn, *Romans*, 1:416; Wilckens, *Römer*, 2:122–123

21 Dunn, *Romans*, 1:416. This translates to "the commandment that leads to life + the law is spiritual = the law of the Spirit of life."

22 See Frank Thielman, *From Plight to Solution: A Jewish Framework for Understanding Paul's View of the Law in Galatians and Romans* (NovTSup 61; Brill, 1989), 88–89. Cf. Cranfield, *Romans*, 1:383–385, who argues it is through faith in addition to the Spirit that the law is fulfilled. Contra Karl Barth (*The Epistle to the Romans* [6th ed.; trans. Sir Edwyn Hoskyns; Oxford University Press, 1968], 273), who states that the law is the Spirit.

23 Käsemann, *Romans*, 217–218.

24 Cf. Schreiner, *Romans*, 400. Contra Douglas Moo, *The Epistle to the Romans* (NICNT; Eerdmans, 1996), 507.

jects both as "unnatural," which is certainly true of the latter.[25] The former would only make sense if the phrase were instrumental, such that the Spirit is life or brings life by the work of Christ.[26] In order to articulate such a concept, however, Paul would likely have utilized another article in order to place the prepositional phrase into the second attributive position. Dunn argues for the connection with the verb, envisioning a continuation of previous Pauline thought rather than something new.[27] Cranfield makes two points in support of this position.[28] First, he asserts that this understanding is the more natural way to read the Greek. Second, he thinks the context of God sending the Son shows specifically this option to be better supported by the context. Both Cranfield and Dunn note how Rom 6:23 parallels the significance of the link between ἐν Χριστῷ Ἰησοῦ and τῆς ζωῆς, thus making this interpretation fit in line with previous Pauline thought. In addition, Rom 6:11 also points in the same theological direction (ζῶντας δὲ τῷ θεῷ ἐν Χριστῷ Ἰησοῦ). Therefore, the objection by Dunn and Cranfield fails at this point.

Cranfield's second objection, that of context, can support both sides. One need only describe the movement of thought (τῆς ζωῆς ἐν Χριστῷ Ἰησοῦ) as reference to eternal or eschatological life.[29] Cranfield's objection regarding the ease of grammar, however, also has a major weakness. First, he notes only the "more natural" understanding of the Greek without demonstrating how it is more natural.[30] In the Pauline epistles, however, ἐν Χριστῷ Ἰησοῦ rarely modifies whatever follows it, instead modifying whatever precedes the phrase. In the twelve other occurrences in Romans, the phrase always modifies what it follows.[31] Contrary to Cranfield and Dunn, the more natural and contextual way of understanding the phrase is to take ἐν Χριστῷ Ἰησοῦ as modifying τῆς ζωῆς and not ἠλευθέρωσεν.[32] Jewett argues that the entire phrase that functions as the subject only makes syntactical sense if it is all taken together as

---

25 Cranfield, *Romans*, 1:374. Contra Frederic Louis Godet, *Commentary on Romans* (Kregel, 1977), 296–297.

26 Cf. Adolf Schlatter, *Romans: The Righteousness of God* (trans. Siegfried S. Schatzmann; Hendrickson, 1995), 173.

27 Dunn, *Romans*, 1:418.

28 Cranfield, *Romans*, 1:374–375.

29 Eschatological referring to the climax of salvation–history, not necessarily the end of time itself. Cf. Thielman (*From Plight to Solution*) who consistently uses "eschatology" and "eschatological" to allude to the time of the Spirit after the resurrection of Christ.

30 Cranfield, *Romans*, 1:375.

31 See Rom 3:25; 6:11, 23; 8:39; 9:1; 12:5; 15:17; 16:3, 7, 9–10.

32 Cf. C. H. Dodd, *The Epistle of Paul to the Romans* (MNTC; Harper & Row, 1932), 118–119; Marie–Joseph Lagrange, *Saint Paul Épitre aux Romains* (Études Biblique; Gabalda, 1916), 191; Otto Michel, *Der Brief an die Römer* (KEK; 4th ed.; Vandenhoeck & Ruprecht, 1966), 189. This is also supported by Longenecker, *Romans*, 686.

a single idea and not broken into pieces.³³ All of this evidence works together to build a case that Paul posits a direct link between the work of Christ and the work of the Spirit.³⁴

The occurrence of νόμος in 8:3 carries through the thought of Paul from 8:2 concerning the law, namely that the law is not an agent itself. In 8:3, Paul emphasizes the inability of the law (ἀδύνατον τοῦ νόμου) to do anything, to accomplish anything, a strand of thought carried in from Romans 7. Paul focuses on this inability as a contrast to what God accomplished in sending Jesus. This lack of ability characterizes the law and is intrinsic to it, as made manifest by ἐν ᾧ when one understands the phrase as modal.³⁵ The law was not weak on its own, rather the impact of the flesh (διὰ τῆς σαρκός) made the law weak due to how humanity was unable to keep the law. The ability to fulfill the law comes about only through the work of Christ, as he functions as the περὶ ἁμαρτίας. Apart from the work of Christ, Paul views the law as weak.³⁶ Paul does not describe the law in contact with the Spirit as weak, however.³⁷ Instead Paul answers the problem of the flesh (διὰ τῆς σαρκός replaced by κατὰ σάρκα in 8:4) with the Holy Spirit (κατὰ πνεῦμα). Christ's work has set the believer free, yet the Spirit functions as the one who makes the work of Christ available to the believer in life (as evidenced by περιπατοῦσιν).³⁸

The next occurrence of νόμος comes in the same sentence, with Paul discussing the fulfillment of the δικαίωμα τοῦ νομοῦ.³⁹ Paul does not look to abrogate the law for Christians, rather he seeks the fulfillment of it (πληρωθῇ), something that God does as evidenced by the divine passive, especially in light of the work of the Spirit.⁴⁰ Martin argues against a divine passive, pushing for the importance of human responsibility, then notes only those with the Spirit are able to fulfill the law anyway.⁴¹ The reason the text goes against

---

33 Jewett, *Romans*, 481.
34 Contra Grant Osborne, *Romans* (IVPNTCS 6; InterVarsity, 2004), 196. He sees life from the Spirit as strictly Christian living and not related to conversion. See below for more discussion on this point.
35 Cf. Käsemann, *Romans*, 216; William Sanday and Arthur C. Headlam, *The Epistle to the Romans* (ICC; 5th ed.; T&T Clark, 1980), 192.
36 Cf. Dunn, *Romans*, 1:438; Fee, *God's Empowering Presence*, 533–534; Schreiner, *Romans*, 401.
37 J. F. Bayes, "The Translation of Romans 8:3," *ExpTim* 111 (1999): 14–16, here 14. Cf. Dunn, *Romans*, 1:440–441.
38 Dunn, *Romans*, 1:439–441; Fee, *God's Empowering Presence*, 534–545; Fitzmyer, *Romans*, 488.
39 For more on δικαίωμα and πληρωθῇ, see 4.1.2 below.
40 Brendan Byrne, "Living out the Righteousness of God: The Contribution of Rom 6:1-8:13 to an Understanding of Paul's Ethical Presuppositions," *CBQ* 43 (1981): 557–581.
41 Martin, *Christ and the Law*, 152. Cf. E. P. Sanders, *Paul, the Law, and the Jewish People* (Fortress, 1983), 98.

his case is because the Spirit comes due to the work of Christ, and Christ came because he was sent by God.⁴² The work cannot be done by humanity, as the ἐν ἡμῖν phrase⁴³ functions as a locative since the agent of a passive is either unstated or in a ὑπό phrase⁴⁴ (e.g. Rom 15:15). Wilckens thinks both the locative and instrumental uses are in view,⁴⁵ yet this is hardly persuasive since the context militates against rather than for an instrumental understanding. Therefore, God does not act alone in this fulfillment. God sent the Son (ἑαυτοῦ υἱὸν πέμψας), and this phrase anticipates and points toward the work of the Spirit (κατὰ πνεῦμα) by whom God fulfills the law. Dunn recognizes the combined work of the Son and Spirit, seeing a continuity between God's use of the law and use of the Son and Spirit.⁴⁶ Paul does not argue for Christians to observe the law (which would be the direct antithesis to Galatians), rather by his use of πληρόω he makes the point that Christians have met the intended goal of the law.⁴⁷ The law for Paul does not stand in opposition to God's plan, nor does it stand as something no longer in use, rather it stands as a guide for the Christian life that God upholds through the Son and Spirit.

The last time Paul uses νόμος in Romans 8 occurs in 8:7. Feuillet advances his idea that Paul here speaks of God's demands rather than the Mosaic law.⁴⁸ Such an interpretation is dubious since the immediate context does not point in such a direction nor would Paul's original audience have understood it in that way due to the context. The parallel to 8:3–4 cannot be missed, as once again Paul intersperses law language with Spirit language.⁴⁹ In addition, he highlights the inability of the law to save, connecting the idea with both 8:3–4 and 7:14–25.⁵⁰ Again, the law cannot meet God's will⁵¹ (i.e. ἀρέσαι οὐ δύναται) not because of itself, but because of sin⁵² (τὸ φρόνημα τῆς σαρκός harkening

---

42 Jewett, *Romans*, 486.
43 For a slightly different analysis with the same result, see Schreiner, *Romans*, 405.
44 Bertone, *"The Law of the Spirit"*, 183. Cf. Fee, *God's Empowering Presence*, 535; Wilckens, *Römer*, 2:128 n. 525.
45 Wilckens, *Römer*, 2:128, especially n. 525.
46 Dunn, *Romans*, 1:423.
47 See the discussion of both δικαίωμα and πληρωθῇ in Bertone, *"The Law of the Spirit"*, 227–234.
48 A. Feuillet, "Loi de Dieu, loi du Christ et loi de l'Esprit d'après les épitres pauliniennes: Les rapports de ces trois lois avec la Loi Mosaique," *NovT* 22 (1980): 29–65, here 47. Cf. Moo, *Romans*, 488.
49 See Bertone, *"The Law of the Spirit"*, 187. Cf. Jewett, *Romans*, 488.
50 For the latter, see Fee, *God's Empowering Presence*, 542; Schreiner, *Romans*, 412; Fitzmyer, *Romans*, 489 (who links only with 7:22–25).
51 Walter Schmithals, *Der Römerbrief: Ein Kommentar* (Gerd Mohn, 1988), 268.
52 Bertone, *"The Law of the Spirit"*, 187.

back to κατὰ σάρκα[53] in 8:4). In Rom 8:7, Paul stresses the inability of the flesh to submit (οὐχ ὑποτάσσεται) to God's law,[54] a statement that is positive about the law since God's standard has not changed. Bertone argues the opposite view, namely that God has changed from the law to the Spirit such that the law is no longer even a moral guidepost for the believer.[55] The Spirit gives life, and since life comes from the Spirit, the law is useless in ethics since that moral compass would now be located within the believer. Fee does not go as far, simply stating that life apart from the Spirit is under the law and therefore leads to death.[56] The law in fact comes from God (genitive of source).[57] Since only those actually in the Spirit can be subject to the law or submit to it, the line of reasoning proposed by Bertone misses the thrust of the passage and the positive nature of the law that Paul is explaining.[58] Submission to the law is the correct response to it, and therefore the correct response to God.[59] Being subject to the law is the proper state (Dunn's "natural state" likely overshoots the idea) for mankind, a place in which the Spirit puts believers.[60] This activity by the Spirit only occurs in conjunction with the work of Christ, as seen by Paul's use of language in 8:7–9.[61] Paul argues for both a christological and a pneumatological solution to the "problem of the law" posed in Romans 7 and the question of condemnation raised in 8:1–4.[62]

Fee calls the theological aspect of fulfilling the law "christological" and the practical aspect "pneumatological," yet this displays a false dichotomy with respect to Paul's argument in 8:1–8.[63] For Paul, the theological and the practical are entwined. Living according to the flesh or according to the Spirit contains both theological and practical threads. In the same way, Roman readers would want to find application for this life.[64] They did not hold to a split between life and religion,[65] or, in Fee's terms, theological and practical

---

53 Käsemann, *Romans*, 219–220 notes the replacement of the κατά phrases for both flesh and Spirit with other qualifiers after 8:5.
54 Cf. Daniel P. Fuller, "Progressive Dispensationalism and the Law/Gospel Contrast: A Case Study in Biblical Theology," in *Biblical Theology: Retrospect and Prospect* (ed. Scott J. Hafemann; InterVarsity, 2002), 237–249, here 246.
55 Bertone, *"The Law of the Spirit"*, 185–191.
56 Fee, *God's Empowering Presence*, 542.
57 Martin, *Christ and the Law*, 35.
58 Dunn, *Romans*, 1:443; Martin, *Christ and the Law*, 31 n. 61.
59 Käsemann, *Romans*, 219. Cf. Cranfield, *Romans*, 1:387.
60 Dunn, *Romans*, 1:427. Cf. Wilckens, *Römer*, 2:130, especially n. 532.
61 Wilckens, *Römer*, 2:130–131. Cf. Fitzmyer, *Romans*, 490.
62 Lowe, "But Why Not?," 244.
63 Fee, *God's Empowering Presence*, 534 n. 187.
64 Walter Burkert, *Ancient Mystery Cults* (Harvard University Press, 1987), 27.
65 Duncan Fishwick, *The Imperial Cult in the Latin West: Studies in the Ruler Cult of the Western Provinces of the Roman Empire* (3 vols.; Brill, 1987–2002), 1.1.75–76.

aspects. The question Paul seeks to answer in this section (especially Rom 8:3-4) comes from Rom 7:7-25, the question of the law.[66] God responds to condemnation according to the law through both the Son and Spirit. God sent the Son in order to bring about the condemnation of sin itself, whereas the Spirit in turn fulfills the law for the believer,[67] so that sin is condemned in the flesh and believers are freed to fulfill the law they otherwise would not be able to fulfill, since the law itself cannot give life.[68] Paul does not allow a break between theological and practical, nor does he allow for a break between the work of the Son in justification and the Spirit in sanctification in regards to the law. The work of the Son and the work of the Spirit are in lockstep with one another. The cornerstone for this argument remains 8:3-4, where the law needs to be fulfilled by Christians,[69] yet the ability to do so only comes from the combination of the death of Christ (i.e. God sending him) and the work of the Spirit in the believer (walking according to the Spirit). Only in this can one please God, which would echo with the Roman mindset.[70]

4.1.2 Law and Sin

The previous section demonstrated how Paul did not see the law as the problem for humanity, rather he looked at sin (or the sin nature, κατὰ σάρκα, etc.) as the problem. This section will briefly cover sin in 8:1-8, where the concept overlaps the law. The law contains the righteous requirement that must be fulfilled, yet people are unable to do so because of the sin nature, that is the flesh. More specifically, God's righteous requirement cannot be met, a positive take on the law yet a negative take on humanity.[71] In what sense, then, can the law be fulfilled? Sin defeats mankind, yet the law is righteous in what it requires. The law is fulfilled not in the sense of abrogation, for that would contradict the entire line of thought Paul has built to this point and overturn the positive remarks he has made concerning it.[72] The law must be fulfilled in a sense of continuity rather than disjunction. Fee states that the relationship

---

66 Lowe, "But Why Not?," 241.
67 Schreiner, *Romans*, 405.
68 J. Blank, "Gesetz und Geist," in *The Law of the Spirit in Romans 7 and 8* (Monograph Series of Benedicta; ed. L. De Lorenzi; St. Paul's Abbey, 1976), 73-100, here 96.
69 Martin, *Christ and the Law*, 152.
70 Jewett, *Romans*, 488.
71 Dunn, *Romans*, 1:423, who believes, "we must give Paul the credit for seeing a deeper consistency [regarding the positive and negative aspects of the law] than his critics allow."
72 Wilckens, *Römer*, 2:129.

of believers to the Torah is now in the past,[73] yet this hardly fits Paul's appreciation of the law in Romans 7-8. At the same time, Paul does not argue for the believer to do, keep, or submit to the law.[74] The righteous requirement of the law can hardly be the prohibition from coveting, as argued by Ziesler.[75] Though there is limited contextual support (cf. Rom 7:7), Paul uses the command merely as an example and one that is not in the immediate context. Paul uses δικαίωμα in order to stress the continuity between the OT and the present time, as what has changed is not God's law, rather the change centers upon the response to it. Some see the righteous requirement (note the singular) as a summation of the entire law, limited to the act of love in Rom 13:8.[76] One objection to such an understanding comes from Fee, who argues that a forensic sense must be understood because it is a forensic term.[77] The problem with such an interpretation, however, lies in the text itself, as Paul does not lean on forensic terminology in the passage, rather the tone conveys a relational aspect (e.g. ἐν ἡμῖν with a phrase in apposition).[78] Even taking πληρωθῇ as a divine passive does not rule out human activity, as the only way to fulfill the law is to walk κατὰ πνεῦμα. The act of walking or living must be done by the person, yet the Spirit works within one to bring about the fulfillment of the law.[79] The Spirit works in the believer as an agent in the believer's life, but an agent who does so by God's will.[80]

The fulfillment of the law comes from walking in the Spirit, yet what does this entail? Paul defines walking according to the Spirit in Rom 8:5-8.[81] The focus in these verses turn to the mind (φρόνημα) or one's thinking (φρονοῦσιν). The mind characterized by flesh (φρόνημα τῆς σαρκός) leads the person only to death. The genitive is likely qualitative.[82] Living and thinking are equated

---

73 Fee, *God's Empowering Presence*, 535 n. 188. Fee declares that it is not "that we should struggle…to fulfill the law…as though our relationship with the Torah were not really past."

74 A topic introduced by Ben Witherington III with Darlene Hyatt, *Paul's Letter to the Romans: A Socio–Rhetorical Commentary* (Eerdmans, 2004), 215 and given more in-depth coverage by Bertone (*"The Law of the Spirit"*, 243–246).

75 John Ziesler, "The Just Requirement of the Law (Rom 8:4)," *ABR* 35 (1987): 77–82.

76 Mentioned in passing by Moo, *Romans*, 482.

77 Fee, *God's Empowering Presence*, 534–535. Cf. Käsemann, *Romans*, 218; Moo, *Romans*, 481–482.

78 Fitzmyer, *Romans*, 488; Käsemann, *Romans*, 218–219; Schreiner, *Romans*, 405.

79 Brendan Byrne, "Living Out the Righteousness of God: The Contribution of Rom 6:1-8:13 to an Understanding of Paul's Ethical Presuppositions." *CBQ* 43 (1981): 557–581, here 569; Dunn, *Romans*, 1:440; Schreiner, *Romans*, 405.

80 Fitzmyer, *Romans*, 487–488; Moo, *Romans*, 485.

81 Cf. Cranfield, *Romans*, 1:385 who declares οἱ κατὰ σάρκα ὄντες "synonymous with" οἱ κατὰ πνεῦμα.

82 E.g. Moo (*Romans*, 487 n. 84) calls it "descriptive."

in Rom 8:5, with οἱ κατὰ σάρκα ὄντες parallel to τὰ τῆς σαρκὸς φρονοῦσιν.[83] Paul juxtaposes the mind characterized by the flesh with the mind characterized by the Spirit (οἱ κατὰ πνεῦμα and τὰ τοῦ πνεύματος).[84] Grammatically, the second portion elides the verb, yet the construction (οἱ κατά plus a noun with τά and an articular noun) shows a parallel contrasting (δέ) image.[85] The reason living and thinking are equated relies on the idea that whatever the mind is dominated by, the person does, and vice versa.[86] The dichotomy between the flesh and Spirit continues in 8:6, this time pointing to the results of each. Flesh leads to death, but Spirit to life and peace or, as Paul states it, the fleshly mind is death and the mind of the Spirit is life and peace.[87] These key words denote large concepts found throughout all of Romans,[88] yet the significance of each is found in the source of each. The mind of flesh leads to death, and again Paul is describing how sin leads to death, that the result of sin is always death. In contradistinction Paul discusses the Spirit, which leads to life and peace, both the opposite of death. Two different minds exist in Paul's argument just as there are two different results, there is not one mind in two aspects.[89] Paul defines walking in the Spirit negatively in 8:6 as not having a mind of flesh.

The idea of a mind of flesh draws on the paradox of the law. Paul has made it clear that Christians are not under the law, yet he connects pleasing God with being under the law (8:7–8). The importance of the negative statement by Paul (ἀρέσαι οὐ δύνανται) cannot be emphasized enough. Paul links together three characteristics of those who have the mind of the flesh. First, they are enemies of God. Second, they cannot submit to God's law (οὐχ ὑποτάσσεται οὐδὲ γὰρ δύναται, the comma inserted between ὑποτάσσεται and οὐδέ in the NA27 is misleading as it might lead to the reader assuming a break where Paul likely does not intend one). Schreiner argues for two distinct phases: (1) they do not keep the law and (2) they are unable to keep the law.[90] The γάρ is likely

---

83 E.g. C. K. Barrett (*The Epistle to the Romans* [HNTC; Harper and Row, 1957], 157) calls the verse a definition.

84 Jewett (*Romans*, 487) calls them "antithetical orientations."

85 Cf. Moo, *Romans*, 486; Schreiner, *Romans*, 412; Wilckens, *Römer*, 2:130.

86 Cf. Cranfield, *Romans*, 1:385–386 (including 385 n. 1); Fitzmyer, *Romans*, 488–489. Longenecker (*Romans*, 697) points to Phil 2:5-11, where attitude and action are intertwined in the example of Jesus.

87 Jewett, *Romans*, 487; Witherington, *Romans*, 215. Witherington notes that ἔστιν should be provided, a commonly enough elided word that his use of "anacoluthon" overstates the matter.

88 Cf. 3.1. These terms frame the conversation in Romans 5–8, with 5 balanced by 8.

89 Many commentators write against this (e.g. Schreiner, *Romans*, 411–412), yet nobody mentions a scholar who defends the one mind understanding, so it seems a strange fight to pick.

90 Schreiner, *Romans*, 412.

explanatory or causal (as is the γάρ at the beginning of the longer phrase[91]), so the reason they do not keep the law is because they cannot, which is a single step and a reason, not two distinct steps. Third, those who have a mind of flesh are unable to please God. Note that this language of inability echoes 8:3,[92] intentionally locating the problem in the person and not the law. Thus, flesh and Spirit are separated as two distinct options, with Paul presenting life in the Spirit as the only viable option.[93] The paradox of the law, both a good gift from God and something that leads to death, is illustrated in the mind of flesh and the beginning of a solution is in the Spirit. The condemnation believers are freed from stems from sin, not the law.[94]

Paul links the concept of sin to the law within Rom 8:1-8 only in 8:1-4. Paul couples forensic language (8:1, 3; κατέκρινεν) with sacrificial language (8:3; περὶ ἁμαρτίας)[95] in order to further explicate the role of the law in sin. Though already relating the law and sin to each other in Romans 7, Paul continues his connection between sin and death and their relationship to the law. Paul relates sin to the law in 7:5, 8 as an actor to a script: sin seizes the law (7:8, λαβοῦσα) in order to promote itself.[96] Sin uses the law to kill (7:11), thus sin ends in death (7:13).[97] In this sense, sin and death can be equated by Paul since sin in fact ends in death. When Paul speaks of the νόμος τῆς ἁμαρτίας καὶ τοῦ θανάτου, he characterizes sin and death as one since sin always results in death, not two separate aspects or traits of the law. He considers sin and death as unified, though not as a "spirit of sin and death," as if Paul envisions another spirit in contrast to the Holy Spirit.[98] In 8:2, Paul places sin in direct opposition to the Spirit, such that sin and the Spirit are characteristics that cannot be shared. The law can be defined by the Spirit or it can be defined by sin. If the law then cannot solve the problem of sin, since the law only exacerbates it, then another solution must be found.

---

91 Cranfield, *Romans*, 1:386.
92 Peter von der Osten–Sacken, *Römer 8 als Beispiel paulinischer Soteriologie* (Vandenhoeck & Ruprecht, 1975), 152.
93 Cf. J. Ayodeji Adewuya, "The Holy Spirit and Sanctification in Romans 8:1-17," *JPT* (2001): 71-84, note 78–79.
94 Frank Thielman, *From Plight to Solution*, 89.
95 In the NT, this phrase only occurs in John 8:46; 16:8, 9; Hebrews 10:6, 8, 18; 13:11 and here. The phrase in Hebrews carries the sacrificial idea whereas the usage in John does not. Cf. 3.4 above for the OT uses.
96 Moo, *Romans*, 435–436. He declares that "Paul again personifies sin" as it "works actively and purposefully" (436).
97 Bertone, *"The Law of the Spirit"*, 163.
98 Cf. Osten–Sacken, *Römer 8*, 228. Contra Lagrange, *Romains*, 191–192, who sees πνεῦμα as a spirit and not the Holy Spirit.

Sin leads to death, yet the Spirit is characterized by life. The Spirit answers the problem of sin for the law, as the law cannot give life as the Spirit does.[99] The Spirit, though, provides a solution only when in the believer, so how does the Spirit enter into the believer?[100] The Spirit enables the law to give life only by the work of Christ. The phrase ἐν Χριστῷ Ἰησοῦ modifies life. Paul does not refer to the location of life, though that would little alter the point, rather he uses the prepositional phrase to describe how life comes about. In other words, ἐν Χριστῷ Ἰησοῦ functions instrumentally.[101] This fits within the context of Christ's death, which is why God sent him to be περὶ ἁμαρτίας, and in overcoming sin God overcomes death through or by use of Christ and the Spirit. Paul combines the Son and the Spirit as the answer to the problem of the law and sin.

How does the term σάρξ fit into the relationship between the law and sin? In Romans 7 and 8:1-3, Paul posits sin as the force that turned the law from being God's gracious gift to an instrument used against humanity. Sin, in turn, is synonymous with death in Pauline terminology, for sin inevitably leads to death.[102] If sin exerts control over the functionality of the law, then Paul relates a similar relationship for flesh, since he states in 8:3 that the inability of the law comes about διὰ τῆς σαρκός. The phrase carries agency, in that the law did not become weak on its own, rather sin weakened it through the flesh. Paul uses the term σάρξ to relate the "fallen nature" of people.[103] The pre–salvific condition of humanity Paul labels as κατὰ σάρκα, a phrase employed in contradistinction to κατὰ πνεῦμα. If walking κατὰ πνεῦμα leads to life, then walking κατὰ σάρκα leads to death. This gives the result that sin and the flesh come to the same end.[104] Thus, σάρξ becomes a synonym for sin with respect to the outcome, even though σάρξ stands as a condition (κατὰ σάρκα) and sin as a state (e.g. Rom 7:20 ἐν ἐμοὶ ἁμαρτία).[105] Sin uses the flesh as a way

---

99 Roger L. Hahn, "Pneumatology in Romans 8: Its Historical and Theological Context," *Wesleyan Theological Journal* 21 (1986): 74-90, here 77; Michel, *Römer*, 192 (though stated positively); Moo, *Romans*, 489; Schreiner, *Romans*, 413.

100 The longer answer to this question for Romans 8 awaits in 4.3.

101 E.g., one could translate this as, "the law of the Spirit of life by Christ Jesus set you free."

102 Moo, *Romans*, 476 n. 31. Moo states that the phrase in 8:2 can be understood as "the power exercised by sin that leads to death."

103 Cranfield, *Romans*, 1:379; Eduard Schweizer, "σάρξ, σαρκικός, σάρκινος," *TDNT* 7:98–151; C. Spicq, "σάρξ, σαρκικός, σάρκινος," *TLNT* 3:231–241. Cf. Moo, *Romans*, 478, who defines the word as "the 'this–worldly' orientation that all people share," and Jewett, *Romans*, 483, who views it through the lens of honor and shame, with this referring to turning "the law into an instrument of status acquisition." As for the question regarding Christ's taking on flesh, see 4.3 below.

104 Bertone, *"The Law of the Spirit"*, 186–187.

105 Contra ibid., 182.

to hinder the law,[106] and thus the flesh functions as an instrument of sin to disable people from fulfilling the law. Sin and the flesh are not identical, as Paul uses them differently in 8:3 twice, with sin modifying flesh (ἐν ὁμοιώματι σαρκὸς ἁμαρτίας) and with flesh being the location of the condemnation of sin (κατέκρινεν τὴν ἁμαρτίαν ἐν τῇ σαρκί).[107] Sin uses the flesh to thwart the goodness of the law.[108]

Paul strengthens this conclusion throughout his description of the one who walks according to the flesh and the one who walks according to the Spirit in 8:5–8 by placing the flesh and Spirit at odds. The first portion of Rom 8:5 sets the stage for the rest of the section, as Paul defines the one who lives according to the flesh (with οἱ κατὰ σάρκα ὄντες as a direct parallel to τοῖς κατὰ σάρκα περιπατοῦσιν).[109] Cranfield notes that there is little distinction between εἰμί and περιπατέω in this instance, with the latter referring to one's conduct and the former essentially reiterating the same concept.[110] Paul paints a contrast between flesh and Spirit based upon which one of these two dominates one's life. Either one has the mind of flesh, signifying the dominance of the flesh in a person, or else one is dominated by the Spirit.[111] The person dominated by each is defined by each, since whatever dominates causes one to think on or desire actions and attitudes within their sphere.[112] In other words, having the mind of something (φρόνημα) means being "completely given to" that something.[113]

The flesh has no way to please God, and thus cannot fulfill the law. Paul's dichotomy between flesh and Spirit paves the way for a solution to the problem of the law's good nature yet inability to grant life.[114] The law cannot grant life because sin took over the law by use of the flesh and thus turned the law into an instrument of death. Paul puts this forth as the reason why those in the flesh are unable to please God. Sin has misappropriated the law, and God's solution is not to eliminate the law but to open a new way for the law to be fulfilled. This new way is enabled by the sending of the Son and the work of the Holy Spirit.

---

106 Osten-Sacken, *Römer 8*, 229.
107 Contra Bertone, *"The Law of the Spirit"*, 182.
108 N. T. Wright, *The Climax of the Covenant: Christ and the Law in Pauline Theology* (Fortress, 1993), 208.
109 Cranfield, *Romans*, 1:385.
110 Cranfield, *Romans*, 1:385, and see n. 1.
111 Fitzmyer, *Romans*, 489–490; Käsemann, *Romans*, 219; Moo, *Romans*, 486.
112 Lagrange, *Romains*, 195–196.
113 Fee, *God's Empowering Presence*, 541.
114 Byrne, *'Sons of God'*, 93.

In Romans 7, Paul outlined the problem of sin and the law. Paul details God's response to this problem, foreshadowed in 7:6, in Romans 8.[115] In recognizing both the problem and solution as stated in Romans, the purpose of God's action through the Son and the Spirit becomes clear.

4.2 Son, Spirit, and Recreation

God cursed the entire world due to sin, and thus God's response must include the entire world lest creation stay marred.[116] In overcoming sin, God intends to break or undo the curse he laid upon the world. Creation suffers in the present circumstances due to the curse, looking to a time when the curse no longer affects it and God remakes creation into what it should be. Paul calls this event ἀποκάλυψις τῶν υἱῶν τοῦ θεοῦ. The adoption culminates in the future.[117] In turn, this adoption brings about the glory Paul speaks of in Rom 8:18.[118] The movement from adoption to glory, from heir to inheritance, answers the problem of the suffering of creation. Both the Son and the Spirit are actively involved in this process of recreation.

4.2.1 Son, Spirit, and Adoption

God calls people to adoption.[119] Paul makes it explicit throughout that God initiates the action for adopting his heirs. However, God uses the Son and the Spirit to accomplish this adoption. Paul argues that adoption occurs through the presence of the Spirit in the life of the believer. In turn, Christ retains his status as the non-adopted Son of God, differentiating him from the rest of the sons of God.[120]

The Spirit brings about the adoption of believers through indwelling them. The ultimate goal of adoption in Romans 8 remains the redemption of physical bodies (Rom 8:23, ἀπολύτρωσιν τοῦ σώματος). It is only through the work of the Spirit that this occurs. Paul states in 8:11 that God will give life to τὰ θνητὰ σώματα ὑμῶν διὰ τοῦ ἐνοικοῦντες αὐτοῦ πνεύματος ἐν ὑμῖν ("your mortal bodies through the indwelling of his Spirit in you"). God uses the Holy

---

115 Cranfield, *Romans*, 1:373; Morrison and Woodhouse, "Coherence," 9.
116 See above 3.2 and 3.3.
117 Susan Eastman, "Whose Apocalypse? The Identity of the Sons of God in Romans 8:19," *JBL* 121 (2002): 263–277, here 266.
118 Byne, *'Sons of God'*, 104–105.
119 See 3.3.1.
120 Kyu Seop Kim, "Another Look at Adoption in Romans 8:15 in Light of Roman Social Practices and Legal Rules," *Biblical Theology Bulletin* 44 (2014): 133–143, here 138.

Spirit as his agent for the resurrection of mortal bodies, as evidenced by the διά phrase.[121] The redemption does not refer to the corporate redemption of Israel, however, as Paul refers explicitly to creation and to the sons of God.[122] Eastman argues for a corporate sense based upon the plural in 8:11, σώματα, turning to a singular in 8:23, σώματος.[123] She contends that the plural refers to Israel as a whole. Instead, Paul more likely intends the singular usage to convey what he already mentioned in 6:6 and 7:24, namely, the interaction of the physical natures of believers with the present age as opposed to the eschatological age.[124] Believers do not leave behind the physical world once they have the Spirit, they are inextricably linked with the created order.[125] This goal of redeeming bodies lies at the heart of what the Spirit does. Paul eliminates the divide between ethics and theology in his discussion of believers having the Spirit living in them, as walking according to the Spirit becomes the way toward a redeemed body.

Paul employs the metaphor of walking according to the Spirit as the antithesis of being controlled by the flesh. Just as sin and the flesh leads to death, so does the Spirit lead to life.[126] Paul allows this differentiation to control the argument in 8:5–8, much like the parallel passage in Gal 5:13–26.[127] The believer does not wield the Spirit in order to defeat the flesh, rather the Spirit actively functions within the believer in order to overcome the believer's obligation (ὀφειλέται).[128] The obligation is not to the flesh, but then to whom or what is obligation owed? While many commentators understand this section as referring only to the lack of obligation to the flesh,[129] Paul does not state it that way. Rather, Paul admits an obligation, but not one to the flesh.[130] Were Paul to have objected to all obligation, the negative particle would proceed the verb (ὀφειλέται οὐκ ἐσμὲν τῇ σαρκί), yet Paul places it so to negate only the prepositional phrase (ἐσμὲν οὐ τῇ σαρκί). The flesh no longer holds power over the believer by way of the law, instead the Spirit has freed (8:3, ἠλευθέρωσεν) the believer completely from its power such that there is no longer any debt.

---

121 Cranfield, *Romans*, 1:392; Dunn, *Romans*, 1:445–446; Schreiner, *Romans*, 416.
122 Contra Eastman, "Whose Apocalypse?," especially 268–270.
123 Eastman, "Whose Apocalypse?," 268.
124 See especially Anders Nygren, *A Commentary on Romans* (trans. Carl C. Rasmussen; Fortress, 1949), 333–334 and Dunn, *Romans*, 1:475.
125 Dunn, *Romans*, 1:445–446; Klaus Haacker, *The Theology of Paul's Letter to the Romans* (New Testament Theology; Cambridge University Press, 2003), 75. Cf. Barth, *Romans*, 289–291.
126 Hahn, "Pneumatology in Romans 8," 80.
127 Paulsen, *Römer 8*, 66–68.
128 Richard J. Dillon, "The Spirit as Taskmaster and Troublemaker in Romans 8," *CBQ* 60 (1998): 682–702, here 695.
129 E.g. Dunn, *Romans*, 1:448; Schreiner, *Romans*, 419.
130 Barth, *Romans*, 291–292; Fee, *God's Empowering Presence*, 556–557; Michel, *Römer*, 195.

Paul illustrates this in 8:13 while continuing the dichotomy of flesh leading to death and the Spirit to life, with the Spirit as the instrument (note the dative, πνεύματι) that enables life.[131] In completing the thought (note the explanatory γάρ),[132] Paul elucidates on this theme by acknowledging that the Spirit actively defeats (literally "by the Spirit put to death," πνεύματι τὰς πράξεις τοῦ σώματος θανατοῦτε) the deeds of the flesh and gives life (ζήσεσθε) instead.[133]

Paul states that the evidence of adoption consists of a life lived πνεύματι θεοῦ (8:14, cf. 4.3.1). This stands in contrast to the future tense of the previous verse (ζήσεσθε), such that a life by the Spirit now gives evidence of a life to come.[134] Paul does not hint at a life that is "driven" by the Spirit,[135] nor about a life of holiness per se,[136] rather he continues his train of thought from 8:5-11 contrasting Spirit and flesh.[137] The uncertainty of the verse, i.e. the conditional particle εἰ, precludes Käsemann's interpretation of this section pertaining to the "enthusiasts" since they would be completely controlled by the Spirit, thus lacking volition. Submission to the Spirit reveals who are the sons of God.[138] Schreiner also holds the converse true, that those who do not demonstrate being led by the Spirit are thus not sons of God,[139] a possibility but it is not something Paul is discussing. The Spirit acts in and through the believer, as evidenced by the passive voice of the verb.[140] Ἄγονται can be middle or passive, yet the form occurs most often in the passive and the middle voice would make nonsense of Paul's argument and use of the dative πνεύματι. Paul stresses throughout the first half of Romans 8 the importance of the Spirit in defeating the flesh and walking as a Christian,[141] and this merely reiterates that theme.

The Spirit enables believers to have two contiguous and overlapping statuses, that of son and of heir. The Spirit of adoption (8:15) is the same Spirit about which Paul has been talking. Adoption is the process by which one who is not a son is made into a son. Thus, if the Holy Spirit is the evidence of one

---

131 See Bertone, "*The Law of the Spirit*", 190–191; Fitzmyer, *Romans*, 493. Cf. Michel, *Römer*, 196.
132 Fee, *God's Empowering Presence*, 557–558; Schreiner, *Romans*, 422.
133 Cf. Adewuya, "The Holy Spirit and Sanctification," 81; Fitzmyer, *Romans*, 493, Wilckens, *Römer*, 2:135.
134 Dillon, "Taskmaster and Troublemaker," 697. Cf. Moo, *Romans*, 498–499.
135 Contra Dunn, *Romans*, 1:450; Käsemann, *Romans*, 226.
136 Contra Adewuya, "The Holy Spirit and Sanctification," 82.
137 Dillon, "Troublemaker and Taskmaster," 696; Moo, *Romans*, 498; Murray, *Romans*, 293; Schreiner, *Romans*, 422.
138 Dunn, *Romans*, 1:450; Moo, *Romans*, 499; Schreiner, *Romans*, 421–422.
139 Schreiner, *Romans*, 422.
140 Cranfield, *Romans*, 1:395.
141 Lowe, "But Why Not?," 246–247.

who has become a son of God, then the same Spirit can rightfully be called πνεῦμα υἱοθεσίας. The elimination of the old life along with its debts and the beginning of a new life with a new *paterfamilias*[142] occurs only through the power of God, namely the Holy Spirit. The Spirit enables believers to call God Father (ἐν ᾧ). The prepositional phrase ἐν ᾧ can either be a direct link to the Spirit (with Spirit as the antecedent to the pronoun) or else a temporal phrase. The difference comes about due to the uncertain punctuation, as a full stop could be appropriate after υἱοθεσίας.[143] The objection to such a reading, though, derives from the problematic break in thought. Paul has been elucidating the importance of the Spirit in the life of the believer for adoption, so why would he suddenly place the onus on the person rather than on the Spirit?[144] The most likely understanding of the prepositional phrase, then, is that the Spirit functions as the instrument by which believers are able to call on God as Father. Paul contrasts this statement on sonship with a statement on slavery, namely that the Spirit dwelling in believers will not put them back into slavery.[145] The implied previous slavery would be to sin, as found in Rom 7:14–20.

The ability to call God "Father" carries two consequences. First, it establishes who has the right to be called children of God. This does not mean the act of crying out activates the Spirit nor does Paul refer simply to the Spirit giving this ability to believers,[146] rather it is a witness to the indwelling of the Spirit.[147] The Spirit enables a change in status, for believers are no longer slaves, but are now children.[148] This adoption elevates the status of believers, which is a typical function that the institution was used for amongst the Romans.[149] No longer are believers slaves, instead they have become sons, a direct contrast to their previous state. In turn, this would clear any doubts about Paul's terminology in the minds of his readers. Upon hearing the phrase "son(s) of god," the typical Roman would think of a human who has the lineage to become a god, especially due to the imperial cult.[150] Paul overturns this idea for

---

142 Francis Lyall, "Roman Law in the Writings of Paul—Adoption," *JBL* 88 (1969): 458–466, here 465–466.

143 See J. Christiaan Beker, "Vision of Hope for a Suffering World: Romans 8:17-30," *The Princeton Seminary Bulletin* 3 (1994): 26-32, here 30.

144 Cf. Cranfield, *Romans*, 1:398–399. Most commentators cite Cranfield here, e.g. Moo, *Romans*, 502; Schreiner, *Romans*, 425.

145 Fee, *God's Empowering Presence*, 566. Though Fee has a strange analysis of the grammar, he still highlights the contrast appropriately.

146 Contra Hahn, "Pneumatology in Romans 8," 82–83.

147 See Byrne, *'Sons of God'*, 100–101.

148 Schreiner, *Romans*, 424–425.

149 James M. Scott, *Adoption as Sons of God* (WUNT II/48; Mohr Siebeck, 1992), 9.

150 Leonard L. Thompson, *The Book of Revelation: Apocalypse and Empire* (Oxford University Press, 1990), 223.

believers by stressing the adoptive act, an act that allows them to have the inheritance of God without being God or gods themselves.

Second, the indwelling of the Spirit enables the new children of God to be heirs of God. Calling on God as Father suggests a change in status not only from slave to child, but from destitution to heir.[151] Paul traces a line of thought that moves from slavery, to sonship, to inheritance in Rom 8:14–17. The spirit of the believer witnesses in conjunction to the Holy Spirit that this trajectory is true.[152] In 8:16–17, Paul explicitly links being a child of God to being his heir (εἰ τέκνα καὶ κληρονόμοι). In Roman law, being an heir is a status enacted throughout the life of the *paterfamilias* rather than becoming an active title only upon his death (as in Jewish or Greek law).[153] In drawing on the Roman understanding of adoption (see 3.3.1), both being an heir and being a child are present experiences, each a status to be enjoyed in this age.[154]

Movement from being a child to being an heir involves a change of status with respect to Jesus as well as with respect to the Father. The Spirit moves the slave to sin into being an adopted son of God. In turn, this alters the relationship with Jesus. Paul notes three times in Romans 8 that Jesus is God's special son (8:3, 29, 32), yet this does not separate Jesus from his adopted brothers in inheritance status before God.[155] The Spirit makes believers not just heirs of God, but even coheirs with Christ (8:17, συγκληρονόμοι Χριστοῦ), an idea that parallels and completes the concept of being an heir of God. Paul is not arguing that one is a coheir with Christ in order to become an heir of God.[156] In fact, Paul's argument projects exactly the opposite concept. The Spirit brings about adoption, adoption brings about the status of being a child, being a child includes inheritance rights from the father who is God, and if one is God's heir then one is a coheir of Christ. Paul's logic follows a very straight path in this section.[157] The μέν...δέ construction only enhances this linear path of thinking as it draws the reader to the natural conclusion of being an heir of God and thus a coheir with Christ.[158] The first readers of the letter would have understood the legal logic, since the *paterfamilias* and heir relationship

---

151 Cf. Byrne, 'Sons of God', 101.
152 Fee, *God's Empowering Presence*, 567–568; Schreiner, *Romans*, 426–427; Wilckens, *Römer*, 2:137–138.
153 Francis Lyall, *Slaves, Citizens, Sons: Legal Metaphors in the Epistles* (Zondervan, 1984), 102–103. Cf. Scott, *Adoption*, 10.
154 Hahn, "Pneumatology in Romans 8," 82.
155 Fitzmyer, *Romans*, 502; Schreiner, *Romans*, 428.
156 Cranfield, *Romans*, 1:407; Moo, *Romans*, 505. Contra Schreiner, *Romans*, 427–428.
157 Cf. Dunn, *Romans*, 1:455. Dunn notes the logic of Paul's argument and then concludes that being a coheir of Christ was Paul's starting point instead of the goal of his argument.
158 Wilckens, *Römer*, 2:138. Contra Byrne, 'Sons of God', 102. He believes the construction only shows simple apposition, but then there would be no need for the construction at all.

dominates the concept of adoption rather than the identity or existence of siblings. The recipients of this letter would have understood the difference in status between Jesus and themselves, as Paul makes a distinction between the adopted sons and the only Son. In fact, Paul introduces the idea of being a fellow heir with Christ in order to speak about what that inheritance is.[159] Thus, the Spirit changes the relationship of the believer through adoption not only with the Father but also with the Son.

4.2.2 *Son, Spirit, and Glory*

What the believer stands to inherit is glory. God has given the believer the status of son and heir through the work of the Spirit and the Son. Adoption leads to glorification, yet the path to glorification comes via the Son instead of the Spirit. The Spirit is the main agent in God adopting believers, yet the relationship to the Son carries more significance with respect to glorification. Paul initially makes this point in 8:17. Romans 8:17 continues the clarification or definition of the new status a believer has due to the work of God. Though some see the introduction of glory in 8:18–30 as the major theme of the section,[160] it is only a part of what Paul discusses, albeit a large part since so many of the themes intersect.[161] Paul continues to unpack the implications and results of believers being adopted by God.[162] The section has a three-fold structure based upon the subjects who are groaning. Thus, 19–22 focuses on creation, 23–25 on the sons, and 26–27 on the Spirit with 18 as the introduction and 28–30 as the conclusion.[163] In 8:17, Paul links suffering with glorification, such that whoever suffers with Christ will be glorified with him as well (cf. 3.3.2). Paul intends the reader to focus on the glorification rather than the suffering, as 8:18 makes clear.[164] This verse conveys the lack of importance

---

159 Byrne, 'Sons of God', 102–103.
160 E.g. Moo, *Romans*, 508.
161 Schreiner (*Romans*, 433) begins his discussion by calling this section one of "hope of future glory and a new creation." Glory occurs only three times in the passage (8:18, 21, 30), though this just lends evidence rather than being conclusive since a subject can be discussed without the presence of the lexeme.
162 See the analysis of Byrne ('*Sons of God*', 103-4) even though he concludes that the section refers mostly to glory. Cf. Wilhelm Thüsing, *Gott und Christus in der paulinischen Soteriologie: Band I Per Christum in Deum: Das Verhältnis der Christozentrik zur Theozentrik* (Aschendorff, 1986), 119.
163 The first to dissect the text based upon the groaning was Nygren, *Romans*, 330–331. With respect to the shifting subjects, see Byrne, '*Sons of God*', 104. Most modern commentators follow this taxonomy.
164 E.g. Byrne ('*Sons of God*', 104) who states with respect to glory that Paul "affirms its overwhelming superiority" over suffering.

that Paul gives suffering when compared to what one gains, which can be seen through the structure of the statement, as the only word negated is ἄξια (worthy), which directly proceeds τὰ παθήματα ("the sufferings").[165] Suffering is a present reality for the believer and glory will be the future reality.[166] Paul mentions suffering as a parallel with Christ, for just as he suffered and then attained glory so will those who follow him.[167] Paul connects all of this to the thought of being adopted by God.

The description of glory does not end here, as Paul continues his line of thought in explaining what the glory of the sons of God will be and how it interacts with creation (see 3.3.2 above and 4.2.3 below). The end goal for the sons of God, though, is to become like the singular Son of God (8:29–30). The language Paul uses in this passage draws attention to the significance of the Son of God over against the sons of God. Paul began addressing the sons of God in the first-person plural in 8:22 and continued this through 8:28. The first-person plural can only refer to the sons of God for a simple reason: they have the Spirit as first fruits already. Any sense of having the Spirit connects the person so having with being a son or child of God. Only those led by the Spirit can be called God's sons (8:14). Since Paul in 8:29–30 speaks to those who have the first fruits of the Spirit,[168] then he can only be speaking to those who are already sons of God.[169] Thus, when Paul moves from the first person to the third person to describe a singular son whom he describes as God's, the only possibility is that of Jesus. Combined with the other uses in this chapter (8:3, 32), Paul is singling Jesus out for special status over against the other sons of God. This special status also becomes plain as the sons, now called brothers (ἀδελφοί), are intended to become like the Son.

What does it mean for the other sons to be made συμμόφους τῆς εἰκόνος τοῦ υἱοῦ αὐτοῦ ("same form as the image of his son")? The phrase by itself conveys two truths. Cranfield notes that the Son is the εἰκὼν τοῦ θεοῦ rather than being κατ' εἰκόνα.[170] In other words, Jesus does not give an approximation of the Father, instead he is the actual image.[171] Cranfield also comments that this phrasing points in the direction of a process of conforming to him

---

165 Dunn (*Romans*, 1:468) asserts that the οὐκ ἄξια...πρός comprises a typical Greek idiom of comparison, yet his citation of LSJ does not support his statement. However, see BDF § 239.
166 Byrne, '*Sons of God*', 103–104; Moo, *Romans*, 506; Schreiner, *Romans*, 428.
167 Lagrange, *Romains*, 203.
168 Cf. Schreiner, *Romans*, 438.
169 Cf. Thüsing, *Gott und Christus*, 121. Thüsing connects the language here with the language of adoption from earlier in the passage. Schreiner (*Romans*, 438–439) connects adoption with first fruits, and thus the link moves all the way through the text.
170 Cranfield, *Romans*, 1:432. Cf. Fitzmyer, *Romans*, 525.
171 Cf. Moo, *Romans*, 534; Thüsing, *Gott und Christus*, 146–147.

as opposed to an instantaneous event.¹⁷² There are three points that will begin to answer the question posed above. First, one should note that Paul has used different language than in 8:3 when describing the coming of Jesus.¹⁷³ Believers are not to be made ἐν ὁμοιώματι of Jesus, rather they are προώρισεν συμμόρφους τῆς εἰκόνος, his image. The shift in language mitigates that a different idea is present in this verse than in 8:3. Second, to be made into the image of Christ carries obvious soteriological implications, yet the stress lies in the eschatological dimension, as Paul's use of glory and hope emphasize.¹⁷⁴ Conformity to Christ carries through the concept of glory from earlier in the section (most notably 8:17–18) and points toward the future (cf. Rom 6:5).¹⁷⁵ Third, the imagery intentionally draws on the metaphor of adoption, since Paul defines συμμόρφους τῆς εἰκόνος as Jesus being the firstborn among all his brothers. The final result, or one could call it purpose, of God conforming the believer to the image of Christ is bound up in two parts of a whole, namely it magnifies his status as the firstborn while also enabling them to become his brother.¹⁷⁶ This sets the idea of inheritance onto a new path, as the firstborn in legal terms had the right to hand out the inheritance. While the preeminence of Christ over his adopted siblings can be seen here, it is hardly the point Paul wants to make by calling Jesus the firstborn.¹⁷⁷ The concept of sonship has been directly linked throughout the chapter with inheritance, and thus any understanding of "firstborn" without the implications for inheritance does not convey Paul's intention nor does it encompass what the first readers would have understood by such language due to the implicit connection.¹⁷⁸ It is this inheritance that the readers would typically associate with the concept of firstborn.¹⁷⁹ Conforming to the image of Christ goes beyond an ethical injunction to an eschatological reality of inheritance.

What in Rom 8:29–30 makes Jesus special enough that the sons are to become like the Son? One would think that God himself would be the more appropriate image into which believers would be conformed. There are two answers to this question. First, God conforms believers into the image of Jesus

---

172 Cranfield, *Romans*, 1:432. This point will be taken up again below.
173 See 4.3 for the significance and theological import of Rom 8:3.
174 Moo, *Romans*, 535, especially n. 155. Wilckens, *Römer*, 2:164. Contra Käsemann, *Romans*, 244.
175 Schreiner, *Romans*, 453. Schreiner's contention that the good of 8:28 finds its definition here is unlikely. Cf. Dunn, *Romans*, 1:484; Wilckens, *Römer*, 2:164. See also 4.3 below.
176 See Cranfield, *Romans*, 1:432. Cf. Dunn, *Romans*, 1:485.
177 Contra Schreiner, *Romans*, 454.
178 Fitzmyer, *Romans*, 525. Contra Dunn, *Romans*, 1:484–485. Dunn sees only a Jewish eschatological concept and disregards how the language would affect the audience to which Paul is writing.
179 Cf. Wilhelm Michaelis, "πρωτότοκος, πρωτοτοκεῖα," *TDNT* 6:871–881.

because Jesus is the firstborn. Dunn is one of the more recent scholars who has stressed the importance of Adam Christology.[180] Though only the topic of Romans in 5:12–21 and named only once (in 5:14), Paul does intersperse Adam Christology throughout Romans. Paul argues in Romans 5 for a single human failure bringing sin to all humanity just as one single triumph can remove the failure for all who believe. Adam was the former, Christ was the latter, the last Adam (cf. 1 Cor 15:45).[181] Just as the first Adam began a new line of descent, namely humanity, so does the last Adam, namely believers. In this sense, both Adam and Christ are the firstborn of their brothers, only Adam's choice leads to death and Christ's to life. Being firstborn for Jesus is not a status or title limited to his resurrection from the dead, as many commentators seem to understand.[182] Schreiner notes how this title sets Jesus apart, and thus refers also to his preeminence.[183] The term has two meanings in the Pauline corpus, referring both to the ability to inherit and to the unique status of a person. In Col 1:15, 18, Paul covers both aspects. First, the phrase ὅς ἐστιν εἰκὼν τοῦ θεοῦ τοῦ ἀοράτου πρωτότοκος πάσης κτίσεως ("who is the image of the invisible God, firstborn of all creation") signifies the place of Christ over all things, a special status. Second, the parallel phrase, πρωτότοκος ἐκ τῶν νεκρῶν ("firstborn from the dead"), notes the eschatological nature of God raising him, a clue to the type of inheritance. The last clause then reorients towards his special status again, as Paul states this is ἵνα γένηται ἐν πᾶσιν αὐτὸς πρωτεύων ("in order that he would be first among all"). Dunn notes how this conveys both immanence and transcendence, a tension Paul intentionally uses.[184] To make the link from Rom 8:29 to Col 1:15–18 even stronger, one should note the language used in Col 1:15 that Jesus is εἰκὼν τοῦ θεοῦ τοῦ ἀοράτου, a parallel phrase to εἰκὼν τοῦ θεοῦ. Thus, in Colossians Paul directly ties together the concept of Jesus as firstborn with the idea of being the image of God.[185] In contrast to those adopted into the family of God, Jesus is the natural son, the firstborn, the one with the right to execute God's will in handing out the inheritance, namely

---

180 See especially James D. G. Dunn, *The Theology of Paul the Apostle* (Eerdmans, 1998), 199–204, 208–212, 241–242, and 288–293.

181 Cf. especially Gordon Fee, *The First Epistle to the Corinthians* (NICNT; Eerdmans, 1987), 788–790; Anthony Thiselton, *The First Epistle to the Corinthians: A Commentary on the Greek Text* (NIGTC; Eerdmans, 2000), 1281–1285.

182 E.g. Dunn, *Romans*, 1:484; Moo, *Romans*, 535.

183 Schreiner, *Romans*, 454. Unfortunately, Schreiner does not take his analysis further. Cf. Fitzmyer, *Romans*, 525.

184 James D. G. Dunn, *The Epistles to the Colossians and to Philemon* (NIGTC; Eerdmans, 1996), 90.

185 See Peter O'Brien, *Colossians, Philemon* (WBC 44; Nelson, 1982), 42–45.

life.[186] Therefore, since Jesus is the last Adam, the firstborn of God's sons, God will conform his children to the image of the Son.

The second reason God conforms believers to Jesus' image instead of his own is because Jesus is the sent one. While the language of sending in John carries great weight since it is more prominent than Paul's usage, one must note the significance it holds in Paul's argument. In John, sending language only occurs when Jesus speaks of himself and his mission (e.g. 3:16–17). Dunn cautions scholars from reading the presumably later Johannine tradition back into the Pauline tradition.[187] While Dunn makes a good point, one must also not eviscerate Paul's terminology because of how robust John's is, as the assumption of a dichotomy between John and Paul is as dangerous as the assumption of none. Dunn argues that the sending in Rom 8:3 does not have an ontological character as this idea of sonship connects to the crucifixion and resurrection, not to the act of sending.[188] However, he contradicts his own point in using Luke 20:13 and Mark 12:7–9 as examples since the motif in these passages assumes sonship before sending, in turn eliminating the need for a sonship based upon the resurrection. Dunn also believes Rom 8:3 echoes various phrases and words found "in the book of Wisdom and including the sending of Wisdom and of the Spirit in 9.10 and 9.17."[189] Neither of these examples, though, makes his case stronger. The sending of a person assumes the existence of the person in order for them to be sent. God does not create the Son, rather he sends the Son.[190] Dunn responds to this point by explaining that the passage has such strong Adam Christology undertones it could only point toward Jesus' death and subsequent resurrection, though his death is more likely in view.[191] Yet Dunn continues, linking the sending not just with the crucifixion but even with Jesus' "whole life,"[192] a phrase which overturns his argument. Dunn's point could have been that Paul was speaking of Jesus being sent to the cross after already being in the world, and thus have avoided any hint of preexistence with respect to the incarnation. Instead, by allowing that Jesus' entire human experience is in view, Dunn must concede the case since a sending that points to such includes the incarnation and cruci-

---

186 Morris, *Romans*, 332–333. Cf. above 3.3.2 and below 4.3.
187 James D. G. Dunn, *Christology in the Making: A New Testament Inquiry into the Origins of the Doctrine of the Incarnation* (2nd ed.; Eerdmans, 1989), 44; and *Theology of Paul*, 278.
188 Dunn, *Christology in the Making*, 44–45.
189 Dunn, *Theology of Paul*, 277. Cf. Dunn, *Christology in the Making*, 44. For more on the links with Wisdom, see his *Theology of Paul*, 277–279.
190 Haacker, *Römer*, 152; Fitzmyer, *Romans*, 484–485. Haacker argues for this point while Fitzmyer only asserts it.
191 Dunn, *Christology in the Making*, 45.
192 Dunn, *Christology in the Making*, 45.

fixion.[193] Dunn also defines preexistence is decidedly "Johannine in formulation,"[194] as he posits preexistence as referring to a real being with God but separate from God.[195] The problem with such an understanding (other than Dunn not clearly defining "preexistence" in the work, so one must look for places where he makes his position plain) is that it assumes either that there are many gods or else that there can be no plurality within the one God.[196] Thus, Dunn concludes that preexistence is not a category Paul would have used, but he defines it such that it could only fit the Johannine corpus anyway. If one understands preexistence simply as referring to existence before physical instantiation (with no artificial tags of existing with God or as a separate being or anything else), then Paul certainly holds to the preexistence of Christ.

If the entire crucifixion event is in view without limiting it strictly to the resurrection in this passage, then Rom 8:3 links directly to 8:32.[197] Since both passages comment on the special status of Jesus' sonship (i.e. ἑαυτοῦ and ἰδίου respectively), there is a link amongst all three passages (including 8:29). In 8:32, Paul alludes to the binding of Isaac (Gen 22:12, 16) in comparison to the relationship between the Father and Son.[198] Paul emphasizes the Father's role in the in the crucifixion of Jesus in 8:32 (the sacrifice that Schreiner calls "the greatest thing imaginable"[199]), with God being the subject of all the verbs (ἐφείσατο, παρέδωκεν ["hand over"], and χαρίσεται ["give graciously"]). This same Father-focus carries into 8:34, though discussing Jesus, the Father still controls the idea of the text since he is at work in and through Christ. In 8:33 Paul answers his question with θεὸς ὁ δικαιῶν, and then describes Jesus as ἐγερθείς ("raised," 8:34). The latter refers to the Father, as the text implies that the Father raised the Son from the dead (note that some important witnesses, such as ℵ* A C Ψ, include the phrase ἐκ νεκρῶν, though it likely was added as an explanatory gloss since there is no discernable reason for it to be dropped).[200] So Jesus became ἐν δεξιᾷ τοῦ θεοῦ ("at the right hand of God"), an obvious allusion

---

193 This last part is the point Moo (*Romans*, 478–481) makes. Moo also mentions the sacrificial tones, something Paul reiterates in 8:32.
194 Arland J. Hultgren, *Christ and His Benefits: Christology and Redemption in the New Testament* (Fortress, 1987), 7.
195 Dunn, *Christology in the Making*, 173, 255–256.
196 Hultgren *Christ and His Benefits*, 7–8. Note that Dunn (*Theology of Paul*, 267–272) does not clear up this confusion in his later work.
197 Fitzmyer, *Romans*, 484; Moo, *Romans*, 478–481.
198 Nils Alstrup Dahl "The Atonement-An Adequate Reward for the Aqedah? (Ro 8:32)" in *Neotestamentica et Semitica: Studies in Honor of Matthew Black* (ed. E. Earle Ellis and Max Wilcox; T&T Clark, 1969), 15–29, here 17.
199 Schreiner, *Romans*, 458.
200 Cranfield (*Romans*, 1:438 n. 5) draws attention to this point.

to Ps 110:1 (109:1 LXX),[201] a position granted by the Father[202] (something inherent in Psalm 110 as well).[203] The very position displays the glory of Christ, as Paul moves explicitly and intentionally from the humiliation of the cross (i.e. Jesus as ὁ ἀποθανών) to the glorification by Jesus' change in status to God's vice-regent.[204] Thus, Jesus being sent connects to his special status, and his special status is why believers are conformed to his image instead of the Father's image.

God conforms believers to the image of the Son as a further form of glory. This reason Paul gives for God making the believers συμμόρφους τῆς εἰκόνος τοῦ υἱοῦ αὐτοῦ is found by following the string of five verbs (i.e. προέγνω, προώρισεν, ἐκάλεσεν, ἐδικαίωσεν, and ἐδόξασεν) in 8:29-30.[205] The first verb, προέγνω, often gains the most attention due to its notoriety in the Arminian-Calvinist debates over the nature of mankind's free will balanced with God's sovereignty.[206] The lexeme is rare in the NT, occurring only six other times.[207] The emphasis lies on God's knowledge of whom he will save.[208] The second verb, προώρισεν, carries through the action of the first, moving from God's knowledge to God's action.[209] The third verb, ἐκάλεσεν, refers to the act of calling.[210] One should note, however, that "calling" was often used in Jewish writings to refer to sonship,[211] though this reference might have been too subtle for Paul's readers. The fourth verb, ἐδικαίωσεν, often carries great significance in Romans, yet displays the status with which God gifts believers.[212] The final verb, ἐδόξασεν, makes manifest the goal toward which this entire chain has been working, the glorification of the believer.[213] The emphasis in this chain of

---

201 See Dunn, *Romans*, 1:503–504. Cf. Ziesler, *Romans*, 229 n. x.
202 Schlatter, *Romans*, 196–197.
203 See the remarks in Dunn, *Romans*, 1:504.
204 Cf. Moo, *Romans*, 542–543.
205 Paul-Gerhard Klumbies, *Die Rede von Gott bei Paulus in ihrem zeitgeschtlichen Kontext* (Vandenhoeck & Ruprecht, 1992), 203. Klumbies introduces this as "the life of God in Christ."
206 E.g. Tom McCall and Keith D. Stranglin, "S. M. Baugh and the Meaning of Foreknowledge: Another Look," *Trinity Journal*, n.s., 26 (2005): 19–31.
207 The verb is found in Acts 26:5; Rom 11:2; 1 Pet 1:20; 2 Pet 3:17; and the noun in Acts 2:23; and 1 Pet 1:2.
208 Rudolf Bultmann, "προγινώσκω, πρόγνωσις," *TDNT* 1:715–716. Cf. Moo, *Romans*, 532–533; Schreiner, *Romans*, 451–453; Witherington, *Romans*, 228–229.
209 Paul J. Achtemeier, *Romans* (Interpretation. John Knox, 1985), 176; Schreiner, *Romans*, 453. Schreiner's contention that the two are nearly synonyms (452) falls short when one considers the progression inherent in the two verses. Cf. Peter von der Osten–Sacken, *Römer 8 als Beispiel paulinischer Soteriologie* (Vandenhoeck & Ruprecht, 1975), 71.
210 The issue of the perseverance of the saints, brought up in reference to this verb, is not relevant for this discussion. Cf. Moo, *Romans*, 535.
211 Byrne, *'Sons of God'*, 120.
212 Cranfield, *Romans*, 1:433.
213 Byrne, *Romans*, 272; Moo, *Romans*, 535; Schreiner, *Romans*, 454–455. Moo suggests this recaptures the main theme of this section of Romans, bringing the paragraph back to

verbs falls on the last verb, and this can be seen by the doxology that follows in 8:31-39. Paul assures his readers that no outside force can take away the sure future glory of believers. All of this, in turn, is linked back to the concept of sonship (8:29; cf. 8:32), which in turn derives from the concept of adoption.

In the end, glory comes about through the work of both the Son and the Spirit. The Spirit brings believers into glory because he functions as the agent of adoption. God uses the Spirit in believers in order to gather them into his family as sons and heirs. The Son brings believers into glory through being the firstborn, the designated natural heir. Jesus was not adopted as believers were, and so he stands as the executer of God's will. Thus, both the Son and Spirit function as agents of God in bringing God's adopted sons into glory.

4.2.3 Son, Spirit, and Creation

Part of the glory God gives to believers is a redeemed body (8:23, see 3.3.2). This signals God's gracious repeal of the curse in that the physical world is no longer under the curse from Genesis 3. Just as the Son and Spirit are God's agents in adopting and giving glory to believers, so are they his agents in righting creation itself.

Creation fell through no fault of its own (see 3.2). God brought about recreation through his adoption of believers. The Spirit is part of recreation as the active agent in adoption. God will renew creation in the eschatological act of revealing who he has adopted as sons.[214] In the glorious moment, all the sons of God will be made known. The Spirit actually adopts for the Father, and thus the Spirit brings about this moment of revelation.

The Son also has a part in the redemption of creation, yet that has not been spelled out as clearly.[215] The Father conforms all believers to the image of the Son, and so when God reveals them he will be revealing images of the Son. In this sense, Christ as the sent one and the firstborn functions as the template for the other sons for the redemption of their bodies.[216] At the same time, Jesus holds power over all creation as its Lord. Jesus' love cannot be separated from those he loves, and in the same way nothing can separate God's love from those he loves (8:38-39). The love of the Father is ἐν Χριστῷ Ἰησοῦ τῷ

---

where it began, whereas Schreiner mentions that glory "brackets" the text (455).

214 Note the language of birth pangs in 8:22, a typical metaphor for the eschatological happenings. Cf. D. T. Tsumura, "An OT Background to Rom 8.22," *NTS* 40 (1994): 620–621.

215 John Bolt, "The Relation Between Creation and Redemption in Romans 8:18-27," *Calvin Theological Journal* 30 (1995): 34–51, here 45–47.

216 J. Ramsey Michaels, "The Redemption of Our Body: The Riddle of Romans 8:19–22," in *Romans and the People of God: Essays in Honor of Gordon D. Fee on the Occasion of His 65th Birthday* (eds. Sven K. Soderlund and N. T. Wright; Eerdmans, 1999), 92–114, especially 100.

κυρίῳ. While the Son is the lord of believers (κυρίῳ ἡμῶν), this does not limit the domain of his lordship.[217] The use of κύριος at this point in the chapter likely draws on the occurrence at 5:1.[218] The peace of 5:1 (cf. 8:6) finds total fulfillment in the eschaton, as that peace is tantamount to justification.[219] Thus, the work of Christ in redeeming creation lies not in his interaction with creation but with his salvific work for mankind. In order to understand the implications for the relationship between the Father, Son, and Spirit, the topic of salvation in Romans 8 needs to be discussed.

4.3 Son, Spirit, and Salvation

While glory comes from salvation and adoption seems to be a metaphor for it, God opens the way to salvation through his agents, the Son and Spirit. Romans 8 opens with a statement that condemnation no longer obtains for those who are ἐν Χριστῷ Ἰησοῦ. Lowe asks why believers are not judged negatively,[220] and the answer to this question is interspersed throughout the rest of Romans 8.[221] The answer for Paul begins in the question itself, namely that those who are not condemned are given special status by being ἐν Χριστῷ Ἰησοῦ.[222] At the same time, Paul also includes mention of being in the Spirit. Before one can fully come to an answer to this question, one must understand the implications of being ἐν Χριστῷ Ἰησοῦ and ἐν πνεύματι, while also considering the relationship between the two.

4.3.1 "In Christ" and "In the Spirit"

This section will discuss the significance of "in Christ" and "in the Spirit," with special attention paid to Rom 8:1-4, since Paul uses "in Christ" as an answer to the problem of sin and the law found in Romans 7. Paul often employs the phrase ἐν Χριστῷ Ἰησοῦ (or a variant, leaving out a name or title or substituting a pronoun) throughout his letters.[223] While limited in reference to believ-

---

217 Gibbs, *Creation and Redemption*, 47. See also John Pester, "Glorification," *Affirmation and Critique* 7 (2002): 55–69.
218 Cranfield, *Romans*, 1:444.
219 Cf. Moo, *Romans*, 298–299.
220 Lowe, "But Why Not?," 231.
221 Contra Lowe, "But Why Not?," 231, who only looks to 8:1–15 in answer to this question.
222 Jewett, *Romans*, 480, notes that the phrase τοῖς ἐν Χριστῷ Ἰησοῦ occurs only here in Paul (otherwise only in 1 Pet 5:14), and this special status only through the work of the Holy Spirit, thought he posits an ecstatic experience of the Spirit.
223 See. W. Elliger, "ἐν," *EDNT* 1:447–449, here 448; Albrecht Oepke, "ἐν," *TDNT* 2:537–543, here 541–543. Those occurrences of the phrase including Χριστῷ are Rom 3:24; 6:11, 23; 8:1–2, 39; 9:1; 12:5; 15:17; 16:3, 7, 9–10; 1 Cor 1:2, 4, 30; 3:1; 4:10, 15 (2x), 17; 15:18–19, 22, 31; 16:24; 2 Cor 2:14, 17;

ers, typically the prepositional phrase carries more theological weight than simply identifying a people group.[224] Byrne, for instance, contends that Paul uses it to convey a communal concept of existing within the sphere of influence of Jesus.[225] He even goes so far to say that the entire community is contained within the person of Jesus, pointing to Rom 6:3.[226] Cranfield also looks to Romans 6, though he includes 6:2–11, to identify what Paul signifies by using the phrase.[227] Lowe sees 6:1–11 as a possible link, noting that the answer to why there is no condemnation could be that believers gain "transformational righteousness in union with Christ."[228] Each of these scholars[229] makes this link because of the culmination of Paul's argument in 6:11 referring to ζῶντας τῷ θεῷ ἐν Χριστῷ Ἰησοῦ. In 6:1–11, Paul considers how believers are baptized into Jesus' death and so share the resurrection, such that God replaces death with life in Christ Jesus.[230] The result pictured by this baptism symbolizing death and resurrection is the new life given to the believer. Thus, Cranfield states the ἐν Χριστῷ formula refers to how God sees Jesus' death instead of our sin, leading to the believer living for Christ and God seeing that as the life of Christ.[231] Both Cranfield and Wilckens believe the locative sense of the phrase is therefore excluded.[232] Käsemann connects the formula to the practice of baptism explicitly within mystery cults (noting Isis as a possible example).[233] Though some have contended that water in the Isis cult contains salvific power (due to the resurrection of Osiris after he hid in the water of the Nile),[234] the

---

3:14; 5:17, 19; 12:2, 19; Gal 1:22; 2:4, 17; 3:14, 26, 28; 5:6; Eph 1:1, 3, 10 (with article), 12 (with article), 20 (with article); 2:6–7, 10, 13; 3:6, 11 (with article), 21; 4:32; Phil 1:1, 13, 26; 2:1, 5; 3:3, 14; 4:7, 19, 21; Col. 1:2, 4, 28; 1 Thess 1:1 (conjoined to θεῷ); 2:14; 4:16; 5:18; 2 Thess 1:1 (conjoined to θεῷ) ; 3:12; 1 Tim 1:14; 3:13; 2 Tim 1:1, 9, 13; 2:1, 10; 3:12, 15; Phlm 1:8, 20, 23. Those without Χριστῷ yet using a name or title are Rom 14:14; 16:2, 8, 11, 12 (2x), 13, 22; 1 Cor 1:31; 4:17; 7:22, 39; 9:1–2; 11:11; 15:58; 16:19; 2 Cor 2:12; 10:17; Gal 5:10; Eph 1:15; 2:21; 4:1, 17, 21; 5:8; 6:1 (possibly, as the phrase might be a later addition to the text), 10, 21; Phil 1:14; 2:19, 24, 29; 3:1; 4:1–2, 4, 10; Col 3:18, 20; 4:7, 17; 1 Thess 3:8; 4:1, 17; 2 Thess 3:4, 12; Phlm 1:16, 20.

224 Longenecker (*Romans*, 693–694) seems to struggle with nailing down a solid understanding of this rather slippery and large phrase. Acknowledging it does refer to those who are believers, he then wants to enlarge the idea to incorporate a mystical understanding. Precisely what this entails, however, fits within the sphere of the human–divine relationship in an undefined way.

225 Byrne, *Romans*, 235.
226 Ibid., 190. He connects 8:1 to 6:3.
227 Cranfiled, *Romans*, 1:373.
228 Lowe, "But Why Not?," 233.
229 Cf. Moo, *Romans*, 473; Schreiner, *Romans*, 398.
230 Käsemann, *Romans*, 160, 162–163.
231 Cranfield, *Romans*, 1:315–316.
232 Ibid., 315; Wilckens, *Römer*, 2:121.
233 Käsemann, *Romans*, 160–161.
234 E.g. Sharon Heyob, *The Cult of Isis Among Women in the Greco–Roman World* (EPRO 51; Brill, 1975), 61.

evidence leads to a different conclusion, namely that water is just a symbol.[235] Thus, this idea of baptism being from the mystery cults, and so the phrase ἐν Χριστῷ coming from them as well, is unfounded.

In addition, Käsemann holds that "with Christ" (σὺν Χριστῷ) and "in Christ" (ἐν Χριστῷ) are synonymous.[236] His argument comes from linking 6:8 with 6:11. He also believes that there is "obviously" a connection with God conforming believers "with Christ as God's image, an idea which probably derives from liturgical tradition."[237] While many scholars decide against this position,[238] Käsemann's case cannot be lightly dismissed. In his favor lies the Pauline usage of "in Christ" pointing toward eschatological life, as evidenced in both 6:11 and 8:1-4.[239] This fits with the occurrence of "with Christ" in 6:8, namely that participation in Jesus' death constitutes participation in Jesus' life. Every usage of ἐν Χριστῷ will not be the same,[240] though one should expect some overlap, yet a one-to-one correspondence seems unlikely. Wedderburn notes the "with Christ" language typically complements a specific action (often dying, e.g. Phil 1:23 and Col 2:20).[241] Cranfield rightly holds that the σὺν Χριστῷ idea originates with Paul, and thus Käsemann cannot use tradition history since there is none.[242] Dunn points to the eschatological use of the term, as it typically carries a future notion of life yet to come or an existence not fully realized.[243] Within Romans, the phrase is rare (occurring only in 6:8 and debatable in 8:32 since it is a periphrastic way of compounding the subject of a verb[244]), making it hard to analyze. Dunn, rather than only looking at all occurrences of σὺν Χριστῷ or equivalents in Paul, focuses on the compound words.[245] What makes these profitable lies in the different subjects of the implied prepositional phrases (the συν prefix plus the object of the verb). While typically denoting Christ, the subjects can also be the Spirit

---

235 Ladislav Vidman, *Isis und Sarapis bei den Griechen und Römern: Epigraphische Studien zur Verbreitung und zu den Trägern des ägyptischen Kultes* (Religionsgeshichtliche Versuche und Vorarbeiten; de Gruyter, 1970), 13.

236 Käsemann, *Romans*, 161–162.

237 Ibid., 162.

238 E.g. Dunn, *Romans*, 1:324; Peter Siber, *Mit Christus leben. Eine Studie zur paulinischen Auferstehungshoffnung* (ATANT 61; Theologischer Verlag, 1971), 196–198.

239 E.g. Moo, *Romans*, 380–381.

240 See the chart in Michel Bouttier, *En Christ: etude d'exegese et de theologie Pauliniennes* (Presses Universitaires de France, 1967), 133.

241 E.g. A. J. M. Wedderburn, "Some Observations on Paul's Use of the Phrases 'in Christ' and 'with Christ,'" *JSNT* 25 (1985): 83–97.

242 Cranfield, *Romans*, 1:312.

243 Dunn, *Romans*, 1:321–322. He also thinks this analysis encompasses the συν–compound verbs (321).

244 Cf. Cranfield, *Romans*, 1:311–312.

245 Dunn, *Romans*, 1:313.

(συμμαρτυρέω in 8:16, συναντιλαμβάνομαι in 8:26), possibly God or all things (συνέργω in 8:28), or creation (συνωδίνω and συστενάζω in 8:22).[246] All of these terms circle around the divide between life and death, this world and the one to come.[247] Since Paul occasionally creates his own compounds, it is likely this terminology began with him rather than Paul borrowing the language.[248] The "in Christ" phrase, on the other hand, has a larger domain. In Rom 8:2, 39, Paul attaches the phrase to life, an inherently eschatological concept. This connects "in Christ" to a future oriented life (i.e. at least some portion of the life is in the future if not all of it), and it allows for a communal understanding of the phrase since the number of believers is not limited.[249] The difference, then, seems to be one of emphasis. Whereas σὺν Χριστῷ stresses a function or action the believer can participate in that Christ has already done, the ἐν Χριστῷ phrase includes an eschatological aspect that goes beyond a simple action.[250] Thus in Pauline thought one must first be σὺν Χριστῷ in order to be ἐν Χριστῷ, just as dying with Christ in 6:8 initiates the death to sin and life to God in 6:11.[251]

Ἐν Χριστῷ has now been limited in scope, yet what does it signify in 8:1? Building off of what Paul already stated in 6:1–11, to be ἐν Χριστῷ refers to those identifying with Christ in his death and actively living a life for him.[252] Considering Romans 7 and how Paul equates sin with death (see 4.1), life functions as the key characteristic of those in Christ, so sin needs to be defeated since life is the antithesis of death. This life defines the believer, and what it means to be ἐν Χριστῷ, yet the significance of this life needs to be explained. What follows in 8:2–4 identifies how being ἐν Χριστῷ supersedes condemnation.

In Rom 8:2–4, Paul fleshes out the significance of being ἐν Χριστῷ while also explaining how one attains such status.[253] The law of the Spirit begins the explanation as it contrasts with the law of sin and death.[254] The reason for condemnation, as Paul contends in Romans 7, is not the law but sin. Sin leads directly to death, and it is from death that God seeks to save people. He does so by condemning sin itself rather than those who commit sin. The law then

---

246 Dunn, *Romans*, 1:313.
247 Ibid., 1:313.
248 Contra Käsemann, *Romans*, 161–162.
249 For more on the connection between the eschatological life and the communal aspect of "in Christ," see Wilckens, *Römer*, 2:45–47.
250 Cf. the conclusions of Dunn, *Romans*, 1:321–322, 324.
251 Dunn, *Romans*, 1:324. He concludes that the "ἐν Χριστῷ of v 11 is the result of the σὺν Χριστῷ of v 8."
252 Cf. Moo, *Romans*, 472–473; Schreiner, *Romans*, 399; Witherington, *Romans*, 210.
253 Cf. Cranfield, *Romans*, 1:372; Moo, *Romans*, 471; Schreiner, *Romans*, 399.
254 For the defense of this reading of Paul, see above 4.1.

can be fulfilled by the Spirit within those who walk according to the Spirit. The key for understanding the ἐν Χριστῷ of 8:1 is understanding the significance and intention of πέμψας in 8:3 (cf. 3.4 above). The reason for this is twofold. First, the sending is a Father-focused event such that the Son functions as God's agent to do the work the Father wants done.[255] For believers to be in Christ, God acts decisively to defeat sin since it cannot be defeated without God's direct help.[256] Thus, God breaks into history by sending his Son, the new Adam, to displace the work of the first Adam.[257] Second, closely related to the first, the results of the sending change the course of history (or salvation-history) in that the Spirit comes or is enabled to come through the act of sending.[258] Thus, in analyzing the significance of the Father sending the Son, one can understand the import of ἐν Χριστῷ.

While the emphasis of πέμψας lies on the action of the Father, the immediate results come directly from the work of the Son.[259] The work of the Son sets believers free from death, the result of sin, but how? Paul answers by stating that God sent his Son ἐν ὁμοιώματι σαρκὸς ἁμαρτίας καὶ περὶ ἁμαρτίας. While the latter phrase carries cultic overtones (cf. 3.4 above), the initial words create much debate. Schreiner begins looking at this difficult concept by recalling Rom 6:5, where believers are connected to Jesus τῷ ὁμοιώματι τοῦ θανάτου αὐτοῦ.[260] The likeness cannot be the exact death of Christ, as only he could die his death, yet this likeness does affirm a particular identification between Jesus and believers, hence Paul's use of σύμφυτοι γεγόναμεν.[261] Branick believes that Paul sees a continuity here in 8:3, such that there is no difference between Christ's flesh and sinful flesh.[262] Gillman notes that the work of Branick is flawed because it was based on a flawed study,[263] a study that tried to deduce a single meaning for every occurrence of ὁμοίωμα when

---

255 Moo, *Romans*, 478. Cf. Dunn, *Romans*, 1:420.
256 Moo, *Romans*, 477; Schreiner, *Romans*, 401; Wilckens, *Römer*, 2:124.
257 Dunn, *Romans*, 1:438.
258 Fee (*God's Empowering Presence*, 528) overstates the point saying, "Paul simply will not move on to talk about Spirit activity without grounding it squarely upon the work of Christ." Cf. Dunn, *Romans*, 1:440–441; Schreiner, *Romans*, 405.
259 Cf. Fee, *God's Empowering Presence*, 530. In regard to 8:2–4, Fee acknowledges, "the work of Christ is the obvious central concern of the sentence."
260 Schreiner, *Romans*, 402.
261 Schreiner, *Romans*, 314.
262 Vincent P. Branick, "The Sinful Flesh of the Son of God (rom 8:3): A Key Image of Pauline Theology," *CBQ* 47 (1985): 246–262.
263 The study said to be flawed is that of Ugo Vanni, "*Homoiōma* in Paulo (Rm 1, 23; 5,14; 6,5; 8,3; Fil 2,7). Un interpretazione esegetico-teologica alla luce dell'uso dei LXX," *Greg* 58 (1977): 321–345, 431–470.

a single meaning is not necessary.²⁶⁴ While Branick argues for a direct correspondence between the things compared, Gillman notes the example of Rom 5:14 where there cannot be a one-to-one correspondence simply because the sin of Adam is not repeatable since a first time by definition can only occur once, as she explains that "similarity is certainly intended, but the very changed circumstances do not allow for full congruence with Adam's sin."²⁶⁵ Wilckens tries to push for a third understanding over against either complete identification or moderate congruence by noting that ὁμοίωμα can refer simply to form, yet in the end he reduces his position to "Identität bei Nichtidentität."²⁶⁶ In the final analysis, Gillman's view better explains the data available than Branick's within Romans and does not commit the lexical fallacy of limiting a word to a single meaning. Dunn adds an interesting twist, advocating Adam Christology in the passage while explaining that if Adam Christology is here, then Paul must be understanding Jesus as functioning in an Adamic capacity without actually being Adam, and thus there is identification with distinction.²⁶⁷ In this context, especially considering how flesh is used throughout the ongoing argument in Romans 8, the expression of Jesus as πέμψας ἐν ὁμοιώματι σαρκὸς ἁμαρτίας most likely refers to his identification with humanity as a something slightly different as opposed to a complete congruence.²⁶⁸

Christ came ἐν ὁμοιώματι σαρκὸς, yet how does this answer the problem of condemnation by way of God sending the Son, being "in Christ?" The second phrase offered by Paul carries through the theme of the law and how the problem of sin was dealt with in the law itself, namely περὶ ἁμαρτίας.²⁶⁹ The cultic background previously mentioned sets the tone for what Paul is referencing. For an example outside of the Pentateuch, Neh 10:33 (LXX 10:34) states καὶ τὰ περὶ ἁμαρτίας ἐξιλάσασθαι περὶ Ισραηλ, clearly a discussion of sin offerings since the entire verse is concerned with the cultic issues Jews had

---

264 Florence Morgan Gillman, "Another Look at Romans 8:3: 'In the Likeness of Sinful Flesh,'" *CBQ* 49 (1987): 597–604, here 597–598.
265 Gillman, "Another Look at Romans 8:3," 599.
266 Wilckens, *Römer*, 2:126. For his full discussion, see 2:124–126.
267 Dunn, *Romans*, 1:438–439. Dunn's position on Adam Christology here in 8:1–4 certainly has merit. See below.
268 See the reasonable conclusion of Moo, *Romans*, 479. Moo balances all three views, opting for a position similar to Wilckens, that Paul wants to show "inward and real participation" while also conveying "a note of distinction." Contra Jewett, *Romans*, 484, who posits the idea that the term "sinful flesh" should be "understood as the perverse quest for honor that poisons every human endeavor." The cultic tone of the passage makes this concept unlikely.
269 Michel, *Römer*, 188; Schreiner, *Romans*, 403; Wilckens, *Römer*, 2:126–128.

to abandon due to the exile and were now instituting once again.[270] Following on the heels of the discussion of sin and law from Romans 7 (see 3.2), and considering the issues of condemnation and the law already introduced in 8:1-2, Paul must be linking this phrase with God rescuing people from the power of sin by the person of Jesus as a sacrifice.[271] In order for a sin offering to occur in the OT, blood must be shed and a living being must die (cf. Exod 29:36; Lev 4:25; especially Exod 30:10). Therefore, for Jesus to be a sin offering, he had to be able to die, and thus he came in the flesh.[272] In Roman religion, there existed no parallel to the sin offering since salvation was not from sin but from circumstances.[273]

The other issue in this phrase is why it had to be sinful flesh (σαρκὸς ἁμαρτίας, taking the second genitive as qualitative[274]) as opposed to just flesh. While some scholars immediately jump to the conclusion that this refers to humanity as fallen rather than humanity as sinful (and therefore the conclusion that Jesus himself sinned),[275] this needs to be analyzed without prejudging the results. The issue of note is that Paul qualifies his use of σάρξ with ἁμαρτίας, thus immediately demonstrating that this type of flesh differs in moral substance from his following uses of the word (e.g. 8:4). Here flesh signifies physicality, otherwise sinful flesh (if flesh refers to the "sin nature") is redundant (sinful sin nature), rather it refers to the physical body constrained by the results of sin (e.g. illness, death, etc.).[276] In turn, ἁμαρτίας describes σάρξ as sinful, such that Jesus did not escape the results of the fall (e.g. loss of innocence, the curses of Gen 3, death). The addition of ἁμαρτίας clarifies σάρξ as purely physical, so how does ὁμοίωμα help Paul's argument? It helps by limiting the identification of Jesus and the flesh constrained by sin to congruence rather than total equivalence.[277] Adding together the significance of the entire set of phrases, πέμψας ἐν ὁμοιώματι σαρκὸς ἁμαρτίας καὶ περὶ ἁμαρτίας refers to God sending Jesus as one identified with sinful flesh as a sin offering,

---

270 The full verse reads εἰς ἄρτους τοῦ προσώπου καὶ θυσίαν τοῦ ἐνδελεχισμοῦ καὶ εἰς ὁλοκαύτωμα τοῦ ἐνδελεχισμοῦ τῶν σαββάτων τῶν νουμηνιῶν εἰς τὰς ἑορτὰς καὶ τὰ ἅγια καὶ τὰ περὶ ἁμαρτίας ἐξιλάσασθαι περὶ Ισραηλ καὶ εἰς ἔργα οἴκου θεοῦ ἡμῶν ("for the bread of presence, the regular sacrifice, the regular burnt offering, the Sabbaths, the new moons, for the feasts and the holy days, and the sin offerings to make propitiation for Israel").
271 Moo, *Romans*, 480; Wilckens, *Römer*, 2:127. Cf. Barth, *Romans*, 277–278.
272 Richard H. Bell, "Sacrifice and Christology in Paul," *JTS* 53 (2002): 1–27, here 7–8.
273 Burkert, *Ancient Mystery Cults*, 27–28.
274 E.g. Cranfield, *Romans*, 1:379.
275 Cf. Gillman, "Another Look at Romans 8:3," 602–603. Gillman simply quotes Dunn for her reasoning without showing her exegesis to arrive at such a conclusion, though to be fair her article concerns a different portion of the passage. Cf. Dunn, *Romans*, 1:421–422.
276 Cf. Dunn, *Romans*, 1:421–422; Fitzmyer, *Romans*, 485; Schreiner, *Romans*, 403.
277 Moo, *Romans*, 479–480; Schreiner, *Romans*, 402–403.

a sacrifice. In other words, God caused Jesus to become human and die for the sins of others. This in turn defines ἐν Χριστῷ as more than union with Christ, it defines it as all believers and all believers as ἐν Χριστῷ.[278]

What, then, does it mean to be ἐν πνεύματι? Paul builds his description of the sending of the Son with the dichotomy between walking κατὰ σάρκα and walking κατὰ πνεῦμα. Paul continues detailing the differences between the two types of people throughout 8:5–8.[279] Paul concludes the section with the summary of the negative aspects of humanity as ἐν σαρκί in 8:8.[280] The contrasting concept Paul uses to overcome ἐν σαρκί is ἐν πνεύματι in 8:9.[281] The conflicting lifestyles of κατὰ σάρκα and κατὰ πνεῦμα from 8:4 Paul renames ἐν σαρκί and ἐν πνεύματι.[282] Just as 8:5–8 defines what κατὰ σάρκα signified, so does 8:9-11 do the same for κατὰ πνεῦμα.[283] Thus, for ὑμεῖς to be ἐν πνεύματι the reverse is true, as the Spirit must be ἐν ὑμῖν, a reversal rather than a restatement of the first half of 8:9.[284] If living ἐν σαρκί leads to death, and ἐν πνεύματι is the opposite of ἐν σαρκί then living ἐν πνεύματι leads to life (cf. 8:2). Life for Paul carries an eschatological flavor, and thus ἐν πνεύματι brings in an eschatological flavor as well.[285] Hahn's contention that ἐν πνεύματι references two eras in eschatological terms and κατὰ πνεῦμα does not[286] misses the import of the function of κατὰ πνεῦμα with respect to salvation–history, as both can only be used of someone who is a believer.

The reason ἐν πνεύματι describes only believers comes from the context. The indwelling of the Spirit signifies belonging to God.[287] This can be seen from 8:9, yet Paul supports this assertion with his reasoning in 8:11. God raised Jesus from the dead, a fact Paul takes for granted as already established to his readers (not to mention its implicit presence in 8:1-4).[288] In the same way, believers have the Spirit of resurrection within them so that the resurrection of Christ is tied closely with that of believers, since the same Spirit works for

---

278 Cf. Wright, *Climax of the Covenant*, 216. This conclusion allows for other, more nuanced meanings to be understood at various junctures, as this is proposed simply for 8:1–2.

279 Cf. 4.2.1 above.

280 Dunn, *Romans*, 1:428; Fee, *God's Empowering Presence*, 542.

281 Fitzmyer, *Romans*, 490; Michel, *Römer*, 192; Moo, *Romans*, 489–490.

282 Fee, *God's Empowering Presence*, 545. Cf. Dunn, *Romans*, 1:428.

283 Dillon, "Taskmaster and Troublemaker," 693. Cf. Longenecker, *Romans*, 697; Arthur Skevington Wood, *Life by The Spirit* (Zondervan, 1963), 45.

284 Contra Schreiner, *Romans*, 413. While if p then q is true, that does not normally mean if q then p. Paul's argument here in Rom 8:9 states if p then q and if q then p, thus p = q in a logical sense.

285 Cf. Hahn, "Pneumatology in Romans 8," 78–79. Hahn argues that Paul's use of ἐν πνεύματι always draws in eschatological notions throughout Romans, as in 2:29 and 7:6.

286 Ibid., 78.

287 See 3.3.1.

288 Cf. Dunn, *Romans*, 1:432; Schreiner, *Romans*, 415–416; Wilckens, *Römer*, 2:133.

both.[289] Only those who are children and heirs should look for their own resurrection and attendant glory, for if the glory of Christ comes after his resurrection so will that of believers.[290]

Ἐν πνεύματι does point in the direction of ethics (keeping in mind that neither Paul nor his readers would think in terms of ethics as separated from theology[291]), a set of standards only for believers. Just as Paul uses "the flesh" as a description and sign of unbelievers (or at least those not yet believing), so the Spirit must be descriptive of those who do believe (cf. 8:4 and the opposition of κατὰ σάρκα κατὰ πνεῦμα).[292] Paul explicitly states the ethical concern in terms of putting the flesh to death by the Spirit (8:13, πνεύματι)[293] The obligation of those Paul calls ἀδελφοί[294] in 8:12 is to live by the Spirit in 8:13.[295] Paul then moves into his discussion of adoption from the ethical implications of having the Spirit.

Ἐν πνεύματι does not refer to ethics alone (even though the phrase contrasts with ἐν σαρκί in 8:9), for the Spirit carries more than ethical power for Christians. The Spirit enables adoption, as Paul illustrates in 8:15–16.[296] This act of adoption is part of someone being ἐν πνεύματι. In 8:14, Paul is defining those who have the Spirit as sons of God, not making sonship logically prior to the reception of the Spirit.[297] The term ὅσοι does not convey conditionality, rather it carries an inclusive sense.[298] This sonship is larger than some sort of ethical norm: rather sonship denotes heir, and heir conveys the sense of inheritance, and the inheritance is glory.[299] Therefore, the concept of ἐν πνεύματι points toward the reality of being a believer.

How, then, do ἐν Χριστῷ and ἐν πνεύματι relate to each other? The first step is to pay attention to what Paul does not mean, specifically the difference

---

289   Fee, *God's Empowering Presence*, 552; Wilckens, *Römer*, 2:134.

290   See both 3.3.2 and 4.2.2.

291   See both 4.1.1 with respect to the discussion about Fee and 2.3 with respect to ethics or the practical in the Imperial Cult. Cf. Jewett, *Romans*, 490. Jewett discusses how Seneca wrote to Lucilius and spoke of a spirit indwelling them, showing that this idea would not be foreign to the Roman congregations.

292   Cranfield, *Romans*, 1:390; Dunn, *Romans*, 1:444; Schreiner, *Romans*, 411.

293   Fee, *God's Empowering Presence*, 558.

294   Likely this address is used intentionally to transition from the negative aspects of the Spirit with respect to the flesh in order to move onto the positive, namely adoption.

295   Hahn, "Pneumatology in Romans 8," 81; Moo, *Romans*, 494; Murray, *Romans*, 294.

296   Cf. Moo, *Romans*, 500; Schreiner, *Romans*, 424; Nigel Watson, "And If Children, Then Heirs' (Rom 8:17)–Why Not Sons?" *ABR*, 49 (2001): 53–56, here 53.

297   Jewett, *Romans*, 497; Scott, *Adoption*, 260. Cf. Schreiner, *Romans*, 427.

298   Cf. Cranfield, *Romans*, 1:395; Walter Schmithals, *Die theologische Anthropologie des Paulus. Auslegung von Röm. 7,17–8,39* (Kohlhammer Taschenbücher 1021; Kohlhammer, 1980), 128. Contra Michel, *Römer*, 196–197.

299   Cf. 3.3 and 4.2.

God and the Son and the Spirit

between flesh and Spirit is not the difference between Adam and Christ,[300] even though Adam Christology is in view at the beginning of Romans 8.[301] "In Christ" language carries a sense of unity, a sense of belonging to a being that ties into the typical understanding of what it means to be a member of a mystery religion due to the way the cults rely upon select membership.[302] "In the Spirit" carries ethical connotations that are not at the fore of "in Christ" language, yet being "in the Spirit" relates directly to sonship just as being "in Christ" does. In other words, the concepts for both overlap at a specific point, namely the issue of life.[303]

4.3.2 Life

Paul's use of the term "life" (ζωή) in Romans 8 can lead to two different understandings. First, life appears to be something lived out on the earth through the power of the Spirit. Second, Paul intimates that life is an eschatological existence, the opposite of which is not just death but also flesh and sin.[304] Throughout Romans 8, Paul connects life with the Spirit (8:2, 6, 10, 11, 13, 23), interlacing the two without equating them. Paul also connects Jesus to life (8:2, 10, 11, 17, 29–30), making an overlap between the functions of the Son and Spirit with respect to how life, and therefore salvation, operates.[305]

In 8:2, Paul connects life to both the Son and the Spirit.[306] Dodd paraphrases a portion of 8:2 as "the law of the Spirit brings the life which is in Christ Jesus."[307] Dodd understands ἐν Χριστῷ as functioning as a locative, which is unlikely. Rather, an instrumental sense fits the argument Paul is making, since this discussion stems from Paul giving an explanation as to why believers are no longer condemned. They are no longer condemned because they are "in Christ," and as condemnation leads to death so does being "in Christ" lead

---

300 Ben Witherington, *Paul's Narrative Thought World: The Tapestry of Tragedy and Triumph* (Westminster/John Knox, 1994), 251.
301 Cf. Dunn, *Romans*, 1:434–435.
302 Witherington, *Romans*, 211. Cf. John M. Court, "Mithraism Among the Mysteries," in *Religious Diversity in the Greco-Roman World: A Survey of Recent Scholarship* (ed. Dan Cohn-Sherbok and John M. Court; Sheffield Academic Press, 2001), 182–195.
303 Longenecker, *Romans*, 698. He notes that the three persons all work together in the believer to promote life as the resurrection of Jesus functions as both precedent and promise. Cf. Käsemann, *Romans*, 213. He sees the overlap as due to the lordship of Christ over the believer.
304 On the overlap of death, sin, and flesh, see 4.1.2.
305 This connection between life and salvation will be justified below.
306 See the discussion on what the prepositional phrase modifies in πνεύματος τῆς ζωῆς ἐν Χριστῷ Ἰησοῦ ἠλευθέρωσεν in 4.1.1 above.
307 Dodd, *Romans*, 118–119.

to life.³⁰⁸ Dying with Christ opens the way to life in the Spirit (cf. Rom 7:4–6).³⁰⁹ The Spirit then applies life to the believer, so the believer obtains life by Christ.³¹⁰ Thus, the work of the Spirit and of Christ overlap.

The results of being in Christ and in the Spirit lead to life in Rom 8:6, 10. Paul states that the end of having the mind of the Spirit is ζωὴ καὶ εἰρήνη.³¹¹ The end of the mind of flesh is death and enmity with God.³¹² Murray thinks this points toward sanctification being the issue over against justification, since life in the Spirit must refer to how one lives.³¹³ However, one must assume that death here refers to separation from God rather than actual death, otherwise Paul's contrast of life and death holds little to no significance as an antithesis. Instead, Paul is pointing toward an eschatological reality, a position made all the stronger by understanding that one's relationship to the law is determinative for one's relationship with God (cf. 8:2–4).³¹⁴ While some opt for this being a temporal act, with death meaning separation from God and life being equated with peace, both defined as a relational standing with God,³¹⁵ Paul continually points toward a future reality where the relationship with God becomes finalized, such that one's status before him will not change.

Paul points toward a future understanding of life in 8:10, as the Spirit is ζωὴ διὰ δικαιοσύνην. Some scholars argue for an understanding of πνεῦμα in this verse as the human spirit,³¹⁶ with Wright pointing out a possible parallel between body and spirit as both being part of a human.³¹⁷ Bertone rightly notes that this would force ζωή to function adjectivally instead of as a noun, something that Paul does not do with the word, as he typically uses a form of ζάω to denote the state of being alive or coming back to life.³¹⁸ The statement by Paul that σῶμα νεκρὸν διὰ ἁμαρτίαν carries future not present significance in that the body will die yet this is not the end,³¹⁹ and the readers of this letter are obviously not dead yet. Thus, considering the two phrases as parallel, the life Paul is referencing must be future also since it runs counter to death be-

---

308   Hahn, "Pneumatology in Romans 8," 77.
309   Lowe, "But Why Not?," 240. Cf. Käsemann, *Romans*, 218–219.
310   Hahn, "Pneumatology in Romans 8," 77–78; Schreiner, *Romans*, 413.
311   Hahn, "Pneumatology in Romans 8," 78; Dunn, *Romans*, 1:442; Moo, *Romans*, 487–488.
312   Cf. Moo, *Romans*, 488; Osten-Sacken, *Römer 8*, 235; Schreiner, *Romans*, 412.
313   Murray, *Roans*, 285–286. He calls this "knowledge and fellowship of God" the "apex of true religion."
314   Byrne, *Romans*, 239; Moo, *Romans*, 487–488.
315   Cf. Bertone, *"The Law of the Spirit"*, 186–187, especially 187 n. 82.
316   See especially Sanday and Headlam, *Romans*, 198; Wright, *Climax of the Covenant*, 202.
317   Wright, *Climax of the Covenant*, 202. Yet see in N. T. Wright, "The Letter to the Romans," in *The New Interpreter's Bible* (12 vols.; Abingdon, 2002), 584, where he seemingly disagrees with this conclusion.
318   Bertone, *"The Law of the Spirit"*, 187–188. He counts 23 uses of ζάω in Romans alone.
319   Dunn, *Romans*, 1:445; Moo, *Romans*, 491–492; Schreiner, *Romans*, 414.

cause of sin. In addition, 8:11 continues the discussion of life as resurrection life, a life that can only be future.[320] This is borne out in 8:13 through the use of μέλλω and the future indicative of ζάω.[321] All of this highlights life as a future oriented idea in Paul's thought. A future life would not fit within the typical worldview of a Roman. Life ended with death, and salvation was about this life.[322] Romans did not hold a strong view of life after death, instead they hoped for either another chance at life, a lack of existence, or else a drab life in the grave.[323] Paul's contrast to this would offer an unforeseen hope, a future living without the fear of punishment or existence in a tomb.[324] Even the mystery cults in general (the cult of Dionysus is a possible exception) offered no future hope.[325] A resurrected life would be a wonderful contrast to what the typical Roman believed.

Paul combines the Son and Spirit in the giving of life in Rom 8:10–11. First, those who receive life must have "Christ in you" (Χριστὸς ἐν ὑμῖν), a reversal of the standard ἐν Χριστῷ formula.[326] Fee notices that in reading these verses (8:9–10), one would expect to find a reference to the Spirit instead of to Christ.[327] Paul's language here deviates from his norm then, demonstrating to the reader that something atypical is occurring in this thought. The connection of Christ to believers can be expressed in multiple ways, including them being in Christ and Christ being in them.[328] This is important because Paul transitions immediately back into Spirit language by the end of the thought, such that the "indwelling of Christ" (admittedly altered Pauline terminology) has commonality and overlap with the Spirit giving life to the believer.

Second, the Spirit also dwells within the believer. Paul makes this explicit by stating πνεῦμα οἰκεῖ ἐν ὑμῖν as a condition for ζῳοποιέω ("I make alive," 8:11). This verse does not imply that the Spirit raised Jesus from the dead,[329] rather it explicitly credits the Father for this action.[330] While there is a strong identification between believers and Jesus with respect to the nature of their res-

---

320 Hahn, "Pneumatology in Romans 8," 80; Schreiner, *Romans*, 415.
321 Cf. Dunn, *Romans*, 1:430; Fitzmyer, *Romans*, 493.
322 Robert Turcan, "Salut mithriaque et sotriologie noplatoncienne," in *La soteriologia dei culti oriental nell' Impero Romano* (ed. Ugo Bianchi and Maarten J. Vermaseren; Brill, 1982), 173–191, here 173–174.
323 John Ferguson, *The Religions of the Roman Empire* (Aspects of Greek and Roman Life; Thames and Hudson, 1970), 132–136.
324 Cf. Ferguson, *Religions of the Roman Empire*, 133–134.
325 Ferguson, *Religions of the Roman Empire*, 135–138.
326 Cf. Moo, *Romans*, 491.
327 Fee, *God's Empowering Presence*, 548.
328 Moo, *Romans*, 491; Schreiner, *Romans*, 413–414. Cf. Dunn, *Romans*, 1:430.
329 Contra Scott, *Adoption*, 256.
330 Schreiner, *Romans*, 415–416. He rightly notes the stress Paul places upon this by the double use of ἐγείρω in 8:11.

urrections,³³¹ Paul's statements reject the need for the Spirit to be the agent of the Son's resurrection as Paul stresses the Father's role.³³² The Spirit dwelling in the believer points toward the future bodily resurrection of the believer. The Spirit is God's agent in giving life to τὰ θνητὰ σώματα, as seen by the διά phrase. Cranfield discusses the textual variant (an accusative object instead of the genitive reading adopted above), and rightly sides with the genitive reading due to manuscript evidence (א A C* Pc 81 for the genitive against B D F G Ψ for the accusative), the likelihood of the genitive becoming accusative due to the surrounding accusative phrases (e.g. διὰ δικαιοσύνην), and because agency is the most likely concept.³³³ In addition, God uses the Spirit as an agent for bringing about adoption (cf. 8:15), and adoption also leads to a future redemption of physical bodies (see 3.3 and 4.2 above).

Life, then, is a future-oriented concept in the argument of Romans 8. This means the idea of salvation (which is the opposite of condemnation) is also future oriented. This goes against the backdrop of typical Roman religion in that sacrifice to the gods should bring about salvation in this lifetime, a salvation from current troubling circumstances or possibly future physical circumstances.³³⁴ For example, some people sacrificed to Isis for healing.³³⁵ Paul overturns this paradigm by speaking of present suffering and a salvation that comes after death instead of being saved from death by having their lives prolonged. The cults employed magic as a means to preserve their lives and to affect the world around them.³³⁶ Most religions in Rome focused on extending life as a reward for proper adherence to the god invoked by the worshippers.³³⁷ At the same time, Paul uses participation language that would at least be familiar to inhabitants of Rome, even if Paul has a different way of speaking about it.³³⁸ The most intriguing aspect of Paul's concept of salvation in Romans 8 stems from his discussion of agency, namely that the same function can be performed at different times by different beings. Most importantly,

---

331 Scott, *Adoption*, 256.
332 Byrne, *Romans*, 241; Dunn, *Romans*, 1:432–433; Schreiner, *Romans*, 415–416. Byrne thinks Paul is referencing God's oversight of the entire resurrection process, whereas Dunn believes Paul is trying to limit the divine status of Jesus.
333 Cranfield, *Romans*, 1:392. For an updated discussion, see Longenecker, *Romans*, 677–678.
334 Fishwick, *Imperial Cult*, 2.1.375–376 n. 2; Turcan, "Salut mithriaque et sotériologie néoplatonicienne," 173–174. Cf. Seneca, *Tranq.*, 14.9.
335 Burkert, *Ancient Mystery Cults*, 15.
336 France Le Corsu, *Isis: myth et mystères* (Les Belle Letters, 1977), 192–193.
337 Mary Beard, John North, and Simon Price, *Religions of Rome* (2 vols.; Cambridge University Press, 1998), 1:290.
338 Cf. Käsemann, *Romans*, 161.

God and the Son and the Spirit

Paul blurs the lines between the Father, Son, and Spirit throughout the chapter and highlighted by 8:9–11.

4.4 Son, Spirit, and God

Throughout Romans 8, Paul speaks of God drawing on the Son and the Spirit to perform different tasks. The Father sends the Son in order to save people while also using the Spirit within the lives of believers. The Father employs adoption as a way of redeeming people, yet adoption is accomplished by the Spirit's work and represents a change in status with the Son as believers become coheirs with Christ. In addition, the different functions of both the Son and Spirit point beyond them simply being "other gods" and toward a more complex relationship with the Father. While the idea of a triad would fit within the Roman theological landscape of the first century,[339] Paul seems to be pointing beyond a triad (three gods associated with each other) and to a trinity (one god unified in three beings).

Many scholars look only at a few specific verses from Romans 8 to find some sort of nascent trinitarian thought,[340] yet the entire chapter pushes in such a direction.[341] In order to analyze Paul's thoughts about God, the relationship between the Son and Father along with the relationship between the Son and Spirit will be analyzed.

4.4.1 Son and Father

Paul constantly notes the work of God through Christ in Romans 8, particularly in the process of salvation. Paul associates Jesus with life in Rom 8:1–4, yet the more important issue is God sending his Son. The purpose of God sending Jesus includes the opening of salvation to people through Jesus' death and resurrection. It also includes the concept of inheritance and glorification, both results of the sending. The sending ends with Jesus as the vice-regent of God.

---

339 See 2.4.
340 E.g. Schreiner, *Romans*, 414. He indicates that texts like Romans 8:9–10, "provided the raw material form which the church later hammered out the doctrine of the Trinity," thus seeming to assume a lack of developed Trinitarian thought in Paul. Some scholars (e.g. Dunn, *Christology in the Making*, 44) either deny the Trinity outright or deny some integral part (e.g. preexistence of Jesus).
341 Note the usage of Romans 8 in Francis Watson, "The Triune Divine Identity: Reflections on Pauline God Language, in Disagreement with J. D. G. Dunn," *JSNT* 80 (2000): 99–124, especially 121–122.

Sending in the NT often carries overtones of preexistence. Dunn believes this is the correct Johannine understanding,[342] but that it does not in fact work for Paul's utilization of the motif.[343] He goes on to caution the exegete from reading John into Paul. While this is a valid point, one must not also deny what Paul is saying because of John. Dunn comments on the parallel language found in "the book of Wisdom including the sending of Wisdom and of the Spirit in 9.10 and 9.17."[344] He connects sonship only with the resurrection, due to Rom 1:4, and denies that sonship is in any way connected to sending in Romans 8.[345] Paul does connect sending with sonship, as Jesus is sent in order to provide an opportunity for people to become sons (or more importantly, heirs).[346] The obvious objection to Dunn's case is that if one is sent rather than created for a specific purpose, one must already exist.[347] Dunn counters this objection by referring to the strength of the Adam Christology inherent in 8:1–4, an Adam Christology that is so prevalent that Paul could only be referring to the death (and possibly resurrection) of Jesus and nothing else.[348] He believes that this link is so strong that Jesus' sonship then refers, like Adam's, to "his whole life."[349] If indeed the entire life of Jesus is in view, then Paul must be implying the preexistence of Christ since God is then sending the Son for the purpose of living his entire life.[350]

Moo thinks that the purpose of sending goes beyond the incarnation and even the crucifixion, pointing toward the glorification of the Son in the future.[351] If the idea of sending points toward the crucifixion and resurrection, then 8:3 connects directly with 8:32 in that the Son functions as the agent of the Father in his death.[352] Paul carries through the idea of sonship from 8:29 to 8:32, focusing on the special relationship the Father has with the Son. This special relationship is evident due to the use of ἰδίου instead of ἀγαπητοῦ, which a direct quotation of the LXX (Gen 22:12, 16) would need. Rather than quoting directly, Paul changes his language in order to differentiate the importance of Christ from the other sons of God (who would also be loved by

---

342 E.g. John 3:17.
343 Dunn, *Christology in the Making*, xvii. Cf. his *Theology of Paul*, 278–279. In the latter, Dunn leaves the verdict open only for Wisdom Christology.
344 Dunn, *Christology in the Making*, 44.
345 Ibid., 44–45.
346 See 4.2.1.
347 Haacker, *Römer*, 152. Cf. Fitzmyer, *Romans*, 484–485.
348 Dunn, *Christology in the Making*, 45.
349 Ibid.
350 The same can be said of Gal 4:4–5, with the link to the entire life of Jesus being more obvious (γενόμενον ἐκ γυναικός, "born of a woman").
351 Moo, *Romans*, 478–481.
352 Fitzmyer (*Romans*, 484) also makes the connection between 8:3 and 8:32.

God).³⁵³ This change also more closely reflects the Masoretic text of יְהִידְךָ.³⁵⁴ Paul's use of ἰδίου carries the uniqueness of Jesus' relationship with the Father, stressing the difference between God's adopted sons or children and the one Son.³⁵⁵ This special status of Jesus makes him specially qualified as God's sacrifice, paralleling Abram's sacrifice of Isaac. In both cases the focus is on the father giving up his son (note the use of παραδίδωμι in 8:32³⁵⁶). Schmithals argues that Isaac is a type of Christ and thus Jesus' sonship comes only from his function as God's sacrifice, and this is Paul's point here.³⁵⁷ The problem is that Jewish literature does not focus on Isaac, rather it speaks of Abram's faithfulness.³⁵⁸ Paul uses the Aqedah motif simply as an illustration, making a point slightly different from the typical Jewish understanding, though it varies only in upon whom it focuses instead of any other matters.³⁵⁹ Dahl thinks that Paul could not possibly be focusing on God here, as Jewish literature never used this to focus on God only on Abram.³⁶⁰ His argument stems from the fact that Isaac was never seen as a type of Messiah in Jewish literature, but many texts in the OT that Christians use to understand the Messianic work of Jesus do not fit into Jewish literature. The sending of the Son by the Father looked beyond his death, however, and toward the future. The handing over of the Son only began the trajectory.

Why did the Father hand over his Son? While Paul answers this question by viewing the benefits for believers, he also draws in the glorification of the Son. Yes, the Father handed over the Son to die, but then God also raised him and elevated him (8:34). The language Paul uses is intentional: he stresses the person of Christ but the actions of God, such that God's actions are seen primarily in what happens to Jesus. There is a singular structure to Rom 8:31–39, a structure based on a question and answer format.³⁶¹ This pericope conveys a

---

353 Origen, *The Fathers of the Church: Origen, Commentary on the Epistle to the Romans, Books 6–10* (vol. 104; trans. Thomas P. Scheck; The Catholic University of America Press, 2001), 93. He says, "lest it should be thought that he handed over one of these who appeared to be adopted amongst his sons, by the general sense of 'sons,' he has added, 'his own Son,' in order to point to him who alone is begotten by an ineffable generation from God himself."

354 Cf. Dahl, "The Atonement," 17.

355 Cf. especially Cranfield, *Romans*, 1:436; Dunn, *Romans*, 1:501; Fitzmyer, *Romans*, 530–531; and Moo, *Romans*, 520.

356 Cf. Wilckens, *Römer*, 2:172–173.

357 Schmithals, *Römerbrief*, 308.

358 Dunn, *Romans*, 1:501; Fitzmyer, *Romans*, 531–532; Talbert, *Romans*, 228.

359 Dunn, *Romans*, 501; Fitzmyer, *Romans*, 530–531.

360 Dahl, "Atonement," 18. He argues "it is unlikely that Abraham's act of obedience was ever considered a typological prefiguration of God's act of love."

361 Cf. Cranfield, *Romans*, 1:437–438; Moo, *Romans*, 541; Schreiner, *Romans*, 461–462; Richard B. Hays, *Echoes of Scripture in the Letters of Paul* (Yale University Press, 1989), 59. Achtemeier, *Romans*, 148–149; Barrett, *Romans*, 172–173; Fitzmyer, *Romans*, 528–530; and John

courtroom setting,³⁶² with 33–34 directly alluding to Isa 50:9 (50:8 LXX).³⁶³ The passage in Isaiah also unfolds in a court setting (remembering that court can refer to either the throne room of a ruler or a trial setting), and thus the backdrop of Rom 8:33–34, and therefore 8:31–39, becomes more clear.³⁶⁴ In this setting, the Father stands in as the ruler, and the believer is the defendant. No accuser is mentioned, and for good reason, since nobody has the ability to bring charges against believers since God is the one who justifies (θεὸς ὁ δικαιῶν) and Jesus intercedes "on our behalf" (ἐντυγχάνει ὑπὲρ ἡμῶν). God declares the person just and Jesus pleads the case before God on the behalf of believers (hence ὑπὲρ ἡμῶν) based upon his own death.³⁶⁵

Moo thinks this intercession fits the role of Jesus as high priest,³⁶⁶ yet this metaphor does not appear anywhere in Romans (though Jesus functions as a sacrifice in 8:3–4), and Moo has to draw on Heb 7:25 to even make the connection. Schreiner opts for the intercession of Jesus being his death.³⁶⁷ While this does fit in the context of the passage (Jesus' death plays a large role in 8:31–39), the present tense of the verb indicates an iterative sense, which would contradict Paul's stance that Jesus died only once as a sin offering. In addition, this would also break the natural progression in 8:34 that moves from Jesus' death, to his resurrection, to his glorification (on Ps 110:1, see below), and finally to his function in his glorified state, and thus Jesus' death is not in view. Instead of a court scene, Dunn posits this as another occurrence of Adam Christology and possibly parallel to the role of angel intercessors in Jewish apocalyptic literature.³⁶⁸ He does not move beyond stating these points as possibilities, as the textual support for his position is weak. The im-

---

D. Moores, *Wrestling with Rationality in Paul: Romans 1–8 in a New Perspective* (SNTSMS 82; Cambridge University Press, 1995), 122; all claim 8:33–34 being entirely composed of questions (though in various ways).

362 For the full impact of the court scene in Romans 8:31–39, see Isabelle Parlier, "La Folle Justice de Dieu: Romains 8, 31–39," *FoiVie* 5 (1992): 103–110.

363 Cranfield, *Romans*, 1:437; Dunn, *Romans*, 1:503; Moo, *Romans*, 542 n. 32 (Moo's grammar is confusing, but his comments on 5:9–10 indicates he must be referring to this allusion); Schreiner, *Romans*, 462; Schmithals, *Römerbrief*, 310–311; and Hays, *Echoes*, 59–60; all see the echo. See especially Shiu-Lun Shum, *Paul's Use of Isaiah in Romans: A Comparative Study of Paul's Letter to the Romans and the Sibylline and Qumran Sectarian Texts* (WUNT II/156; Mohr Siebeck, 2002), 201–202.

364 For the legal language in Isa 50:8–9, see Claus Westermann, *Isaiah: A Commentary* (OTL; trans. David M. G. Stalker; Westminster, 1969) 2:231, and J. Alec Motyer, *The Prophecy of Isaiah: An Introduction and Commentary* (InterVarsity, 1993), 400. John D. Watts, *Isaiah* (2 vols; WBC 24–25; Word, 1985–1987), 2:204, calls this political language, but his continued analysis fits a legal understanding instead.

365 Osten-Sacken, *Römer 8*, 312.

366 Moo, *Romans*, 542–543. Cf. Cranfield, *Romans*, 1:439; Murray, *Romans*, 329–330.

367 Schreiner, *Romans*, 463.

368 Dunn, *Romans*, 1:504.

agery in Rom 8:31–39 contains nothing that would point to Adam, especially since the court metaphor dominates the foreground. In the end, Paul stresses the ability of the Son to entreat the Father, but the only reason he can do so is because of his exalted position. God does not raise the Son and leave him be, instead God exalts Jesus and places Christ at his right hand (ἐστιν ἐν δεξιᾷ τοῦ θεοῦ). This is a clear allusion to Ps 110:1 (109:1 LXX), as David says εἶπεν ὁ κύριος τῷ κυρίῳ μου κάθου ἐκ δεξιῶν μου ἕως ἂν θῶ τοὺς ἐχθρούς σου ὑποπόδιον τῶν ποδῶν σου. The entire Psalm is one of exaltation and glorification of an individual, here applied to Jesus the Messiah.[369] This phrase is used throughout the NT as a metaphor for power and authority given by God specifically for Jesus' unique status.[370] Dunn makes two important notes about the use of the Psalm.[371] First, this Psalm gives credence to the understanding of the king (or to whomever this is applied) being God's vice-regent on earth. Second, Jesus alone attains such an honor of those who are not ancient heroes but rather were recent figures in history as compared to the exaltation of Adam, Enoch, and Melchizedek against the lack of exaltation for the Teacher of Righteousness or any of the failed Messianic pretenders. Jesus alone reaches this exalted status of being at the right hand of God, just as he alone died for sin, just as he alone was raised by God, just as he alone of humans can intercede before God (for the issue of the intercession of the Holy Spirit, see 4.4.2 below). Why did God hand over his Son? God handed him over to ensure salvation for his people while also glorifying the Son, two purposes that worked together.

God sending his Son carries the notion of preexistence and leads to the glorification of the Son (among other results). Why would God conform believers into the image of his Son instead of into an image of himself? The answer concerns the importance of Jesus as firstborn and that he was sent by God (cf. 4.2.2). The firstborn language, as noted above, covers both how Jesus is the natural Son of God (as opposed to adopted sons) and his ability to inherit (see 4.2.1). The special status of Jesus as the singular Son of God carries vast import.[372] To a Roman, the title "son of god" carries the notion of the imperial cult. Jesus would be understood not just as a man, but as a ruler of special authority so designated by his familial relationship to an already extant God. In using this idea for both believers and Jesus, Paul removes the separation between God and man (since God adopts humans) yet widens the

---

369 For a bibliography on the understanding of this allusion, see Ziesler, *Romans*, 229 n. x.
370 Cf. David M. Hay, *Glory at the Right Hand: Psalm 110 in Early Christianity* (SBLMS 18; Abingdon, 1973).
371 Both in Dunn, *Romans*, 1:504.
372 N. T. Wright, *The Resurrection of the Son of God* (Christian Origins and the Question of God 3; Fortress, 2003), 723–725.

separation between man and God by elevating Jesus. Barth notes this act of elevation especially in 8:33–39 (i.e. the glorification and exaltation of Christ to God's right hand) as Jesus accomplishes what no person alone could.[373] Paul using the title Son of God does not affirm the deity of Jesus, yet it does stress the unique nature of the Son and special relationship he has with the Father.[374] The Father glorifies the Son because of their relationship to one another and because of the unique status of Jesus.

Another key to understanding the relationship between the Father and Son lies in Rom 8:39. Within this verse, Paul takes two important steps in developing the identity of Jesus. First, Jesus is named κύριος ἡμῶν. Paul does not use this title for Jesus throughout the rest of the chapter, saving it for the moment of climax. Dunn notes that this sense of assurance Paul gives to his readers flows through this title since it stresses Jesus' dominion over all even though he is both under God and died.[375] While Bousset believed the extreme importance of the title stemmed from later Hellenistic reflection upon it,[376] and given the various backgrounds of the title this makes sense, there is likely more to it. Paul drew on both the Greco-Roman world and the Jewish one, creating a multicultural identifier for the significance of Jesus. The Romans in particular would understand this as a possible identifier for divinity, especially the titular use of certain words for a human reserved for the emperors.[377] At the same time, the Jewish literary background (note the use in the LXX) points toward an overlap with the One God.[378] Κύριος itself is used for both God (e.g. 4:8) and Jesus (e.g. 1:4) in Romans. Writing to a Jewish group, this could be construed as giving someone else the honor due to God, but then Paul has already been explicit in displaying how God has given glory to the Son due himself. Writing to Romans, this could be construed as divine honors accorded to a man, and maybe a form of apotheosis since Paul was writing after the death of Jesus. The apotheosis had to occur and needed attestation for the person to become divinized.[379] However, apotheosis does not fit as Jesus came back while the emperors (and their divinized family members)

---

373 Barth, *Romans*, 329.

374 Cf. Douglas J. Moo, "The Christology of the Early Pauline Letters," in *Contours of Christology in the New Testament* (ed. Richard N. Longenecker; Eerdmans, 2005), 169–192, here 187–188.

375 Dunn, *Romans*, 1:513.

376 This is a main thrust of Wilhelm Bousset, *Kyrios Christos: A History of the Belief in Christ from the Beginnings of Christianity to Irenaeus* (trans. J. E. Steely; Abingdon, 1970), especially 139–148, 151–152.

377 Cf. 2.3 above.

378 Though brief, see the results of Dieter Zeller, "New Testament Christology in Its Hellenistic Reception," *NTS* 48 (2001): 312–333, here 316–321.

379 Cf. Dio Cassius, *Roman History*, 59.11.3.

did not.[380] Domitian in particular coupled κύριος with divine forms of address such as θεός. For example, Juventius Celsus called him "lord" and "god" in person and in writing.[381] These various titles were used in Rome for the emperors in the first century.[382] However, there is a qualitative difference between the lordship of Jesus and that of either the emperors on the one hand, since Jesus came back from the dead, and God on the other, since Jesus derives his power and status from the Father.

The second step of developing the identity of Jesus in 8:39 consists of Paul discussing ἡ ἀγάπη τοῦ θεοῦ τῆς ἐν Χριστῷ. Paul has changed his language slightly in 8:31-39, as 8:35 begins the subject of ἀγάπη τοῦ Χριστοῦ, not ἀγάπη τοῦ θεοῦ. Yet the argument of 8:35-39 covers the same concept, as Paul considers all the various trials (8:35-36) and everything that exists (8:38-39) that can keep believers from this love. Again, this section focuses on the reader as a believer and therefore safely ensconced in this love,[383] and Paul defines what it means to be in Christ and thus no longer under condemnation (cf. 8:1).[384] The assurance for the believer rests in the unchanging nature of God's love,[385] and thus having it embodied in Christ shows the extent of it. God's love is Christ's love, they are one and the same in Paul's argument, otherwise it does not make sense.[386] In fact, some manuscripts (א B [which adds τῆς ἐν Χριστῷ Ἰησοῦ] 365 1506) have ἀγάπης τοῦ θεοῦ in 8:35 instead of ἀγάπης τοῦ Χριστοῦ (supported by C D F G Ψ 33 1739), which caused Chrysostom to note that Paul is able to use their names (or titles) interchangeably.[387] Thus, this change in names or titles carried significant weight for the proclamation of the early church, and since Paul chose his language carefully, it carried significance for him as well. There is another significant exchange of titles in Romans 8, once again involving the Father and Son, but in 8:9 the Spirit is the central focus.

The relationship between the Father and Son in Romans 8 is complex. Paul describes Jesus as God's Son, a unique status setting him apart from

---

380 Cf. Wright, *Resurrection of the Son*, 55–57, 724–725.

381 Dio Cassius, *Romans History*, 67.5.7 and 67.13.4.

382 Andreas Alföldi, *Die monarchische Repräsentation im römischen Kaiserreiche* (Wissenschaftliche Buchgesellschaft, 1970), 49–53.

383 Moo, *Romans*, 546; Schreiner, *Romans*, 466–467; A. H. Snyman, "Style and the Rhetorical Situation of Romans 8:31–39," *NTS* 34 (1988): 218–231, here 227.

384 Parlier, "La Folle Justice," 106–107. Cf Wilckens, *Römer*, 2:177.

385 Dunn, *Romans*, 1:508; Moo, *Romans*, 547; Francis C. Rossow, "The Hound of Heaven, A Twitch upon the Thread, and Romans 8:31–39," *Concordia Journal* 23 (1997): 91–98, here 91.

386 Moo, *Romans*, 547; Osten-Sacken, *Römer 8*, 52.

387 See Barbara Aland, "Trustworthy Preaching: Reflections on John Chrysostom's Interpretation of Romans 8," in *Romans and the People of God: Essays in Honor of Gordon D. Fee on the Occasion of His 65th Birthday* (ed. Sven K. Soderlund and N. T. Wright; Eerdmans, 1999), 271–282, here 272–273; Cranfield, *Romans*, 1:439–440.

God's adopted sons. Jesus is sent to fulfill God's work on earth, so he functions as God's agent. At the same time, Paul uses titles and functions typically denoting divine status. Paul seems to be including the Father and Son as God, yet a determination at this point would be premature.

4.4.2 Son and Spirit

Paul has demonstrated that God has solved the problem of sin interfering with the law by sending the Son and the Spirit.[388] The question that comes to mind due to Paul's arguments concerns the overlap of the Son and Spirit. Throughout Romans 8, the Son and Spirit perform many of the same functions or functions so close in results that it is difficult to distinguish the actions of each as separate things. So, are they separate beings or the same being?[389] Up until now, this work has assumed the separation of the Son and Spirit, yet the relationship must be explored in order to determine if they are two or one, and if two, to what extent are they differentiated.

The consistent overlap between the results of a person being ἐν Χριστῷ and ἐν πνεύματι displays at the very least a closeness between the Son and Spirit (see 4.3.1). This comes across most strongly in the uses of ἐντυγχάνω in 8:27 for the Spirit and 8:34 for the Son. The Spirit intercedes for the holy/the saints (ἐντυγχάνει ὑπὲρ ἁγίων). Thus, the Spirit intercedes on behalf of those who are in Christ and the intercession takes place before God (cf. 8:26).[390] Jesus is at δεξιᾷ τοῦ θεοῦ where he ἐντυγχάνει ὑπὲρ ἡμῶν. Jesus is sitting at God's right hand (which means given a place of authority in God's presence) and intercedes on behalf of "us" referring to believers.[391] The larger picture makes for strong similarities between the Son and Spirit, yet one must examine the details in order to complete the analysis.

In 8:26–27, Paul speaks twice of the Spirit interceding for believers. While the words are technically different (ὑπερεντυγχάνω and ἐντυγχάνω), the semantic domain for each is approximately the same.[392] Paul references the Spirit as an aid to those unable to pray for what they should pray for, an aid in terms of presenting what they need to bring to God. This does not mean, as

---

388 The language of sin interfering with the law comes from the law's goodness combined with sin perverting the law in Romans 7 into something harmful rather than helpful.

389 See Cranfield, *Romans*, 2:843; Schreiner, *Romans*, 413–414. Cf. Moo, *Romans*, 491.

390 Haacker, *Römer*, 168; James E. Rosscup, "The Spirit's Intercession," *The Masters Seminary Journal* 10 (1999): 139–162, here 149–150.

391 Schreiner (*Romans*, 463) goes so far as to rename "us" as "saints."

392 Respectively, BDAG, 1033 and 341; L&N 33.348 compared to 33.169 and 33.347.

some have argued,³⁹³ that the Spirit enables glossolalia (speaking in tongues) in order to facilitate communication with God. The thrust of Paul's diction aims at the communication between the Father and the Spirit. The Jewish background points toward this conclusion.³⁹⁴ The Spirit also knows what is going on in God's mind, and it is to his mind that the Spirit is attuned.³⁹⁵ Only the Spirit knows God's mind (1 Cor 2:11), and it is by this that the Spirit can appropriately intercede for believers since the Spirit knows both the mind of the believer and the mind of God.³⁹⁶ The Spirit links the believer and God more than just soteriologically (ἐν πνεύματι) and ethically (περιπατοῦσιν κατὰ πνεῦμα), the link also includes a mode of communication.³⁹⁷ Intercession in this instance involves the Spirit bringing the requests a believer cannot express directly to the Father, those requests that are made according to God's will (κατὰ θεόν).³⁹⁸

Jesus intercedes for believers as the vice-regent on behalf of his people before the ruler in Rom 8:34. The allusion to Isa 50:9 paints the picture of a royal court setting. The roots δικ– and κρινο– are the key to the allusion, as both function within the two respective texts as the cruxes of the matter:

Isaiah 50:9 (50:8 LXX)
ὅτι ἐγγίζει ὁ <u>δικαιώσας</u> με τίς ὁ <u>κρινόμενός</u> μοι ἀντιστήτω μοι ἅμα καὶ τίς ὁ <u>κρινόμενός</u> μοι ἐγγισάτω μοι

Romans 8:33–34
τίς ἐγκαλέσει κατὰ ἐκλεκτῶν θεοῦ θεὸς ὁ <u>δικαιῶν</u> τίς ὁ <u>κατακρινῶν</u> Χριστὸς Ἰησοῦς ὁ ἀποθανών

Figure 4.1: Allusion to Isaiah 50:9 in Romans 8:33–34

In both cases no accuser has the ability to come forward.³⁹⁹ Note the reversal here, as Isaiah has the suffering servant as supplicant, yet Paul turns that on its head as the sufferer is now glorified.⁴⁰⁰ In the case of the Isaiah passage, the main idea is the nearness of the Lord to the accused such that no charges

---

393 Cf. especially Fee, *God's Empowering Presence*, 577; John Bertone, "The Experience of Glossolalia and the Spirit's Empathy: Romans 8:26 Revisited," *Pneuma* 25 (2003): 54–65.
394 E. A. Obeng, "The Origins of the Spirit Intercession Motif in Romans 8:26," *NTS* 32 (1986): 621–632.
395 Cf. Cranfield, *Romans*, 1:423–424; Julie L. Wu, "The Spirit's Intercession in Romans 8:26–27: An Exegetical Note," *ExpTim* 105 (1993): 13.
396 David E. Garland, *1 Corinthians* (BECNT; Baker, 2003), 98–99.
397 See Geoffrey Smith, "The Function of 'Likewise' (ΩΣΑΥΤΩΣ) in Romans 8:26," *TynBul* 49 (1998): 29–38. On the last, cf. Peter O'Brien, "Romans 8:26, 27. A Revolutionary Approach to Prayer?," *RTR* 46 (1987): 65–73.
398 Dunn, *Romans*, 1:480; Fitzmyer, *Romans*, 520; Rosscup, "The Spirit's Intercession," 162.
399 Motyer, *Isaiah*, 400.
400 Wilckens, *Römer*, 2:174. Cf. Dunn, *Romans*, 1:503; Schreiner, *Romans*, 462.

brought against them will stand.[401] The same holds true for the entire passage of Rom 8:31–39.[402] The intercession of Jesus is on behalf of those who are declared innocent by God.[403] Dunn comments on an important nuance in 8:34, namely that Jesus has already been granted some of God's power to judge in that he is able to condemn yet withholds from doing so.[404] This strengthens the understanding that the allusion to Psalm 110:1 coupled with the courtroom scene places Jesus in the position of vice-regent.[405] Therefore, Jesus appears in the court scene as both a person of great, albeit derived, authority and as one who takes the part of supplicants before the greater authority.

Since both the Spirit and Son intercede for believers before God, are these two different functions or one and the same? Wilckens notes an important difference, namely one of setting.[406] The Spirit intercedes for believers from within them, explicitly from their hearts since he is ἐραυνῶν τὰς καρδίας ("the one who searches hearts").[407] If the Spirit searches the heart then his prayers to the Father are located there or comes from there. Paul locates Jesus, on the other hand, ἐν δεξιᾷ τοῦ θεοῦ, in other words "das interzessorische Wirken Christi" is "im Himmel" ("the intercessory work of Jesus is in heaven").[408] Thus, Christ does the external work of intercession while the Spirit simultaneously covers the internal.[409] The work of the Son and Spirit overlap to a great degree here, as with the "in Christ" and "in the Spirit" language (see 4.3.1). Just as being "in Christ" and being "in the Spirit" reference salvation within the individual (and the results of it as well) without being identical in all respects,[410] so does this intercession come from both the Son and Spirit on behalf of believers. Though Paul approaches the intercession of each differently,[411] he posits a functional equivalence between the two. Therefore, Paul describes two sep-

---

401   Motyer, *Isaiah*, 400–401.
402   Parlier, "La Folle Justice," 110.
403   Cf. Dunn, *Romans*, 1:511; Fitzmyer, *Romans*, 533; Moo, *Romans*, 541–543.
404   Dunn, *Romans*, 1:503. This assumes splitting the θεὸς ὁ δικαιῶν τίς ὁ κατακρινῶν into two separate phrases, something some of the early fathers did not do (cf. Lagrange, *Romains*, 219).
405   So Cranfield, *Romans*, 1:438–439; Moo, *Romans*, 542–543.
406   Wilckens, *Römer*, 2:174–175. "Setting" is not the word Wilckens would use to speak of his position.
407   Cranfield, *Romans*, 1:424; Moo, *Romans*, 527; Schreiner, *Romans*, 446.
408   Wilckens, *Römer*, 2:175.
409   Hanh, "Pneumatology in Romans 8," 86. Cf. Haacker, *Römer*, 168. He notes, "An eine Fürsprache des Geists vor dem Thron Gottes zu denken, liegt weniger nahe, weil V. 27a dann unmotiviert erschiene und eine Konkurrenz zur Rolle Christi in V. 34 entstünde."
410   See Gordon Fee, "Christology and Penumatology in Romans 8:9-11 – and Elsewhere: Some Reflections on Paul as a Trinitarian," in *To What End Exegesis? Essays Textual, Exegetical, and Theological* (Eerdmans, 2001), 218–239, here 222 n. 18.
411   Haacker, *Römer*, 168.

arate beings (since they are in different places) who perform the same task (intercession). From a Roman perspective, this would be a quandary as gods who hold similar functions tend to become a single entity, either by one being eliminated or the two combining. For example, Apollo replaced Helios and Isis merged with Demeter.[412] Paul, however, has more to say about the Son and Spirit.

Rom 8:9 is a significant passage for understanding the relationship between the Son and Spirit, including the role of the Father. The first and most significant aspect of 8:9 for this discussion lies in Paul's description of the Holy Spirit as both πνεῦμα θεοῦ and πνεῦμα Χριστοῦ. If the Spirit intercedes before God, then the Spirit cannot be God. More importantly, if the Spirit is "of God" the same way the Spirit is "of Christ," then the Spirit cannot be Christ either.[413] What does Paul intend to signify by these qualifiers? If the Spirit belongs to or comes from God,[414] then the Spirit in some way serves God or is functionally subordinate to God. In the same way it is true for the Spirit belonging to or coming from Christ. While the congruence between the Father and Son is significant (see 4.4.3 below), here the Spirit functions as the surety of both God and Christ in the believer.[415] The Spirit guarantees life by its presence, a life that can only be granted by God through the death and resurrection of the Son.[416] This life also includes peace with God.[417] The Spirit gives the effects of the cross to the believer even though the work is that of Christ.[418] The qualifiers point toward the Spirit as the actuality of life in the believer given by God through Christ, such that Hab 2:4 (quoted in Rom 1:17) could be rewritten "the righteous by the Spirit shall live."[419] The indwelling of the Spirit comes from God and being the Spirit of Christ solidifies the believers adoption by God.

Does this mean the Spirit is divine? In one sense, combining 8:26–27 with 1 Cor 2:11, the Spirit must be divine if he can know God's will and enable the prayers of believers to come before God.[420] The Spirit also has to be a separate

---

412 Euripides, *Phaethon*, 781 and Herodotus, *Histories*, II, 171.2–3, respectively.
413 Cf. Moo, *Romans*, 491. Contra Dunn (*Romans*, 1:429), who thinks that "Spirit of Christ" is just a narrower classification within the category of "Spirit of God."
414 It is too difficult to distinguish between a genitive of possession or source here with any certainty.
415 Fee, "Christology and Pneumatology," 233. Cf. Rom 8:23.
416 Achtemeier, *Romans*, 134–135. Cf. Dunn, *Romans*, 1:429–430; Moo, *Romans*, 491.
417 Friedrich Wilhelm Horn, "Wandel im Geist: Zur pneumatologischen Begründung der Ethik bei Paulus," *KD* 38 (1992): 149-70, here 167.
418 Fee, *God's Empowering Presence*, 552.
419 Cf. Cranfield, *Romans*, 2:841.
420 Schreiner, *Romans*, 446–447.

being[421] in order for him to complete the functions Paul lists for him in Romans 8. For example, if the Spirit intercedes before the Father (8:26–27), then the Spirit must have some sort of separation from the Father.[422] If the Spirit is "of Christ," then the Spirit has some sort of relationship with Christ, yet the two intercede from different locales. If Jesus has the right to intercede before the Father due to his exalted status, a status that points toward his divinity, then the Spirit must have the same status. All of this points toward Paul understanding the Spirit as divine.

4.5 Triunity?

Two questions are left at this point, and they have slightly different scopes. The first question applies directly to Paul and his own thought. Does Paul understand God as a triunity in Romans 8? In order to answer this question, some words need to be defined and some perspective included. If this first question is answered positively, then a second question follows, and it pertains to Paul's readers. Would the Roman recipients of Paul's letter have understood Paul's writing as describing a God who is a triunity?

The first question has to be defined before it can be answered. What is meant by the term "triunity" when applied to Paul? Historically, the church has understood the Trinity as "God eternally exists as three persons, Father, Son, and Holy Spirit, and each person is fully God, and there is one God."[423] The early church struggled with how to integrate these various concepts they found in Scripture together into a unified, logically consistent set.[424] The largest problems came in deciding the terminology to use with respect to the relationship between the Father and Son, with the divergence in the early church stemming toward separate theologies.[425] Therefore, while theologians today use such words as "person" or "essence," specific meanings are in mind that would be anachronistic to search for in Paul's writing, especially since he

---

421 "Person" in this context would carry too much theological baggage.

422 Cf. Dunn, *Romans*, 1:479–480. Dunn ponders how this "conception of God" can "stretch" first century "Jewish monotheism" while he still denies any sort of Trinitarian thought within Paul and Romans in particular.

423 Wayne Grudem, *Systematic Theology: An Introduction to Biblical Doctrine* (Zondervan, 1994), 226. Cf. John S. Feinberg, *No One Like Him* (Foundations of Evangelical Theology; Crossway, 2001), 438; Ronald H. Nash, *The Concept of God: An Exploration of Contemporary Difficulties with the Attributes of God* (Zondervan, 1983), 87–88.

424 Cf. William G. Rusch, ed. and trans., *The Trinitarian Controversy* (Sources of Early Christian Thought; Fortress, 1980); Aloys Grillmeier, *Christ in Christian Tradition Volume One: The Apostolic Age to Chalcedon (451)* (2nd ed.; trans. John Bowden; John Knox, 1975).

425 E.g. Grillmeier, *Christ in Christian Tradition*, 551–554. Cf. Richard A. Norris, Jr., ed. and trans., *The Christological Controversy* (Sources of Early Christian Thought; Fortress, 1980).

God and the Son and the Spirit 133

does not employ the same vocabulary. Therefore, Paul was not a trinitarian as the church would speak of today for the simple reason that his terminology would be incorrect.

The more pressing matter in this case lies in whether Paul's theology was consistent with Trinitarian thought such that he held to and propagated a belief in a triune God, though without anachronistically employing the jargon (e.g. ὁμοούσιος) of the later church. This means that Paul has to hold to one God in three beings, a statement that Dunn would deny and Watson would uphold.[426] Paul was a monotheist, so his belief in one God is a given (cf. 1.2). The issue of congruence between the Son and Spirit and also the Father and Spirit has already been discussed, so there is no problem in terms of each one existing as a separate being (Paul clearly posits Jesus as separate from God). The last question left is whether Paul considered the Son and Spirit (the Father is a given) to be God, in other words did Paul teach a triune identity of God?

In terms of Jesus being divine, there are many indications of this throughout Romans, some of which occur in Romans 8. The name or title of κύριος holds distinctive importance both for the Roman background as well as for how Paul quotes from the OT with this title is a replacement for God's name.[427] God gives Jesus the power to intercede as vice-regent on behalf of believers (8:34; cf. 4.2.2 and 4.4.1), a magnified place of authority. God sends Jesus as his agent for defeating sin in the flesh, a defeat only God could give. God's love is found in the death of Jesus as is the love of Jesus (8:39; cf. 5:8), showing a level of equality between them.[428] The most direct piece of evidence, however, comes from Rom 8:9, where πνεῦμα θεοῦ and πνεῦμα Χριστοῦ are used interchangeably.

One of the main actants in Romans 8 is the Holy Spirit, and this is referred to by the expressions πνεῦμα θεοῦ and πνεῦμα Χριστοῦ. Contrary to James Dunn, this book found that there is no difference in how the genitives function in those two phrases, so there can be and should be no distinction in

---

[426] Dunn, *Theology of Paul*, 252–260, especially 260; Watson, "Triune Divine Identity," 117–123, especially 123.

[427] David B. Capes, "YHWH Texts and Monotheism in Paul's Christology," in *Early Jewish and Christian Monotheism* (ed. Loren T. Stuckenbruck and Wendy E. S. North; JSNTSup 263; T&T Clark, 2004), 120–137, here 124–132. Cf. David B. Capes, *Old Testament Yahweh Texts in Paul's Christology* (WUNT II/47; Mohr Siebeck, 1992), 88–89.

[428] Richard B. Hays, "The God of Mercy Who Rescues Us from the Present Evil Age," in *The Forgotten God: Perspectives in Biblical Theology* (eds. A. Andrew Das and Frank J. Matera; Westminster John Knox, 2002), 123–143, here 135.

terms of authority of God or Christ over the Spirit.[429] Indeed, the movement from God to Christ is so seamless that Cranfield states, "the ease with which Paul can pass from one expression to the other is one more indication of his recognition of the divine dignity of Christ."[430] This leaves the reader of Paul with a binitarian concept, as the Son and Father are both God. The position of the Spirit in turn must be clarified.

The Spirit functions in much the same way that the Son does in Romans 8, though with different emphases. Dunn argues that *"no distinction can be detected in the believer's experience between the exalted Christ and Spirit of God"*[431] (emphasis original). What Dunn does not do, however, is look at the functions of each instead of just the experience of each. For God to bring about salvation, humanity needs to be freed from the law because of sin, a freedom that can be found only in Christ and his work, yet fulfillment of the law which introduces salvation into the believer's life comes only through walking in the Spirit.[432] Being ἐν Χριστῷ and ἐν πνεύματι brings about the same result, namely salvation for the person who is both, showing a functional equivalence between the Son and Spirit.[433] The Spirit, like the Son, has the ability to intercede before the Father, something that is a function of the divine.[434] Most importantly, nobody apart from God himself can grant people the right to call him "Abba," and yet the Spirit is the one who does so.[435] The Spirit functions as the agent of adoption even though God is the one who is adopting since they become children of God and not children of the Spirit.[436] No Jew who studied the Scriptures would have a problem thinking of the Holy Spirit as God or as the agent of God's power, the problem would be in seeing the Spirit as separate from God.

Paul is a monotheist. He does, however, see both the Son and Spirit as divine, so the only way to reconcile this is to posit one God existing in three beings. While this could point toward modalism, the interaction between the beings disallows such a construct. Some verses are more explicit in this matter than others (e.g. 8:9–11),[437] yet Paul indicates the Father, Son, and Spirit as

---

429 Contra Dunn, *Romans*, 1:429. Dunn believes that being "of Christ" is intentionally a narrower definition of the Spirit, even though Paul returns to "of God" in 8:14. Cf. 4.4.2 above.
430 Cranfield, *Romans*, 1:388. Cf. his further discussion in 2:838–840.
431 Dunn, *Christology in the Making*, 145–147, here 146.
432 Neil Elliott, *The Rhetoric of Romans: Argumentative Constraint and Strategy and Paul's Dialogue with Judaism* (JSNTSup 45; JSOT Press, 1990), 258–259.
433 Cranfield, *Romans*, 2:843. He looks especially at 8:1 for the Son and 8:9 for the Spirit.
434 Haacker, *Römer*, 148.
435 Cranfield, *Romans*, 2:842.
436 Ibid., 842–843.
437 Schreiner, *Romans*, 413–414.

God each independently and when functioning in his argument together.[438] Therefore, Paul does have an understanding of God as a triunity in Romans 8, though it is implicit in his wording rather than explicit.[439]

The second question, and the heart of this work, is to consider if Paul's original readers, the Roman recipients of the letter, would have understood Paul's argument as triune in nature. The theology of the people of Rome in the first place is polytheistic, so in order to even evangelize the Roman people one would need to discuss the monotheistic nature of God (cf. Rom 3:27–31).[440] The Roman Christians would understand that Paul holds to only a single god, the God of the OT. The language Paul invokes in Romans 8, however, brings to mind issues within the Roman religious context.

In the epistle to the Romans, Paul does not write in order to fortify the pagan mindset of the Roman Christians. Instead his writing both draws on the Roman theological landscape of the first century as well as overturns it in order to convey his message.[441] For example, Roman adoption is what Paul draws on in 8:15,[442] not Jewish. In contrast, Paul speaks of a resurrection from the dead for Jesus into a physical existence, something that is not part of Roman mythology, as even the resurrection of Osiris places him as heavenly judge and forced him to cede his kingship to Horus.[443] Paul can also take a middle ground with respect to Roman theology, however, where he affirms some aspects while overturning others such as in his discussion of life. In Romans 8, Paul describes a salvation, that is "life," that is both present and future. The present aspect is found in the ethical working of the Spirit in believers.[444] The future aspect is the adoption as sons toward a future resurrection and life with God[445] (not to deny the ethical aspect of adoption[446]). One must understand that Paul has taken into consideration the mindset of his readers, some of it to draw upon for his case and some of it to contradict.

---

438 Cranfield, *Romans*, 2:843.
439 Frances Young and David F. Ford, *Meaning and Truth in 2 Corinthians* (Eerdmans, 1987), 255–260. This section explores the Trinity in 2 Corinthians.
440 C. H. Giblin, "Three Monotheistic Texts in Paul," *CBQ* 37 (1975): 527–547, here 543–545.
441 Jewett, *Romans*, 48–49. Jewett argues, "that Paul criticizes and reverses the official system..." and, "[s]everal aspects of the civic cult are reflected in the way the argument of the Epistle to the Romans proceeds."
442 Lyall, "Adoption," 465–466.
443 Cf. Le Corsu, *Isis*, 7–13. See also Wright, *Resurrection of the Son*, 82–83.
444 Abdón Moreno Garcia, "La Sabduría del Espíritu es Biógena. Hacia una Sintaxis de la Alteridad (Rm 8,6 y Flp 2,2)," *Estudios Biblicos* 60 (2002): 3–30, here 19–20. Garcia compares Rom 8:6 and Phil 2:2 as ethical injunctions.
445 Cf. Eastman, "Whose Apocalypse?," 265–270. Though she thinks this future redemption is for Israel alone, she does make a convincing case for the life and redemption to be future.
446 Burke, "Adoption and the Spirit," 318–320.

Naming Jesus as the Son of God would not be a blasphemous issue among Romans, only a political one. Many of the Roman emperors were deified after death, and some claimed to be the sons of a god (whether deifying an ancestor, as Augustus did, or claiming physical descent from a classic god, as Julius Caesar did).[447] A man could be the son of a god in this life without offending Roman sensibilities. The problem comes in Paul giving Jesus divine status not while dead but while Christ is alive (e.g. 8:3 and the sending motif). The resurrection of Jesus would be a bigger problem in terms of the theology of the Roman people, since resurrection did not fit into the apotheosis model of humans–becoming–gods in the Roman mindset.[448] Jesus as a man after his death creates a disjunction for a Roman reader, as once a human obtains godhood, there is no need for flesh anymore.[449] The gods of the pantheon in fact took on flesh only for sport (i.e. to hide their identities), including those who had once been mortal. The deity of Christ would not be a problem for a Roman, rather his incarnation and ongoing humanity would.

The Holy Spirit does not have a parallel in Roman mythology with respect to being bodiless, yet Paul's description would fit within the Roman mindset. Within the mystery cults, the participant would go through an induction ceremony to become part of the cult proper.[450] As one continued through the various levels of the cult, one would learn more and more about what the cult really stood for and thus the rewards would shift. The theology of the Spirit overturns this notion, however, as Paul demonstrates that the Spirit intercedes for all believers and that there is no difference among believers since all are now coheirs with Christ. The Romans would likely understand the Spirit as salvation in terms of the current earthly reward received from a god, since this is what they sought.[451] For example, when people were relieved of debt, they would describe that individual who helped them as being from the god, referring to whichever one they worshipped or to whom they had sacrificed.[452] Paul tempers this expectation by speaking of the suffering of the believer (8:17-18) and all of creation (8:22) such that full salvation is

---

[447] Cf. Alföldi, "Die zwei Lorbeerbäume des Augustus," 403-22; and Stefan Weinstock, *Divius Julius* (Clarendon, 1971), especially 270–317, respectively.

[448] See Wright, *Resurrection of the Son*, 76–77, 81–84. Wright also includes Greek examples, so this more accurately could be called the Greco–Roman mindset.

[449] The example of Heracles fits this well, as in Apollodorus, *The Library*, 2.7.7. Cf. Wright, *Resurrection of the Son*, 55, 57.

[450] See 2.2. Some cults had different levels of initiation, e.g. Mithras. Cf. David Ulansey, *The Origins of the Mithraic Mysteries: Cosmology and Salvation in the Ancient World* (Oxford University Press, 1989), 67–124.

[451] Burkert, *Ancient Mystery Cults*, 27.

[452] Weinstock, *Divus Julius*, 300.

God and the Son and the Spirit

an eschatological hope (8:24) whereas the Spirit is but a taste of that hope (8:23). In fact, the only use of σῴζω in Romans 8 is in conjunction with hope (8:23). Thus, the Roman recipients of the letter would have understood the Holy Spirit as divine.

Taking into consideration the views on Christ and the Spirit that Paul expressed to his readers and the way in which he expressed them, would the first readers of his letter have understood Paul's language in Romans 8 to be consistent with a triune identity for God? Dunn would say no, citing Jesus as separate from God in Paul's theology and the Spirit as just another name for God.[453] Dunn looks for explicit unity with explicit separation, something that does not fit the description of God that Paul gives. Yet Paul does not argue for a triunity so much as "presuppose" it in his argumentation.[454] Romans is an occasional letter, not an apologetic for Paul's theology proper (see 1.2 and 1.3). Thus, when Paul builds his case using the Father, Son, and Spirit, one needs to examine the usage in order to determine if it can be considered a triune understanding of God.

The last major Roman theological piece that coincides with Paul's argument is that of the history of triads in the Roman theological landscape (see 2.4 in particular). Some triads had members whose functions were completely scattered, for example Jupiter, Quirinius, and Mars. Other triads had members who functioned against each other, as with Ormuzd, Ahriman, and Mithras, since Ormuzd and Ahriman battled while Mithras was the balance.[455] A triad would fit within the Roman understanding of how gods interact, yet the counter-cultural aspect would be the congruence of functions. In Roman mythos, when one god overlapped with another, the greater would absorb the lesser (e.g. Isis and Demeter, Apollo and Helios). Paul does not allow for this kind of absorption; instead he describes coinciding functions while keeping them separated.

This book concludes that Paul argues as a triunitarian and intentionally uses the Roman pagan theological mindset of his readers both for support and as a foil for his discussions. The coincidental functions of the Son and Spirit strengthen the identification of the two rather than causing a theological "hostile takeover," which was the norm for the Roman pagan deities. They both were active in giving life to the believer, and neither dominated the other. Instead, the Son opened the way througwh his death and the Spirit finalized the act through indwelling. The same can be said of adoption as well.

---

453 For the latter, see Dunn, *Theology of Paul*, 271.
454 Fee, "Christology and Pneumatology," 235.
455 Finegan, *Myth and Mystery*, 103.

Taking this into consideration along with Paul's monotheism and identification of both the Son and Spirit as God, the Roman recipients of Paul's letter would have understood the arguments in Romans 8 as implicitly conveying Paul's triune theology.

Conclusion

The thesis of this book is, *when taking into account his Jewish background and the Roman context into which he was writing, Paul communicates the Father, Son, and Spirit as a triunity to his readers in Romans 8*. This in turn gave two separate problems to address. The first issue, which dominated chapter 3 and much of chapter 4, was whether Paul held to a Trinitarian view of God at all. The second issue, which dominated chapter 2 and appeared briefly in chapter 3 and more in chapter 4, was that if Paul held to a triune identity of God, would his readers have understood his writing as such.

Chapter 2 began by addressing the second issue first in order to keep the information it raised in the back of one's mind as the exegesis of Romans 8 commenced. The greatest of the Roman pagan gods and the head of their pantheon was described, starting with some of the statues and accompanying imagery. While Jupiter ruled over the entire pantheon, he typically was seen in special relationship with two other gods (Quirinius and Juno), called the Capitoline Triad. Those three gods were the greatest of the Roman pantheon and held a special place in the heart of Rome's citizens.

The chapter progressed then to cover the mystery cults, focusing on Isis and Mithras. A common thread through all mystery cults, including the two surveyed, was the lack of future orientation with respect to salvation. Salvation focused on the immediate life of the person participating in the cult and not on a future existence. Isis also came to be seen as an earth goddess, taking over from Demeter and occasionally Hestia. She was a member of a group of three gods, including her husband Osiris and son Horus. The cult of Mithras had the same characteristics, with an earthly orientation and his own triad.

Though Isis had a heroic quest, Mithras had only his usurpation of the Perseus myth with respect to slaying the great bull.

After recognizing the accretion and significant characteristics within the mystery cults, the chapter covered the imperial cult of Rome. The cult began with Julius Caesar, as Octavian and the Senate worked to keep his divine honors intact after his death. In turn, Octavian used his relationship with Julius to become the son of a god, helping both himself and Rome politically in dealing with outside nations and people groups. After the Senate granted him a new name, the newly-minted Augustus used the cult outside of Rome to cement his status and that of Rome by employing altars with the inscription of "Roma and Augustus." The following emperors all continued the cult, acclaiming the previous ruler as a god (if they were related) in order to boost their own power by either being the son of a god or else claiming divinity on their own. Domitian claimed divine status for himself while alive, claiming the title of κύριος, and other emperors were worshipped during their lifetimes. This worship often included sacrifices asking for favor from the emperor or from Rome (Roma) for the one who asked.

This chapter gave an overview of the Roman pagan theological landscape of the first century. Gods, especially ruling ones, appeared in triads. They had humanistic characteristics in many respects, yet when one god looked like another, the greater would absorb the lesser. Salvation for all types of Roman religion was temporally aspected, with the supplicants looking for help in their current circumstances. Humans could be worshipped as divine, since the deceased emperors ascended to divine status through apotheosis (and a confirming vote of the Senate) and some emperors claimed divine status during their own lifetimes, both abroad as a political tactic and at home. It is into this religious climate that Paul wrote.

Chapter 3 addressed the first question, looking at Paul's use of and understanding of God in Romans 8. In order to set the stage for exegeting Romans 8, this work took a brief look at Romans 1–7, with special emphasis on 5 and 7. Romans 5 overlaps with 8 in terms of vocabulary and some of the main themes, especially the pair of life and death. Romans 7 develops the problem of sin with an emphasis on sin's usurpation and corruption of the law. The solution to the problem of sin is what Paul sets out to discuss in Romans 8, both a short-term and a long-term solution.

The next three sections of the chapter are closely related, as Paul examines God's relationship with creation and recreation in Romans 8. God is lord over creation, he is the creator who wants only good for what he has made, yet at the same time he is the one who cursed creation because of Adam's sin.

This curse is the result of sin, and therefore to remove the curse God must remove the root cause of the curse, sin. In order to bring about the removal of the curse, God must renew creation by bringing about recreation. Recreation occurs at the revelation of the sons of God. The sons of God are those whom God adopts through the work of Christ and the Holy Spirit, with adoption in Romans 8 adhering to the legal Roman institution of adoption. God uses these agents to do his work throughout Romans 8. This process of adoption moves from enlarging God's family to bringing about recreation through the glory of his new adopted sons. The glory in turn is the new physical bodies with which God gifts his sons, based upon the likeness of Christ. Salvation is the final answer to sin, and adoption and recreation are two of the images Paul employs to speak of this event. God causes salvation through the sending of his own special son and the work of the Spirit.

Chapter 4 built off the foundation of the two previous chapters. Paul describes God as the Father of Jesus, his Son, and his other children, believers. At the same time, Jesus is the special Son of God, a title that would have resonated in Roman pagan minds as an announcement of the divine status of Jesus. In his role as the sent one, Jesus opens the way for salvation to take place, yet it is the Spirit who brings salvation to the new adopted son of God. The problem of sin and the law displays God's faithfulness, as he abandons neither the law nor the sinner, instead he rehabilitates both through his sending of the Son and the consequent work of the Spirit. The Son and Spirit function as God's agents in reestablishing creation as recreation.

God as Father pursues salvation through his two agents. Paul describes how God enables both "in Christ" and "in the Spirit" within those who believe in him. While these two terms overlap in significant ways, "in the Spirit" carries more ethical connotations whereas "in Christ" carries communal ones. Both, however, stress the life within the believer that comes from the Father through both of his agents. Life then has enormous significance in Romans 8, as Paul uses the term as a counterpoint to sin and death, which two terms he equates. Paul, contrary to the expectations of the Roman recipients, utilizes life as an eschatological and future oriented word, looking for salvation not in this life but in the one to come.

This study then concluded with a look at the relationships among the three principle figures in Romans 8: the Father, the Son, and the Spirit. Paul implicitly gives Jesus the status of divinity through his special status as God's vice-regent. However, Paul explicitly equates Jesus with God through his variance of terms in Rom 8:35, 39 with respect to whose love Paul is discussing as well as the relationship each has to the Spirit, as the Spirit is both πνεῦμα θεοῦ and πνεῦμα Χριστοῦ. The Spirit also has divine status, as Paul intermingles the functions of the Son and Spirit with respect to the work of salvation (e.g. the "in Christ" and "in Spirit" language) and in the work of intercession for believers. Combined with the given of Paul being a monotheist, the only way to understand Paul's theologizing and thus theology is if Paul understood God as a triunity. In turn, the Roman recipients would have understood Paul's argument as triunitarian by including his monotheism with the discussion of Jesus as God's Son, the importance of a triad that is unified, the overlap of functions without absorption of being within these three, and the overall argumentation employed by Paul throughout Romans 8. Thus, this work has proven the thesis that *when taking into account his Jewish background and the Roman context into which he was writing, in Romans 8 Paul communicates the Father, Son and Spirit as a triunity to his readers.*

The purpose of this book was to determine whether or not the recipients of Paul's letter to the Romans would understand his theologizing as coming out of a triune identity theology. In the midst of arguing that this was indeed the case, this work also covered a few other areas. First, there have been an insufficient number of attempts in the last few decades to compare Pauline theology to the Greco-Roman backdrop as opposed to one that is exclusively Jewish. This work has made a step forward in heading back into that field of research without taking a history of religions approach, which looked for borrowing rather than possible intentions or just influence. Second, this work had to argue for the triune nature of Paul's theology before any further progress could be made in ascertaining the understanding of the original readers with respect to Paul's theology proper. If Paul did not hold a triunity to begin with, then obviously his readers could not understand him as doing such.

This book specifically examined the work of God in order to ascertain Paul's own theology. Paul described the different functions of the Father, Son, and Spirit in order to highlight different aspects of each. In doing so, Paul displays his theology concerning who God is. By expressing overlapping functions of Jesus and the Holy Spirit, Paul lets his readers know that this triad is different from any other, as the overlap between them does not cause a collapse into a single god. Instead, Paul maintains the plurality within God while also maintaining the unity.

The most important impact is not what this book argued for or attempted to bring back into prominence, rather the most important aspect is that a study focused on the concept of God in Paul's theology. Paul's theology has too often been discussed in the light of certain themes, such as righteousness or freedom in Christ. Too few works look to the starting point of Paul's theologizing with respect to discerning who Paul thinks God is. If this project can help nudge scholarship into rediscovering the significance and ubiquity of theology proper in the letters and thought of Paul, then the work was well worth the effort. The reason for beginning with God is that all of Paul's discussion of soteriology, creation, life, Christology, pneumatology, hamartiology, the fate of Israel, and his understanding of the law all circle around and are interconnected with Paul's doctrine of God.

One interesting sidebar this work was unable to explore is the nature of the Trinity. In other words, a trajectory in Paul's thought seems to be the subordination of the Son to the Father due to the nature of their interactions. Paul discusses the Father sending the Son and how the Father utilized the Son to fulfill specific purposes. The same is also true of the relationship between the Father and the Spirit. With respect to the Son and Spirit, it seems as if Paul has the Son over the Spirit in terms of authority (or source, depending upon the nature of the genitive), yet the two have very similar and overlapping functions.

Another path that could be taken is reexamining the relationship between Paul's letters and the cultures to which they were written. While the history of religion's school went too far in trying to make Christianity dependent upon first-century religions, due to the concurrent nature of Christianity and certain forms of paganism, it is likely that there was some sort of influence whether direct or indirect between the two. It would be profitable for scholarship to research not just Paul's background and the immediate conflicts in the churches Paul wrote to, but also the theological and cultural landscapes of the various destinations of Paul's correspondence, which would likely yield a greater understanding of why Paul chose some of the language and arguments he employed. This combined with understanding that Paul himself was partially a product of diaspora Judaism would give deeper insight into his works.

In the end, the triune identity of God in Paul's theology is not overly surprising considering how the church's theology developed after the time of Paul. The first great Christian theologian built the foundation upon which modern orthodoxy stands in terms of his theologizing about the nature and work of the Father, Son, and Spirit. While much of the language of Nicea comes from Greek philosophy and the Gospel of John, much of the content and understanding comes from the letters and passages of Paul, letters like Romans and passages like Romans 8.

Bibliography

Achtemeier, Paul J. *Romans*. Interpretation. John Knox, 1985.

———. "Unsearchable Judgments and Inscrutable Ways: Reflections on Romans." Pages 3–21 in *Pauline Theology Volume IV: Looking Back, Pressing On*. Edited by E. Elizabeth Johnson and David M. Hay. Scholars Press, 1997.

Adewuya, J. Ayodeji. "The Holy Spirit and Sanctification in Romans 8:1–17." *Journal of Pentecostal Theology* (2001): 71–84.

Anderson, Graham. "Greek Religion in the Roman Empire: Diversities, Convergences, Uncertainties." Pages 143–63 in *Religious Diversity in the Graeco-Roman World*. The Biblical Seminar 79. Edited by Dan Cohn-Sherbok and John M. Court. Sheffield Academic Press, 2001.

Aland, Barbara. "Trustworthy Preaching: Reflections on John Chrysostom's Interpretation of Romans 8." Pages 271–282 in *Romans and the People of God: Essays in Honor of Gordon D. Fee on the Occasion of His 65th Birthday*. Edited by Sven K. Soderlund and N. T. Wright. Eerdmans, 1999.

Aletti, Jean-Noël. *Israël et la Loi dans la latter aux Romains*. Lectio Divina 173. Les Éditions du Cerf, 1998.

———. "La présence d'un modèle rhétorique en Romains." *Biblica* 71 (1990): 1–24.

———. "La *dispositio* rhétorique dans les épîtres pauliniennes." *New Testament Studies* 38 (1992):385–401.

———. "The Rhetoric of Romans 5–8." Pages 294–308 in *The Rhetorical Analysis of Scripture: Essays from the 1995 London Conference*. edited by Stanley E. Porter and Thomas H. Olbricht. Journal for the Study of the New Testament Supplement Series 146. Sheffield Academic Press, 1997.

———. "Rm. 7.7–25 encore une fois: enjeux et propositions." *New Testament Studies* 48 (2002): 358–76.

Alföldi, Andreas. *Die monarchische Repräsentation im römischen Kaiserreiche*. Wissenschaftliche Buchgesellschaft, 1970.

———. "Die zwei Lorbeerbäume des Augustus." Pages 403–22 in *Römischer Kaiserkult*. Edited by Antonie Wlosok. Wissenschtliche Buchgesellschaft, 1978.

Aune, David E. "The Influence of Roman Imperial Court Ceremonial on the Apocalypse of John." *Biblical Research* 28 (1983): 5–26.

———. *Revelation*. 3 vols. Word Biblical Commentary 52a–c. Thomas Nelson, 1997–1998.

———. "Romans as *Logos Protreptikos*." Pages 278–96 in *The Romans Debate*. Edited by Karl P. Donfried. Hendrickson, 1991.

Balsdon, J. P. V. D. "Die 'Göttlichkeit' Alexanders." Pages 254–90 in *Römischer Kaiserkult*. Edited by Antonie Wlosok. Wissenschaftliche Buchgesellschaft, 1978.

Barclay, John M. G. "Diaspora Judaism." Pages 47–64 in *Religious Diversity in the Graeco-Roman World*. The Biblical Seminar 79. Edited by Dan Cohn-Sherbok and John M. Court. Sheffield Academic Press, 2001.

Barnett, Paul. *The Second Epistle to the Corinthians*. New International Commentary on the New Testament. Eerdmans, 1997.

Barrett, Anthony A. *Caligula: The Corruption of Power*. Yale University Press, 1989.

Barrett, C. K. *The Epistle to the Romans*. Harper's New Testament Commentary. Harper and Row, 1957.

Barrett, C. K. ed. *The New Testament Background: Selected Documents*. Revised edition. Harper & Row, 1989.

Barr, James. "'Abba' Isn't 'Daddy.'" *Journal of Theological Studies* 39 (1988): 28–47.

———. "'Abba, Father' and the Familiarity of Jesus' Speech." *Theology* 91 (1988): 173–9.

Barth, Karl. *The Epistle to the Romans*. Sixth edition. Translated by Sir Edwyn Hoskyns. Oxford University Press, 1968.

Bassler, Jouette M. *Divine Partiality: Paul and a Theological Axiom*. Society of Biblical Literature Dissertation Series 59. Scholars Press, 1982.

Bauckham, Richard. *God Crucified: Monotheism and Christology in the New Testament*. Eerdmans, 1998.

———. *Jesus and the God of Israel: God Crucified and Other Studies on the New Testament's Christology of Divine Identity*. Eerdmans, 2009.

Bauer, Walter, Frederick William Danker, William Arndt, and F. Wilbur Gingrich. *A Greek-English Lexicon of the New Testament and Other Early Christian Literature*. Third edition. University of Chicago Press, 2000.

Bayes, J. F. "The Translation of Romans 8:3." *Expository Times* 111 (1999): 14–16.

Beard, Mary, John North, and Simon Price. *Religions of Rome*. 2 vols. Cambridge University Press, 1998.

Beck, Roger. "The Mysteries of Mithras: A New Account of Their Genesis," *Journal of Roman Studies* 88 (1998): 115–28.

———. "Ritual, Myth, Doctrine, and Initiation in the Mysteries of Mithras: New Evidence from a Cult Vessel," *Journal of Roman Studies* 90 (2000): 145–80.

Beker, J. Christiaan. "Echoes and Intertextuality: On the Role of Scripture in Paul's Theology." Pages 64–69 in *Paul and the Scriptures of Israel*. Journal for the Study of the New Testament Supplement Series 83. Edited by Craig Evans and John Sanders. Sheffield Academic, 1993.

———. "Vision of Hope for a Suffering World: Romans 8:17–30," *The Princeton Seminary Bulletin* 3 (1994): 26–32.

Bell, Richard H. "Sacrifice and Christology in Paul." *Journal of Theological Studies* 53 (2002): 1–27.

Bendemann, Reinhold von. "Die kritische Diastase von Wissen, Wollen und Handeln: Traditionsgeschichtliche Spurensuche eines hellenistischen Topos in Römer 7." *Zeitschrift für die Neutestamentliche Wissenschaft* 95 (2004): 35–63.

Bertone, John A. "The Experience of Glossolalia and the Spirit's Empathy: Romans 8:26 Revisited," *Pneuma: Journal for the Society of Pentecostal Studies* 25 (2003): 54–65.

———. *"The Law of the Spirit": Experience of the Spirit and Displacement of the Law in Romans 8:1–16*. Studies in Biblical Literature 86. Peter Lang, 2005.

Bertram, Georg. "Ἀποκαραδοκία" *Zeitschrift für die neutestamentliche Wissenschaft* 49 (1958): 264–70.

Bickermann, Elias. "Consecratio." Pages 1–25 in *Le Culte des souverains dans l'Empire Romain*. Edited by William den Boer. Entretiens sur l'antiquité classique 19. Hardt, 1973.

──────. "Die römische Kaiserapotheose." Pages 82–121 in *Römischer Kaiserkult*. Edited by Antonie Wlosok. Wissenschaftliche Buchgesellschaft, 1978.

Bindemann, Walther. *Die Hoffnung der Schöpfung: Römer 8,18–27 und die Frage einer Theologie der Befreiung von Mensch und Natur*. Neukirchener Verlag, 1983.

Black, Matthew. "The Interpretation of Romans viii 28." Pages 166–72 in *Neotestamentica et Patristica*. Edited by W.C. van Unnik. Brill, 1962.

──────. *Romans*. New Century Bible Commentary. London: Oliphants, 1973.

Blank, J. "Gesetz und Geist." Pages 73–100 in *The Law of the Spirit in Romans 7 and 8*. Monograph Series of *Benedicta*. Edited by L. De Lorenzi. St. Paul's Abbey, 1976.

Bolt, John. "The Relation Between Creation and Redemption in Romans 8:18–27." *Calvin Theological Journal* 30 (1995): 34–51.

Bornkamm, Günther. "The Letter to the Romans as Paul's Last Will and Testament." Pages 18–28 in *The Romans Debate*. Edited by Karl P. Donfried. Hendrickson, 1991.

Botermann, Helga. *Das Judenedikt des Kaisers Claudius: Römischer Staat und Christiani im 1. Jahrhundert*. Hermes Einzelschriften 71. Steiner, 1996.

Bousset, Wilhelm. *Kyrios Christos: A History of the Belief in Christ from the Beginnings of Christianity to Irenaeus*. Translated by J. E. Steely. Abingdon, 1970.

Bouttier, *En Christ: etude d'exegese et de theologie Pauliniennes*. Presses Universitaires de France, 1967.

Bowersock, G. W. *Augustus and the Greek World*. Clarendon, 1965.

Branick, Vincent P. "The Sinful Flesh of the Son of God (Rom 8:3): A Key Image of Pauline Theology." *Catholic Biblical Quarterly* 47 (1985): 246–62.

Bremmer, Jan. "The Legend of Cybele's Arrival in Rome." Pages 9–22 in *Studies in Hellenistic Religion*. Edited by M. J. Vermaseren. Vol 78 of Études préliminaries aux religions orientales dan l'empire romain. Brill, 1979.

Bruce, F. F. "Christianity Under Claudius." *Bulletin of the John Rylands University Library of Manchester* 44 (1962): 309–26.

──────. *Paul: Apostle of the Heart Set Free*. Eerdmans, 1977.

──────. *Romans*. Tyndale New Testament Commentary 6. Eerdmans, 1985.

Bultmann, Rudolf. *Der Stil der paulinischen Predigt und die kynisch-stoische Diatribe*. Vandenhoeck & Ruprecht, 1910.

Burkert, Walter. *Greek Religion*. Translated by John Raffan. Harvard University Press, 1985.

──────. *Ancient Mystery Cults*. Harvard University Press, 1987.

Burke, Travor J. "Adoption and the Spirit in Romans 8." *Evangelical Quarterly* 70 (1998): 311–24.

Byrne, Brendan. "How Can We Interpret Romans Theologically Today?" *Australian Biblical Review* 47 (1999), 29–42.

———. "Living Out the Righteousness of God: The Contribution of Rom 6:1–8:13 to an Understanding of Paul's Ethical Presuppositions." *Catholic Biblical Quarterly* 43 (1981): 557–81.

———. *'Sons of God'—'Seed of Abraham': A Study of the Idea of the Sonship of God of All Christians in Paul Against the Jewish Background*. Analecta biblica 93. Biblical Institute, 1979.

———. *Romans*. Sacra Pagina 6. Liturgical Press, 1996.

Capes, David B. *Old Testament Yahweh Texts in Paul's Christology*. Wissenschaftliche Untersuchungen zum Neuen Testament II/47. Mohr Siebeck, 1992.

———. "YHWH Texts and Monotheism in Paul's Christology." Pages 120–37 in *Early Jewish and Christian Monotheism*. Edited by Loren T. Stuckenbruck and Wendy E. S. North. Journal for the Study of the New Testament Supplement Series 263. T&T Clark, 2004.

Carson, D. A. *The Gospel According to John*. Pillar New Testament Commentary. Eerdmans, 1991.

Carson, Robert A. G. *Coins of the Roman Empire*. Routledge, 1990.

Chang, Hae-Kyung. "(ἀπο)καραδοκία bei Paulus und Aquila." *Zeitschrift für die neutestamentliche Wissenschaft* 93 (2002): 268–78.

Classen, C. Joachim. "St. Paul's Epistles and Ancient Greek and Roman Rhetoric." Pages 265–291 in *Rhetoric and the New Testament: Essays from the 1992 Heidelberg Conference*. Edited by Stanley E. Porter and Thomas H. Olbricht. Journal for the Study of the New Testament Supplement Series 90. Sheffield Academic Press, 1993.

Clauss, Manfred. *Kaiser und Gott: Herrscherkult im römischen Reich*. Teubner, 1999.

———. *The Roman Cult of Mithras: The God and His Mysteries*. Translated by Richard Gordon. Rutledge, 2001.

Cotter, David W. *Genesis*. Berit Olam. Liturgical Press, 2003.

Court, John M. "Mithraism Among the Mysteries." Pages 182–95 in *Religious Diversity in the Greco-Roman World: A Survey of Recent Scholarship*. Edited by Dan Cohn-Sherbok and John M. Court. Sheffield Academic Press, 2001.

Cousar, Charles B. "Continuity and Discontinuity in Romans 5–8 (In Conversation with Frank Thielman)." Pages 196–210 in *Pauline Theology Volume III: Romans*. Edited by David M. Hay and E. Elizabeth Johnson. SBL, 2002.

Cowan, Christopher. "The Father and Son in the Fourth Gospel: Johannine Subordination Revisited." *Journal of the Evangelical Theological Society* 49 (2006): 115–35.

Craigie, Peter C. *Psalms 1–50*. Word Biblical Commentary 19. Word, 1983.

Cranfield, C.E.B. "Romans 8:28." *Scottish Journal of Theology*. 19 (1966): 204–15.

———. *Romans*. 2 vols. International Critical Commentary. T&T Clark, 1975. Repr., T&T Clark, 2003.

———. "Some Comments on Professor J. D. G. Dunn's *Christology in the Making* with Special Reference to the Evidence of the Epistle to the Romans." Pages 267–80 in *The Glory of Christ in the New Testament*. Edited by L. D. Hurst and N. T. Wright. Clarendon Press, 1987.

Dahl, Nils Alstrup. "The Atonement-An Adequate Reward for the Akedah? (Ro 8:32)." Pages 15–29 in *Neotestamentica et Semitica: Studies in Honor of Matthew Black*. Edited by E. Earle Ellis and Max Wilcox. T&T Clark, 1969.

———. "The Neglected Factor in New Testament Theology." Pages 153–62 in *Jesus the Christ: The Historical Origins of Christological Doctrine*. Edited by Donald H. Juel. Fortress, 1991.

———. "Two Notes on Romans 5." *Studia theologica* 5 (1951): 37–48.

Denton, D. R. "Ἀποκαραδοκία" *Zeitschrift für die neutestamentliche Wissenschaft* 73 (1982): 138–40.

Dillon, Richard J. "The Spirit as Taskmaster and Troublemaker in Romans 8." *Catholic Biblical Quarterly* 60 (1998): 682–702.

Dodd, C. H. *The Epistle of Paul to the Romans*. Moffatt New Testament Commentary. Harper & Row, 1932.

Donfried, Karl Paul. "False Presuppositions in the Study of Romans." Pages 102–25 in *The Romans Debate*. Edited by Karl P. Donfried. Hendrickson, 1991.

Dumézil, Georges. *Archaic Roman Religion*. 2 vols. Translated by Philip Krapp. University of Chicago Press, 1970.

Dunn, James D. G. "Christology as an Aspect of Theology." Pages 202–12 in *The Future of Christology: Essays in Honor of Leander E. Keck*. Edited by Abraham J. Malherbe and Wayne A. Meeks. Fortress, 1993.

———. *Christology in the Making: A New Testament Inquiry into the Origins of the Doctrine of the Incarnation*. 2nd edition. Eerdmans, 1989.

———. "Diversity in Paul." Pages 107–123 in *Religious Diversity in the Graeco-Roman World*. The Biblical Seminar 79. Edited by Dan Cohn-Sherbok and John M. Court. Sheffield Academic Press, 2001.

———. *The Epistles to the Colossians and to Philemon*. New International Greek Testament Commentary. Eerdmans, 1996.

———. "In Quest of Paul's Theology: Retrospect and Prospect." Pages 95–115 in *Pauline Theology Volume IV: Looking Back, Pressing On*. Edited by E. Elizabeth Johnson and David M. Hay. Scholars Press, 1997.

———. *Romans*. 2 vols. Word Biblical Commentary 38a–b. Word, 1988.

———. "Spirit Speech: Reflections on Romans 8:12–27." Pages 82–91 in *Romans and the People of God: Essays in Honor of Gordon D. Fee on the Occasion of His 65th Birthday*. Edited by Sven K. Soderlund and N. T. Wright. Eerdmans, 1999.

———. *The Theology of Paul the Apostle*. Eerdmans, 1998.

Eastman, Susan. "Whose Apocalypse? The Identity of the Sons of God in Romans 8:19." *Journal of Biblical Literature* 121 (2002): 263–77.

Edwards, James R. *Romans*. New International Biblical Commentary. Hendrickson, 1992.

Egelhaaf-Gaiser, Ulrike and Alfred Schäfer. *Religiöse Vereine in der römischen Antike*. Studien und Texte zu Antike und Christentum 13. Mohr Siebeck, 2002.

Elliott, Neil. *The Rhetoric of Romans: Argumentative Constraint and Strategy and Paul's Dialogue with Judaism*. Journal for the Study of the New Testament Supplement Series 45. JSOT Press, 1990.

Esler, Philip F. *Conflict and Identity in Romans: The Social Setting of Paul's Letter*. Fortress, 2003.

_____. "Palestinian Judaism in the First Century." Pages 21–46 in *Religious Diversity in the Graeco-Roman World*. The Biblical Seminar 79. Edited by Dan Cohn-Sherbok and John M. Court. Sheffield Academic Press, 2001.

Evans, John K. *War, Women, and Children in Ancient Rome*. Routledge, 1991.

Fahy, T. "St. Paul's Romans Were Jewish Converts." *Irish Theological Quarterly* 26 (1959): 182–191.

Fay, Ron C. "Greco-Roman Concepts of Deity." Pages 51–80 in *Paul's World*. Pauline Studies 4. Edited by Stanley Porter. Leiden: Brill, 2008.

_____. "Was Paul a Trinitarian? A Look at Romans 8." Pages 327–345 in *Paul and His Theology*. Pauline Studies 3. Edited by Stanley E. Porter. Brill, 2006.

Fee, Gordon D. "Christology and Penumatology in Romans 8:9–11 – and Elsewhere: Some Reflections on Paul as a Trinitarian." Pages 218–39 in *To What End Exegesis? Essays Textual, Exegetical, and Theological*. Eerdmans, 2001.

_____. *The First Epistle to the Corinthians*. New International Commentary on the New Testament. Eerdmans, 1987.

_____. *God's Empowering Presence: The Holy Spirit in the Letters of Paul*. Hendrickson, 1994.

_____. *Pauline Christology: An Exegetical–Theological Study*. Hendrickson, 2007.

Feinberg, John S. *No One Like Him*. Foundations of Evangelical Theology. Crossway, 2001.

Ferguson, Everett. *Backgrounds of Early Christianity*. 3d ed. Eerdmans, 2003.

Ferguson, John. *The Religions of the Roman Empire*. Aspects of Greek and Roman Life. Thames and Hudson, 1970.

Festugière, A. J. "Initée par l'époux," *Monuments Piot* 53 (1963): 135–46.

Feuillet, A. "Loi de Dieu, loi du Christ et loi de l'Esprit d'après les épitres pauliniennes: Les rapports de ces trois lois avec la Loi Mosaique." *Novum Testamentum* 22 (1980): 29–65.

Fiensy, David A. "The Roman Empire and Asia Minor." Pages 36–56 in *The Face of New Testament Studies: A Survey of Recent Research*. Edited by Scot McKnight and Grant R. Osborne. Baker, 2004.

Finegan, Jack. *Myth and Mystery: An Introduction to the Pagan Religions of the Biblical World*. Baker, 1989.

Finn, Thomas M. "The God-fearers Reconsidered." *Catholic Biblical Quarterly* 47 (1985): 74–84.

Fishwick, Duncan. *Imperial Cult in the Latin West: Studies in the Ruler Cult of the Western Provinces of the Roman Empire*. 3 vols. Brill, 1987–2002.

Fitzmyer, Joseph A. *Romans: A New Translation with Introduction and Commentary*. Anchor Bible 33. Doubleday, 1993.

Fox, Robin Lane. *Pagans and Christians*. Harper & Row, 1988.

Freedman, David Noel, ed. *The Anchor Bible Dictionary*. 6 vols. Doubleday, 1992.

Friesen, Steven J. *Imperial Cults and the Apocalypse of John: Reading Revelation in the Ruins*. Oxford University Press, 2001.

Fuller, Daniel P. "Progressive Dispensationalism and the Law/Gospel Contrast: A Case Study in Biblical Theology." Pages 237–49 in *Biblical Theology: Retrospect and Prospect*. Edited by Scott J. Hafemann. InterVarsity, 2002.

Furnish, Victor Paul. "Where Is the 'Truth' in Paul's Gospel? A Response to Paul W. Meyer." Pages 141–77 in *Pauline Theology Volume IV: Looking Back, Pressing On*. Edited by E. Elizabeth Johnson and David M. Hay. Scholars Press, 1997.

Gabriel, Andrew K. "Pauline Pneumatology and the Question of Trinitarian Presuppositions." Pages 347–362 in *Paul and His Theology*. Pauline Studies 3. Edited by Stanley E. Porter. Brill, 2006.

Gaffin, Richard B., Jr. "Glory, Glorification." Pages 348–50 in *Dictionary of Paul and His Letters*. Edited by Gerald Hawthorne, Ralph P. Martin, and Daniel G. Reid. InterVarsity, 1993.

Garcia, Abdón Moreno. "La Sabduría del Espíritu es Biógena. Hacia una Sintaxis de la Alteridad (Rm 8,6 y Flp 2,2)." *Estudios Biblicos* 60 (2002): 3–30.

Garland, David E. *1 Corinthians*. Baker Exegetical Commentary on the New Testament. Baker, 2003.

Gempf, Conrad. "Luke's Story of Paul's Reception in Rome." Pages 42–66 in *Rome in the Bible and the Early Church*. Edited by Peter Oakes. Grand Rapids: Baker, 2002.

Gibbs, John G. *Creation and Redemption: A Study in Pauline Theology*. Novum Testamentum Supplements. Brill, 1971.

Giblin, C. H. "Three Monotheistic Texts in Paul." *Catholic Biblical Quarterly* 37 (1975): 527–47.

Gieniusz, Anrzej. *Romans 8:18–30: "Suffering Does Not Thwart the Future Glory"*. International Studies in Formative Christianity and Judaism. Scholars Press, 1999.

Gillman, Florence Morgan. "Another Look at Romans 8:3: 'In the Likeness of Sinful Flesh.'" *Catholic Biblical Quarterly* 49 (1987): 597–604.

Godet, Frederic Louis. *Commentary on Romans*. Kregel, 1977.

Goell, Theresa. "Nimrud Dagh: The Tomb of Antiochus I, King of Commagene." *Archeology* 5 (1952): 136–44.

Gorday, Peter. *Principles of Patristic Exegesis: Romans 9–11 in Origen, John Chrysostom, and Augustine*. Studies in the Bible and Early Christianity 4. The Edwin Mellen Press, 1983.

Gradel, Ittai. *Emperor Worship and Roman Religion*. Oxford Classical Monographs. Clarendon, 2004.

Grant, Michael. *Nero: Emperor in Revolt*. American Heritage, 1970.

———. *The Roman Emperors: A Biographical Guide to the Rulers of Imperial Rome 31 BC–AD 476*. Charles Scribner's Sons, 1985.

Grappe, Christian. "Qui me délivrera de ce corps de mort? L'Esprit de vie! Romains 7,24 et 8,2 comme éléments de typologie adamique." *Biblica* 83 (2002): 472–92.

Grayston, Kenneth. *Dying, We Live: A New Inquiry into the Death of Christ in the New Testament*. Oxford University Press, 1990.

Greene, John T. "CHRIST in Paul's Thought: Romans 1–8." *Journal of Religious Thought* 49 (1992): 44–58.

Greene, M. Dwaine. "A Note on Romans 8:3." *Biblische Zeitschrift* 35 (1991): 103–6.
Green, Gene L. *The Letters to the Thessalonians*. Pillar New Testament Commentaries. Eerdmans, 2002.
Green, Joel B. *The Death of Jesus: Tradition and Interpretation in the Passion Narrative*. Wissenschaftliche Untersuchungen zum Neuen Testament II/33. Mohr Siebeck, 1988.
Gressmann, Hugo. *Die orientalischen Religionen im hellenistisch-römischen Zeitalter*. W. de Gruyter, 1930.
Griffin, Miriam T. *Nero: The End of a Dynasty*. Yale University Press, 1984.
Grillmeier, Aloys. *Christ in Christian Tradition Volume One: The Apostolic Age to Chalcedon (451)*. 2d edition. Translated by John Bowden. John Knox, 1975.
Gros, Pierre. *Aurea templa: recherches sur l'architecture religeuse de Rome à l'époque d'Auguste*. Palais Farnèse, 1976.
Grudem, Wayne. *Systematic Theology: An Introduction to Biblical Doctrine*. Zondervan, 1994.
Güting, E. "Der geographische Horizont der sogennanten Völkerliste des Lukas (Acta 2:9–11)." *Zeitschrift für die neutestamentliche Wissenschaft* 66 (1975): 149–69.
Haacker, Klaus. *Der Brief des Paulus an die Römer*. Theologischer Handkommentar zum Neuen Testament 6. Evangelische Verlagsanstalt, 1998.
———. *The Theology of Paul's Letter to the Romans*. New Testament Theology. Cambridge University Press, 2003.
Habicht, Christian. "Die augusteische Zeit und das erste Jahrhundert nach Christi Geburt." Pages 39–88 in *Le Culte des souverains dans l'Empire Romain*. Edited by William den Boer. Entretiens sur l'antiquité classique 19. Hardt, 1973.
Hahn, Roger L. "Pneumatology in Romans 8: Its Historical and Theological Context." *Wesleyan Theological Journal* 21 (1986): 74–90.
Hamilton, Victor P. *The Book of Genesis*. 2 vols. New International Commentary on the Old Testament. Eerdmans, 1990–1995.
Hardy, Edward R., ed. *Christology of the Later Fathers*. The Library of Christian Classics. John Knox, 1954.
Hay, David M. *Glory at the Right Hand: Psalm 110 in Early Christianity*. Society of Biblical Literature Monograph Series 18. Abingdon, 1973.
Hays, Richard B. *Echoes of Scripture in the Letters of Paul*. Yale University Press, 1989.
———. "Adam, Israel, Christ—The Question of Covenant in the Theology of Romans: A Response to Leander E. Keck and and N.T. Wright." Pages 68–86 in in *Pauline Theology Volume III: Romans*. Edited by David M. Hay and E. Elizabeth Johnson. SBL, 2002.
———. "The God of Mercy Who Rescues Us from the Present Evil Age." Pages 123–43 in *The Forgotten God: Perspectives in Biblical Theology*. Edited by A. Andrew Das and Frank J. Matera. Westminster John Knox, 2002.
Hellholm, David. "Amplificatio in the Macro-Structure of Romans." Pages 123–51 in *Rhetoric and the New Testament: Essays from the 1992 Heidelberg Conference*. Edited by Stanley E. Porter and Thomas H. Olbricht. Journal for the Study of the New Testament Supplement Series 90. Sheffield Academic Press, 1993.

Hemer, Colin J. *Letters to the Seven Churches of Asia*. The Biblical Resource Series. Eerdmans, 2001.

Hendriksen, William. *Exposition of Paul's Epistle to the Romans*. New Testament Commentary. Baker, 1982.

Heyob, Sharon. *The Cult of Isis Among Women in the Greco-Roman World*. Études Préliminaires aux Religions Orientales dans l'Empire Romain 51. Brill, 1975.

Hill, Wesley. *Paul and the Trinity: Persons, Relations, and the Pauline Letters*. Eerdmans, 2015.

Hinnells, John R., ed. *Mithraic Studies: Proceedings of the First International Congress of Mithraic Studies*. 2 vols. Manchester University Press, 1975.

Hoehner, Harold W. *Ephesians: An Exegetical Commentary*. Baker, 2002.

Horn, Friedrich Wilhelm. "Wandel im Geist: Zur pneumatologischen Begründung der Ethik bei Paulus." *Kerygma und Dogma* 38 (1992): 149–170.

Hultgren, Arland J. *Christ and His Benefits: Christology and Redemption in the New Testament*. Fortress, 1987.

———. "Suffering Together with Christ: A Study of Romans 8:17." Pages 120–6 in *God, Evil, and Suffering: Essays in Honor of Paul R. Sponheim*. Edited by Terence E. Fretheim and Curtis L. Thompson. Word & World Supplement Series 4. Luther Seminary, 2000.

Hurtado, Larry W. *God in New Testament Theology*. Library of Biblical Theology. Abingdon Press, 2010.

———. "Jesus' Divine Sonship in Paul's Epistle to the Romans." Pages 217–33 in *Romans and the People of God: Essays in Honor of Gordon D. Fee on the Occasion of His 65th Birthday*. Edited by Sven K. Soderlund and N. T. Wright. Eerdmans, 1999.

———. *Lord Jesus Christ: Devotion to Jesus in Earliest Christianity*. Eerdmans, 2003.

Jeremias, Joachim. *The Prayers of Jesus*. Translated by John Bowden. SCM, 1967.

Jervis, L. Ann. *The Purpose of Romans: A Comparative Letter Structure Investigation*. Journal for the Study of the New Testament Supplement Series 55. JSOT Press, 1991.

Jewett, Robert. *Romans: A Commentary*. Hermeneia. Fortress Press, 2007.

Jobes, Karen H., and Moisés Silva. *Invitation to the Septuagint*. Baker, 2000.

Jolivet Jr., Ira J. "An Argument from the Letter and Intent of the Law as the Primary Argumentative Strategy in Romans." Pages 309–35 in *The Rhetorical Analysis of Scripture: Essays from the 1995 London Conference*. Edited by Stanley Porter and Thomas H. Olbricht. Journal for the Study of the New Testament Supplement Series 146. Sheffield University Press, 1997.

Käsemann, Ernst. *Commentary on Romans*. Translated and edited by Geoffrey W. Bromiley. Eerdmans, 1980.

Keck, Leander E. "Searchable Judgments and Scrutable Ways: A Response to Paul J. Achtemeier." Pages 22–32 in in *Pauline Theology Volume IV: Looking Back, Pressing On*. Edited by E. Elizabeth Johnson and David M. Hay. Scholars, 1997.

———. "What Makes Romans Tick?" Pages 3–29 in *Pauline Theology Volume III: Romans*. Edited by David M. Hay and E. Elizabeth Johnson. SBL, 2002.

Keesmaat, Sylvia C. *Paul and His Story: (Re)Interpreting the Exodus Tradition*. Journal for the Study of the New Testament Supplement Series 181. Sheffield Academic Press, 1999.

Keresztes, Paul. *Imperial Rome and the Christians: from Herod the Great to about 200 A.D*. Vol. 1. University Press of America, 1989.

Kidner, Derek. *Psalms: An Introduction and Commentary*. 2 vols. Tyndale Old Testament Commentary Series 14a–b. InterVarsity, 1973.

Kim, Kyu Seop. "Another Look at Adoption in Romans 8:15 in Light of Roman Social Practices and Legal Rules," *Biblical Theology Bulletin* 44 (2014): 133–143.

Kittel, Gerhard, and Gerhard Friedrich, eds. *Theological Dictionary of the New Testament*. Translated by Geoffrey W. Bromiley. 10 vols. Eerdmans, 1964–1976.

Klauck, Hans-Josef. *Die religiose Umwelt des Urchristentums*. 2 vols. Studienbucher Theologie 9,1–2. Kohlhammer Verlag, 1995–1996.

———. *The Religious Context of Early Christianity: A Guide to Graeco-Roman Religions*. Translated by Brian McNeil. T&T Clark, 2000.

———. *Religion und Gesellschaft im frühen Christentum. Neutestamentliche Studien*. Wissenschaftliche Untersuchungen zum Neuen Testament I/152. Mohr Siebeck, 2003.

Klein, Günther. "Paul's Purpose in Writing the Epistle to the Romans." Pages 29–43 in *The Romans Debate*. Edited by Karl P. Donfried. Hendrickson, 1991.

Klumbies, Paul-Gerhard. *Die Rede von Gott bei Paulus in ihrem zeitgeschichtlichen Kontext*. Vandenhoeck & Ruprecht, 1992.

Köstenberger, Andreas J. and Scott R. Swain. *Father, Son and Spirit: The Trinity and John's Gospel*. NSBT. InterVarsity, 2008.

Kraabel, A. T. "The Disappearance of the 'God–fearers'." *Numen* 28/2 (1981): 113–126.

Kraftchick, Steven J. "An Asymptotic Response to Dunn's Retrospective and Proposals." Pages 116–39 in *Pauline Theology Volume IV: Looking Back, Pressing On*. Edited by E. Elizabeth Johnson and David M. Hay. Scholars, 1997.

Kraus, Hans-Joachim. *Psalms*. 2 vols. Continental Commentary. Translated by Hilton C. Oswald. Fortress, 1988–1989.

Kraybill, J. Nelson. *Imperial Cult and Commerce in John's Apocalypse*. Journal for the Study of the New Testament Supplement Series 132. Sheffield Academic Press, 1996.

Kruse, Colin. *2 Corinthians*. Tyndale New Testament Commentary 8. InterVarsity, 1987.

Kreitzer, L. Joseph. "Hadrian and the Nero Redivivus Myth." *Zeitschrift für die neutestamentliche Wissenschaft* 79 (1988): 92–115.

Laeuchli, Samuel. "Mithraic Dualism." Pages 46–66 in *Mithraism in Ostia: Mystery Religion and Christianity in the Ancient Port of Rome*. Edited by Samuel Laeuchli. Garrett Theological Studies 1. Northwestern University Press, 1967.

Lagrange, Marie-Joseph. *Saint Paul Épitre aux Romains*. Étudies Biblique. Gabalda, 1916.

Lambrecht, Jan. *The Wretched "I" and Its Liberation*. Louvain Theological and Pastoral Monographs 16. Eerdmans, 1992.

Lampe, Peter. *From Paul to Valentinus: Christians at Rome in the First Two Centuries.* Fortress, 2003.
Latte, Kurt. *Römische Religionsgeschichte.* Beck, 1960.
Lease, Gary. "Mithraism and Christianity." *ANRW* 28.2:1302–32. Part 2. *Principat,* 28.2. Edited by H. Temporini and W. Haase. de Guyter, 1989.
Le Corsu, France. *Isis: mythe et mystères.* Les Belle Lettres, 1977.
Leon, Harry J. *The Jews of Ancient Rome.* Updated edition. Hendrickson, 1995.
Lewers, June E. "The Relationship of Suffering and Hope in Romans 5 and 8." M.A. thesis, Trinity Evangelical Divinity School, 1984.
Lichtenberger, Hermann. *Das Ich Adams und das Ich der Menschheit: Studien zum Menschenbild in Römer 7.* Wissenschaftliche Untersuchungen zum Neuen Testament I/164. Mohr Siebeck, 2004.
Liddell, H. G., R. Scott, and H. S. Jones. *A Greek-English Lexicon.* 9th ed. with revised supplement. Clarendon, 1996.
Lincoln, Bruce. "Mithra(s) as Sun and Savior." Pages 505–23 in *La soteriologia dei culti oriental nell' Impero Romano.* Edited by Ugo Bianchi and Maarten J. Vermaseren. Brill, 1982.
Liou-Gille, Bernadette. *Cultes "Héroïques" romains: Les foundateurs.* Société d'Édition "Les Belles Lettres," 1980.
Lohse, Eduard. "ὁ νόμος τοῦ πνεύματος τῆς ζωῆς Exegetische Anmerkungen zu Rom. 8.2." Pages 101–17 in *Neues Testament und christliche Existenz: Festschrift für Herbert Braun zum 70.* Edited by Hans Dieter Betz and Luise Schottroff. Mohr Siebeck, 1973.
Longenecker, Richard N. "The Focus of Romans: The Central Role of 5:1–8:39 in the Argument of the Letter." Pages 49–69 in *Romans and the People of God: Essays in Honor of Gordon D. Fee on the Occasion of His 65th Birthday.* Edited by Sven K. Soderlund and N. T. Wright. Eerdmans, 1999.
_____. *The Epistle to the Romans: A Commentary on the Greek Text.* New International Greek Text Commentary. Eerdmans, 2016.
Lowe, Chuck. "'There Is No Condemnation' (Romans 8:1): But Why Not?" *Journal of the Evangelical Theological Society* 42 (1999): 231–50.
Louw, Johannes P., and Eugene A. Nida, eds. *Greek-English Lexicon of the New Testament Based on Semantic Domains.* 2d edition. 2 vols. UBS, 1988.
Lyall, Francis. "Roman Law in the Writings of Paul—Adoption." *Journal of Biblical Literature* 88 (1969): 458–66.
_____. *Slaves, Citizens, Sons: Legal Metaphors in the Epistles.* Zondervan, 1984.
Malaise, Michel. *Les conditions de pénétration et de diffusion des cultes égyptiens en Italie.* Études Préliminaires aux Religions Orientales dans l'Empire Romain 22. Brill, 1972.
Martin, Brice L. *Christ and the Law in Paul.* Novum Testamentum Supplement 62. Brill, 1989.
Martin, Ralph P. *2 Corinthians.* Word Biblical Commentary 40. Thomas Nelson, 1986.
Martins, Susan H. "Pauline Didactic use of Literary Technique: An Examination of Antithesis and Contrast in Romans 1–8." M.A. thesis, Trinity Evangelical Divinity School, 1978.

Matera, Frank J. *II Corinthians: A Commentary*. New Testament Library. Westminster John Knox, 2003.
Mays, James Luther. *Psalms*. Interpretation. John Knox, 1994.
McCall, Tom and Keith D. Stranglin. "S. M. Baugh and the Meaning of Foreknowledge: Another Look." *Trinity Journal* 26 (2005): 19–31.
McCasland, S. Vernon. "'Abba, Father.'" *Journal of Biblical Literature* 72 (1953): 79–91.
McKnight, Scot. *A New Vision for Israel: The Teachings of Jesus in a National Context*. Studying the Historical Jesus. Eerdmans, 1999.
Metzger, Bruce. *A Textual Commentary on the Greek New Testament*. 2d ed. German Bible Societies, 1994.
Meyer, Paul W. "Pauline Theology: A Proposal for a Pause in its Pursuit." Pages 140–60 in *Pauline Theology Volume IV: Looking Back, Pressing On*. Edited by E. Elizabeth Johnson and David M. Hay. Scholars Press, 1997.
Michaels, J. Ramsey. "The Redemption of Our Body: The Riddle of Romans 8:19–22." Pages 92–114 in *Romans and the People of God: Essays in Honor of Gordon D. Fee on the Occasion of His 65th Birthday*. Edited by Sven K. Soderlund and N. T. Wright. Eerdmans, 1999.
Michel, Otto. *Der Brief an die Römer*. Kritisch-exegetischer Kommentar über das Neue Testament. 4h ed. Vandenhoeck & Ruprecht, 1966.
Miller, James C. *The Obedience of Faith, the Eschatological People of God, and the Purpose of Romans*. Society of Biblical Literature Dissertation Series 177. SBL, 2000.
Mills, Wayne E. "Sons of God: The Roman View." *Biblical Illustrator* 10/1 (1983): 37–9.
Moberly, R. W. L. *The Bible, Theology, and Faith: A Study of Abraham and Jesus*. Cambridge University Press, 2000.
———. "How Appropriate Is 'Monotheism' as a Category for Biblical Interpretation?" Pages 216–34 in *Early Jewish and Christian Monotheism*. Journal for the Study of the New Testament Supplement Series 263. Edited by Loren T. Stuckenbruck and Wendy E. S. North. T&T Clark, 2004.
Moo, Douglas J. "The Christology of the Early Pauline Letters." Pages 169–92 in *Contours of Christology in the New Testament*. Edited by Richard N. Longenecker. Eerdmans, 2005.
———. *The Epistle to the Romans*. New International Commentary on the New Testament. Eerdmans, 1996.
Moores, John D. *Wrestling with Rationality in Paul: Romans 1–8 in a New Perspective*. Society for New Testament Studies Monograph Series 82. Cambridge University Press, 1995.
Morgan, Robert. *Romans*. New Testament Guides. Sheffield Academic Press, 1995.
Morris, Leon. *The Epistle to the Romans*. Pillar New Testament Commentary. Eerdmans, 1988.
Morrison, Bruce and John Woodhouse. "The Coherence of Romans 7:1–8:8." *The Reformed Theological Review* 47 (1988): 8–16.
Motyer, J. Alec. *The Prophecy of Isaiah: An Introduction and Commentary*. InterVarsity, 1993.

Mounce, Robert H. *Romans*. The New American Commentary 27. Broadman & Holman, 1995.
Moxnes, Halvor. *Theology in Conflict: Studies in Paul's Understanding of God in Romans*. Brill, 1980.
Murray, John. *The Epistle to the Romans*. Eerdmans, 1968. Repr. 1997.
Myers, Charles D., Jr. "Chiastic Inversion in the Argument of Romans 3–8." *Novum Testamentum* 35 (1993): 30–47.
Nash, Ronald H. *The Concept of God: An Exploration of Contemproary Difficulties with the Attributes of God*. Zondervan, 1983.
Norris, Richard A., Jr., ed. and trans. *The Christological Controversy*. Sources of Early Christian Thought. Fortress, 1980.
Nygren, Anders. *Commentary on Romans*. Translated by Carl C. Rasmussen. Fortress, 1949.
Obeng, E. A. "The Origins of the Spirit Intercession Motif in Romans 8.26." *New Testament Studies* 32 (1986): 621–32.
O'Brien, Peter. *Colossians, Philemon*. Word Biblical Commentary 44. Nelson, 1982.
_____. "Romans 8:26, 27. A Revolutionary Approach to Prayer?" *Reformed Theological Review* 46 (1987): 65–73.
Olshausen, Eckart. "Mithradtes VI. und Rom," in *ANRW* 1.806–15. Part 1, 1. Edited by Hildegard Temporini. de Gruyter, 1972.
Origen. *The Fathers of the Church: Origen, Commentary on the Epistle to the Romans*. 2 vols. Vol. 103–104. Translated by Thomas P. Scheck. The Catholic University of America Press, 2001.
Osborne, Grant R. *Romans*. The IVP New Testament Commentary Series 6. InterVarsity, 2004.
Osburn, C.D. "The Interpretation of Romans 8:28." *Westminster Theological Journal* 44 (1982): 99–109.
Osten-Sacken, Peter von der. *Römer 8 als Beispiel paulinischer Soteriologie*. Vandenhoek and Ruprecht, 1975.
Overman, J. Andrew. "The God-fearers: Some Neglected Features." *Journal for the Study of the New Testament* 32 (1988): 17–26.
Parlier, Isabelle. "La Folle Justice de Dieu: Romains 8, 31–39." *Foi et Vie* 5 (1992): 103–10.
Paulsen, Henning. Überlieferung und Auslegung in Römer 8. Wissenschaftliche Monographien zum Alten und Neuen Testament 43. Neukirchener Verlag, 1974.
Penna, Romano. "Les Juifs à Rome au Temps de l'Apôtre Paul." New Testament Studies 28 (1982): 321–47.
Perowne, Stewart. *Roman Mythology*. Library of the World's Myths and Legends. Peter Bedrick Books, 1988.
Pester, John. "Glorification." *Affirmation and Critique* 7 (2002): 55–69.
_____. "The Organic Law in Romans 8." *Affirmation and Critique* 2 (1997): 44–49.
Platner, Samuel Ball. *A Topographical Dictionary of Ancient Rome*. Revised by Thomas Ashby. Oxford University Press, 1929.

Porter, Stanley. "A Newer Perspective on Paul: Romans 1–8 Through the Eyes of Literary Analysis." Pages 366–92 in *The Bible in Human Society: Essays in Honor of John Rogerson*. Edited by M. Daniel Carroll R., David J.A. Clines, and Philip R. Davies. Journal for the Study of the Old Testament Supplement Series 200. Sheffield Academic Press, 1995.

Price, S. R. F. *Rituals and Power: The Roman Imperial Cult in Asia Minor*. Cambridge University Press, 1984.

Rad, Gerhard von. *Genesis: A Commentary*. Old Testament Library. Translated by John H. Marks. Revised edition. Westminster, 1972.

Rawson, Elizabeth. "Caesar's Heritage: Hellenistic Kings and Their Roman Equals." *Journal of Roman Studies* 65 (1975): 148–59.

Reed, Jeffrey T. "Using Ancient Rhetorical Categories to Interpret Paul's Letters: A Question of Genre." Pages 292–324 in *Rhetoric and the New Testament: Essays from the 1992 Heidelberg Conference*. Edited by Stanley E. Porter and Thomas H. Olbricht. Journal for the Study of the New Testament Supplement Series 90. Sheffield Academic Press, 1993.

Rice, David G., and John E. Stambaugh. *Sources for the Study of Greek Religion*. Society of Biblical Literature Sources for Biblical Study 14. Scholars Press, 1979.

Richardson, Neil. *Paul's Language about God*. Journal for the Study of the New Testament Supplement Series 99. Sheffield Academic Press, 1994.

Richardson, Peter. "Augustan-Era Synagogues in Rome." Pages 17–29 in *Judaism and Christianity in First-Century Rome*. Edited by Karl P. Donfried and Peter Richardson. Eerdmans, 1998.

Ridderbos, Herman N. "The Earliest Confession of the Atonement in Paul." Pages 76–89 in *Reconciliation and Hope: New Testament Essays on Atonement and Eschatology*. Edited by Robert Banks. Translated by J. W. Deenick. Eerdmans, 1974.

Riesner, Rainer. *Paul's Early Period: Chronology, Mission, Strategy, Theology*. Eerdmans, 1998.

Roark, C. Mack. "Sin and Evil in Paul's Theology." *Biblical Illustrator* 14/3 (1988): 70–2.

Rodgers, P.R. "The Text of Romans 8:28." *Journal of Theological Studies* 46 (1995): 547–50.

Roland, P. "L'antithèse de Rm 5–8." *Biblica* 69 (1988): 396–400.

Rosscup, James E. "The Spirit's Intercession." *The Masters Seminary Journal* 10 (1999): 139–62.

Rossow, "The Hound of Heaven, A Twitch upon the Thread, and Romans 8:31–39." *Concordia Journal* 23 (1997): 91–8.

Rusch, William G., ed. and trans. *The Trinitarian Controversy*. Sources of Early Christian Thought. Fortress, 1980.

Sanday, William and Arthur C. Headlam. *The Epistle to the Romans*. International Critical Commentary. 5h ed. T&T Clark, 1980.

Sanders, E. P. *Paul, the Law, and the Jewish People*. Fortress, 1983.

Sanders, John W. "Paul and Theological History." Pages 52–57 in *Paul and the Scriptures of Israel*. Journal for the Study of the New Testament Supplement Series 83. Edited by Craig Evans and John Sanders. Sheffield Academic, 1993.

Scherrer, Stephen J. "Signs and Wonders in the Imperial Cult: A New Look at a Roman Religious Institution in the Light of Rev 13:13–15." *Journal of Biblical Literature* 103 (1984): 599–610.

Schiffman, Lawrence H. *From Text to Tradition: A History of Second Temple and Rabbinic Judaism*. Ktav Publishing, 1991.

Schlatter, Adolf. *Romans: The Righteousness of God*. Translated by Siegfried S. Schatzman. Hendrickson, 1995.

Schmithals, Walter. *Die theologische Anthropologie des Paulus. Auslegung von Röm. 7,17–8,39*. Kohlhammer Taschenbücher 1021. Kohlhammer, 1980.

———. *Der Römerbrief als historisches Problem*. Gerd Mohn, 1975.

———. *Der Römerbrief: Ein Kommentar*. Gerd Mohn, 1988.

Schnabel, Eckhard J. *Law and Wisdom from Ben Sira to Paul: A Tradition Historical Enquiry into the Relationship of Law, Wisdom, and Ethics*. Wissenschaftliche Untersuchungen zum Neuen Testament II/16. Mohr Siebeck, 1985.

———. *Early Christian Mission*. 2 vols. InterVarsity, 2004.

Schoeni, Marc. "The Hyperbolic Sublime as a Master Trope in Romans." Pages 171–92 in *Rhetoric and the New Testament: Essays from the 1992 Heidelberg Conference*. Edited by Stanley E. Porter and Thomas H. Olbricht. Journal for the Study of the New Testament Supplement Series 90. Sheffield Academic Press, 1993.

Schreiner, Thomas R. *Romans*. Baker Exegetical Commentary on the New Testament 6. Baker Books, 1998.

Schweizer, Eduard. "Zum religionsgeschichtlichen Hintergrund der 'Sendungsformel' Gal 4,4f. Rm 8,3f. Joh 3,16f. I Joh 4,9." *Zeitschrift für die neutestamentliche Wissenschaft* 57 (1966): 199–210.

Scott, James M. *Adoption as Sons of God*. Wissenschaftliche Untersuchungen zum Neuen Testament II/48. Mohr Siebeck, 1992.

Scott, Kenneth. *The Imperial Cult Under the Flavians*. Arno, 1975.

Seifrid, Mark. "The Subject of Rom 7:14–25." *Novum Testamentum* 34 (1992): 313–33.

Shum, Shiu-Lun. *Paul's Use of Isaiah in Romans: A Comparative Study of Paul's Letter to the Romans and the Sibylline and Qumran Sectarian Texts*. Wissenschaftliche Untersuchungen zum Neuen Testament II/156. Mohr Siebeck, 2002.

Siber, Peter. *Mit Christus leben. Eine Studie zur paulinischen Auferstehungshoffnung*. Abhandlungen zur Theologie des Alten und Neuen Testaments 61. Theologischer Verlag, 1971.

Slingerland, H. Dixon. *Claudian Policymaking and the Early Imperial Repression of Judaism at Rome*. USF Studies in the History of Judaism. Scholars Press, 1997.

Smith, Geoffrey. "The Function of 'Likewise' (ΩΣΑΥΤΩΣ) in Romans 8:26." *Tyndale Bulletin* 49 (1998): 29–38.

Smith, Jonathan Z. *Drudgery Divine: On the Comparison of Early Christianities and the Religions of Late Antiquity*. University of Chicago Press, 1990.

Snyder, Graydon F. "The Interaction of Jews with non-Jews in Rome." Pages 69–90 in *Judaism and Christianity in First-Century Rome*. Edited by Karl P. Donfried and Peter Richardson. Eerdmans, 1998.

Snyman, A. H. "Style and the Rhetorical Situation of Romans 8:31–39." *New Testament Studies* 34 (1988): 218–31.

Söding, Thomas. "Sühne durch Stellvertretung: Zur zentralen Deutung des Todes Jesu im Römerbrief." Pages 375–96 in *Deutungen des Todes Jesu im Neuen Testament*. Edited by Jörg Frey and Jens Schröter. Wissenschaftliche Untersuchungen zum Neuen Testament I/181. Mohr Siebeck, 2005.

Song, Changwon. *Reading Romans as a Diatribe*. Studies in Biblical Literature 59. Peter Lang, 2004.

Spencer, Aida Besancon. *Paul's Literary Style: A Stylistic and Historical Comparison of II Corinthians 11:16–12:13, Romans 8:9–39, and Philippians 3:2–4:13*. Evangelical Theological Society Monograph. Eisenbrauns, 1984.

Spicq, Ceslas. *Theological Lexicon of the New Testament*. Translated and edited by James D. Ernest. 3 vols. Hendrickson, 1994.

Stowers, Stanley K. *The Diatribe and Paul's Letter to the Romans*. Society of Biblical Literature Dissertation Series 57. Scholars Press, 1981.

_____. *Letter Writing in Greco-Roman Antiquity*. Library of Early Christianity 5. The Westminster Press, 1986.

_____. "The Diatribe." Pages 71–83 in *Greco-Roman Literature and the New Testament*. Society of Biblical Literature Resources for Biblical Study 21. Edited by David E. Aune. Scholars Press, 1988.

_____. *Rereading of Romans: Justice, Jews, and Gentiles*. Yale University Press, 1994.

Stuhlmacher, Peter. *Paul's Letter to the Romans: A Commentary*. Translated by Scott J. Hafemann. Westminster John Knox, 1994.

_____. "The Purpose of Romans." Pages 231–42 in *The Romans Debate*. Edited by Karl P. Donfried. Hendrickson, 1991.

Talbert, Charles H. *Romans*. Smyth & Helwys Bible Commentary. Smyth & Helwys, 2002.

_____. "Tracing Paul's Train of Thought in Romans 6–8." *Review and Expositor* 100 (2003): 53–63.

Thielman, Frank. *From Plight to Solution: A Jewish Framework for Understanding Paul's View of the Law in Galatians and Romans*. Novum Testamentum Supplements 61. Brill, 1989.

_____. *Paul and the Law: A Contextual Approach*. InterVarsity, 1994.

_____. "The Story of Israel and the Theology of Romans 5–8." Pages 169–95 in *Pauline Theology Volume III: Romans*. Edited by David M. Hay and E. Elizabeth Johnson. SBL, 2002.

Thiselton, Anthony C. *The First Epistle to the Corinthians: A Commentary on the Greek Text*. New International Greek Testament Commentary. Eerdmans, 2000.

Tinh, Tran tam. "Les empereurs romains versus Isis, Sérapis." Pages 215–30 in *Subject and Ruler: The Cult of the Ruling Power in Classical Antiquity*. Edited by Alastair Small. Journal of Roman Archaeology Supplementary Series 17. Thomson-Shore, 1996.

Thompson, Leonard L. *The Book of Revelation: Apocalypse and Empire*. Oxford University Press, 1990.

Thompson, Marianne Meye. "'Mercy upon All': God as Father in the Epistle to the Romans." Pages 203–16 in *Romans and the People of God: Essays in Honor of Gordon D. Fee on the Occasion of His 65th Birthday*. Edited by Sven K. Soderlund and N. T. Wright. Eerdmans, 1999.

Thrasher, Bill. *The Attributes of God In Pauline Theology*. Eugene, Ore.: Wipf & Stock, 2001.

Thüsing, Wilhelm. *Gott und Christus in der paulinischen Soteriologie: Band I Per Christum in Deum: Das Verhältnis der Christozentrik zur Theozentrik*. Aschendorff, 1986.

Tibbe, Johann. *Geist und Leben*. Biblische Studien 44. Neukirchener Verlag, 1965.

Trocmé, Etienne. "From 'I' to 'We': Christian Life According to Romans, Chapters 7 and 8." Translated by Marie Benedict. *Australian Biblical Review* 35 (1987): 73–6.

Tsumura, D. T. "An OT Background to Rom 8:22." *New Testament Studies* 40 (1994): 620–1.

Tuckett, Christopher M. "Paul, Scripture, and Ethics. Some Reflections." *New Testament Studies* 46 (2000): 403–24.

Turcan, Robert. "Salut mithriaque et sotériologie néoplatonicienne." Pages 173–91 in *La soteriologia dei culti oriental nell' Impero Romano*. Edited by Ugo Bianchi and Maarten J. Vermaseren. Brill, 1982.

Turner, Nigel. *Syntax*. A Grammar of New Testament Greek 3. T&T Clark, 1963.

Ulansey, David. *The Origins of the Mithraic Mysteries: Cosmology and Salvation in the Ancient World*. Oxford University Press, 1989.

VanGemeren, Willem A. "Psalms" in *The Expositor's Bible Commentary* 5. Zondervan, 1991.

Vanni, Ugo. "*Homoima* in Paulo (Rm 1, 23; 5,14; 6,5; 8,3; Fil 2,7). Un interpretazione esegetico-teologica alla luce dell'uso dei LXX." *Gregorianum* 58 (1977): 321–45, 431–70.

Versnel, H. S. *Ter Unus: Isis, Dionysos, Hermes: Three Studies in Henotheism*. Inconsistencies in Greek and Roman Religion 1. Brill, 1990.

Vidman, Ladislav. *Isis und Sarapis bei den Griechen und Römern: Epigraphische Studien zur Verbreitung und zu den Trägern des ägyptischen Kultes*. Religionsgeschichtliche Versuche und Vorarbeiten. de Gruyter, 1970.

Vlachos, Chris Alex. "Exulting in the Hope of Glory: An Exegesis of Romans 8:31–39 and an Analysis of its Function within the Epistle." M.A. thesis, Trinity Evangelical Divinity School, 1995.

Walter, Nikolaus. "Gottes Zorn und das 'Harren der Kreatur'. Zur Korrespondenz zwischen Römer 1,18–32 und 8,19–22." Pages 218–26 in *Christus Bezeugen: Festschrift für Wolfgang Trilling zum 65. Geburtstag*. Edited by Karl Kertelge, Traugott Holtz, and Claus-Peter März. Erfurter theologische Studien 59. St. Benno-Verlag, 1989.

Waltke, Bruce K. with Cathi J. Fredricks. *Genesis: A Commentary*. Zondervan, 2001.

Wanamaker, Charles A. *The Epistles to the Thessalonians*. New International Greek Text Commentary. Eerdmans, 1990.

Wansink, Craig H. "Roman Law and Legal System." Pages 984–91 in *Dictionary of New Testament Backgrounds*. Edited by Craig A. Evans and Stanley E. Porter. InterVarsity, 2000.

Watson, Francis. "The Triune Divine Identity: Reflections on Pauline God Language, in Disagreement with J.D.G. Dunn." *Journal for the Study of the New Testament* 80 (2000): 99–124.

Watson, Nigel. "'And If Children, Then Heirs' (Rom 8:17)—Why Not Sons?" *Australian Biblical Review* 49 (2001): 53–6.

Watts, John D. *Isaiah*. 2 vols. Word Biblical Commentary 24–25. Word, 1985–1987.

Weber, Reinhard. "Die Geschichte des Gesetzes und des Ich in Römer 7,7–8,4: Einige Überlegungen zum Zusammenhang von Heilgeschichte und Anthropologie im Blick auf die theologische Grundstellung des paulinischen Denkens." *Neue Zeitschrift für systematische Theologie und Religionsphilosophie* 29 (1987): 147–79.

Wedderburn, A. J. M. "Some Observations on Paul's Use of the Phrases 'in Christ' and 'with Christ.'" *Journal for the Study of the New Testament* 25 (1985): 83–97.

Weinstock, Stefan. *Divus Julius*. Clarendon, 1971.

Wenham, Gordon J. *Genesis*. 2 vols. Word Biblical Commentary 1–2. Word, 1987–1994.

Westerholm, Stephen. "The 'New Perspective' at Twenty-Five." Pages 1–38 in *Justification and Variegated Nomism: Volume 2–The Paradoxes of Paul*. Baker, 2004.

Westermann, Claus. *Isaiah: A Commentary*. 2 vols. Old Testament Library. Translated by David M. G. Stalker. Westminster, 1969.

———. *Genesis*. 3 vols. Continental Commentary. Translated by John J. Scullion. Fortress, 1995.

White, John L. "Ancient Greek Letters." Pages 85–106 in *Greco-Roman Literature and the New Testament*. Edited by David E. Aune. Society of Biblical Literature Sources for Biblical Study 21. Scholars Press, 1988.

Wiefel, Wolfgang. "The Jewish Community in Ancient Rome and the Origins of Roman Christianity." Pages 85–101 in *The Romans Debate*. Edited by Karl P. Donfried. Hendrickson, 1991.

Wilckens, Urlich. *Der Brief an die Römer*. 3 vols. Evangelisch-Katholischer Kommentar zum Neuen Testament 6.1–6.3. Neukirchener Verlag, 1978–1982.

Witherington, Ben, with Darlene Hyatt. *Paul's Letter to the Romans: A Socio-Rhetorical Commentary*. Eerdmans, 2004.

Witherington, Ben. *Paul's Narrative Thought World: The Tapestry of Tragedy and Triumph*. Westminster/John Knox, 1994.

Witt, R. E. *Isis in the Graeco-Roman World*. Cornell University Press, 1971.

Wood, Arthur Skevington. *Life by the Spirit*. Zondervan, 1963.

Wright, N. T. "New Exodus, New Inheritance: The Narrative Structure of Romans 3–8." Pages 26–35 in *Romans and the People of God: Essays in Honor of Gordon D. Fee on the Occasion of His 65th Birthday*. Edited by Sven K. Soderlund and N. T. Wright. Eerdmans, 1999.

———. "Romans and the Theology of Paul." Pages 30–67 in *Pauline Theology Volume III: Romans*. Edited by David M. Hay and E. Elizabeth Johnson. SBL, 2002.

---. *The Climax of the Covenant: Christ and the Law in Pauline Theology*. Fortress, 1993.

---. "The Letter to the Romans" in *The New Interpreter's Bible* 10. Abingdon, 2002.

---. *The New Testament and the People of God*. Christian Origins and the Question of God 1. Fortress, 1992.

---. *The Resurrection of the Son of God*. Christian Origins and the Question of God 3. Fortress, 2003.

Wu, Julie L. "The Spirit's Intercession in Romans 8:26–27: An Exegetical Note." *Expository Times* 105 (1993): 13.

Young, Frances and David F. Ford. *Meaning and Truth in 2 Corinthians*. Eerdmans, 1987.

Zanker, Paul. *Pompeii: Public and Private Life*. Harvard University Press, 1998.

Zeller, Dieter. "New Testament Christology in its Hellenistic Reception." *New Testament Studies* 46 (2001): 312–33.

---. "The Just Requirement of the Law (Rom 8:4)." *Australian Biblical Review* 35 (1987): 77–82.

Ziesler, John. *Paul's Letter to the Romans*. TPI New Testament Commentaries. Trinity Press International, 1989.

Index

Genesis
3	50 n. 90, 114
3:15	65
3:17	49
3:17–19	47–50
15:2–4	55
22:12	76, 77, 105, 122
22:16	76, 105, 122
48:5	55

Exodus
2:10	55
29:36	114
30:10	114

Leviticus
4:25	114
5:6–7	75 n. 295
5:11	75 n. 295
7:37	75 n. 295
9:2–3	75 n. 295
12:6	75 n. 295
12:8	75 n. 295
14:13	75 n. 295
14:22	75 n. 295
14:31	75 n. 295
15:15	75 n. 295
15:30	75 n. 295
16:3	75 n. 295
16:5	75 n. 295
16:5	75 n. 295
16:9	75 n. 295
23:10	71 n. 261
23:19	75 n. 295

Numbers
6:11	75 n. 295
6:16	75 n. 295
7:16	75 n. 295
7:22	75 n. 295
7:28	75 n. 295
7:34	75 n. 295
7:40	75 n. 295
7:46	75 n. 295
7:52	75 n. 295
7:58	75 n. 295
7:64	75–76 n. 295
7:70	75–76 n. 295
7:76	75–76 n. 295
7:82	75–76 n. 295
7:87	75–76 n. 295
8:8	75–76 n. 295
8:12	75–76 n. 295
15:20–21	71 n. 261
15:24	75–76 n. 295
15:27	75–76 n. 295
18:30	71 n. 261
18:32	71 n. 261
28:15	75–76 n. 295
28:22	75–76 n. 295
28:30	75–76 n. 295
29:5	75–76 n. 295
29:11	75–76 n. 295
29:16	75–76 n. 295
29:19	75–76 n. 295
29:22	75–76 n. 295
29:25	75–76 n. 295
29:28	75–76 n. 295
29:31	75–76 n. 295

29:24	75–76 n. 295
29:38	75–76 n. 295

2 Samuel
7:14	55

2 Kings
12:16	75–76 n. 295

1 Chronicles
28:6	55

2 Chronicles
29:21	75–76 n. 295
29:23–24	75–76 n. 295

Ezra
6:17	75–76 n. 295
8:35	75–76 n. 295

Nehemiah
10:33	75–76 n. 295, 113
10:37	71 n. 261

Job
1:5	75–76 n. 295

Psalms
2:7	55
8:7 (LXX)	49
40:6	75–76 n. 295
73:25–26	59
110:1	106, 124, 125, 130

Proverbs
3:12	69

Isaiah
50:9	124, 129
53:10	75–76 n. 295

Lamentations
3:24	59

Ezekiel
42:13	75–76 n. 295
43:19	75–76 n. 295
43:21	75–76 n. 295

Habakkuk
2:4	131

Mark
12:7–9	104
14:36	58

Luke
20:13	104

John
3:16–17	104
8:46	92 n. 95
16:8	92 n. 95
16:9	92 n. 95

Acts
2	10
2:23	106 n. 207
26:5	106 n. 207

Romans
1–4	40, 40 n. 9
1–8	40, 41
1:1–7	39,
1:1–15	40
1:4	51, 122, 126
1:7	9
1:8–15	39
1:15	9
1:16	51
1:16–17	39, 39 n. 2, 40
1:16–8:39	40
1:17	131
1:18	40, 41
1:18–3:20	39, 41
1:18–4:25	39 n. 3, 40, 42
1:18–11:36	40
1:20	51
1:25	46
2:7	83 n. 15
2:29	115 n. 285
3:20	45
3:21–26	74
3:21–4:25	39, 39 n. 3
3:24	108 n. 223
3:25	85 n. 31
3:26	70
3:27–31	135
4:8	126
4:15	45
4:17	83 n. 15
5	11, 39, 40, 40 n. 9, 42, 43 n. 30, 45, 50 n. 96, 63, 74, 103, 140
5–8	40, 42, 42 n. 20, 43, 50, 74, 91 n. 88
5:1	108
5:1–11	40
5:1–8:39	50
5:3–5	41
5:6	74
5:8	74, 133

Index

5:8–10	74	7:7–8:4	43
5:10	50, 83 n. 15	7:8	92
5:12	50, 83 n. 15	7:10	50, 83, 83 n. 15, 84
5:12–21	40, 41, 42 n. 29, 103	7:11	92
5:12–8:39	41	7:13	45, 50, 83 n. 15, 92
5:13	45, 73	7:13–20	41
5:14	9, 50, 83 n. 15, 103, 113	7:14	84
5:15	74	7:14–20	98
5:16	42 n. 29, 73	7:14–25	44, 44 n. 40, 87
5:17	50	7:20	93
5:17–18	50, 83 n. 15	7:21	45
5:18	42 n. 29, 73	7:21–8:17	41
5:20	45	7:22	45
5:21	50, 83 n. 15	7:24	43, 83 n. 15, 96
6	109	7:24–25	73 n. 273
6–7	40, 42	7:25	43 n. 39, 44 n. 40, 45
6–8	40, 40 n. 9, 41	8	2, 4–7, 9, 11, 39–46, 50 n. 96, 56, 57 n. 147, 63, 73, 81, 82, 95, 108, 117, 120–122, 127, 132–135, 137–143
6:1–11	109		
6:1–14	41		
6:1–8:30	43		
6:2–11	109	8:1	42 n. 29, 43 n. 39, 44 n. 40, 50, 73 n. 274, 92, 111, 112, 127
6:3	109		
6:3–4	44	8:1–2	57, 108 n. 223, 114
6:3–5	50, 83 n. 15	8:1–3	93
6:4	50	8:1–4	9, 81, 88, 92, 108, 110, 122
6:5	102, 112	8:1–8	88, 89, 92
6:6	96	8:1–11	43 n. 30
6:8	110	8:1–13	43 n. 34
6:9	50	8:2	6, 43, 45 n. 49, 50, 73, 78, 83, 84, 86, 92, 93 n. 102, 111, 115, 117
6:9–10	83 n. 15		
6:10	50		
6:11	85, 85 n. 31, 108 n. 223, 110	8:2–4	43 n. 30, 111, 118
6:13	50, 83 n. 15	8:2–8	73
6:15–7:6	41	8:3	59, 75–77, 83, 86, 92–94, 96, 99, 101, 104, 105, 112, 122, 136
6:16	50, 83 n. 15		
6:21	50	8:3–4	74, 87, 89, 124
6:21–23	83 n. 15	8:4	75–77, 83, 84, 86, 88, 114–116
6:22	50	8:5	88 n. 53, 91, 94
6:23	50, 85, 85 n. 31, 108 n. 223	8:5–8	90, 94, 96, 115
7	7, 11, 39, 42–45, 56, 82, 83, 92, 93, 95, 108, 111, 114, 140	8:5–11	97
		8:6	50, 56, 91, 108, 117, 118
7–8	90	8:7	57, 83, 87, 88
7:1	44	8:7–8	91
7:1–6	73	8:7–9	57, 88
7:1–8:17	43, 44	8:8	57, 115
7:4	44, 82	8:9	3, 6, 57, 72, 115, 116, 127, 131, 133
7:4–6	82, 118	8:9–10	119
7:5	44, 45, 50, 92	8:9–11	54, 57, 121, 134
7:5–6	83 n. 15	8:10	117, 118
7:6	43–45, 50, 56, 73, 78, 82, 95, 115 n. 285	8:10–11	50, 56, 119
		8:11	57, 76, 95, 96, 115, 117, 119
7:7	45, 74, 90	8:12	116
7:7–12	41	8:13	97, 116, 117, 119
7:7–24	43 n. 30	8:13–17	54, 56
7:7–25	45, 73, 89		

8:14	56 n. 140, 57, 60, 61, 78, 97, 101, 116	11:5	70, 70 n. 252
8:14–16	56	11:15	83 n. 15
8:14–17	99	12:5	85 n. 31, 108 n. 223
8:14–23	60	13:8	90
8:15	6, 54, 57, 60, 60 n. 171, 97, 120	14:14	108–109 n. 223
8:15–16	116	15:13	51
8:15–17	58	15:15	87
8:16	56 n. 140	15:17	85 n. 31, 108 n. 223
8:16–17	60, 61, 99	15:19	51
8:17	54, 70 n. 251, 72, 99, 100, 117	16	39 n. 2
8:17–18	69, 102, 136	16:2	108–109 n. 223
8:18	70, 72, 95, 100, 100 n. 161	16:3	85 n. 31, 108 n. 223
8:18–30	41, 70 n. 251, 100	16:4	83 n. 15
8:18–39	41, 41 n. 68	16:7	85 n. 31, 108 n. 223
8:19	46, 48, 54, 60, 61, 63	16:8	108–109 n. 223
8:19–22	47, 49, 50, 53, 100	16:9–10	85 n. 31, 108 n. 223
8:19–23	46, 48, 72	16:11	108–109 n. 223
8:20	68	16:12	108–109 n. 223
8:21	60, 61, 68, 100 n. 161	16:13	108–109 n. 223
8:22	47–49, 101, 111, 136	16:22	108–109 n. 223
8:23	47, 48, 54, 59, 60 n. 171, 68, 70–72, 95, 96, 107, 117, 137		
		1 Corinthians	
8:23–25	100	1:2	108 n. 223
8:24	137	1:4	108 n. 223
8:26	111, 128	1:18	51
8:26–27	100, 128, 131, 132	1:30	108 n. 223
8:27	6	1:31	108–109 n. 223
8:28	101	2:4	51
8:28–30	100	2:5	51
8:29	6, 59, 76, 99, 103, 105, 107	2:11	129, 131
8:29–30	101, 102, 106, 117	3:1	108 n. 223
8:30	59, 100 n. 161	3:22	51
8:31–39	5, 8–9, 42, 107, 123–125, 127, 130	4:10	108 n. 223
		4:15	108 n. 223
8:32	6, 76, 77, 99, 101, 105, 107, 110, 122, 123	4:17	108 n. 223
		4:19	51
8:33	79, 105	4:20	51
8:33–34	77, 124	5:4	51
8:33–39	126	6:14	51
8:34	6, 74, 77, 105, 123, 124, 128–130, 133	7:22	108–109 n. 223
		7:29	70 n. 252
8:35	127	7:39	108–109 n. 223
8:35–36	127	9:1–2	108–109 n. 223
8:35–39	127	11:11	108–109 n. 223
8:38	51	12:10	51
8:38–39	47, 50, 53, 107	12:28–29	51
8:39	85 n. 31, 108 n. 223, 111, 126, 133	14:11	51
9–11	42, 45	15:18–19	108 n. 223
9:1	85 n. 31, 108 n. 223	15:22	108 n. 223
9:4	54, 60 n. 171	15:24	51
9:5	3	15:27–28	49
9:17	51	15:31	108 n. 223
11:2	106 n. 207	15:43	51
11:3	83 n. 15	15:45	103
		15:56	51

Index   169

15:58	108–109 n. 223	3:11	108–109 n. 223
16:19	108–109 n. 223	3:16	51
16:24	108 n. 223	3:20	51
		3:21	108–109 n. 223

2 Corinthians

1:8	51	4:1	108–109 n. 223
2:12	108–109 n. 223	4:17	108–109 n. 223
2:14	108 n. 223	4:21	108–109 n. 223
2:17	108 n. 223	4:32	108–109 n. 223
3:14	108–109 n. 223	5:8	108–109 n. 223
4:7	51	6:1	108–109 n. 223
5:17	108–109 n. 223	6:10	108–109 n. 223
5:19	108–109 n. 223	6:21	108–109 n. 223
6:2	70 n. 252		
6:7	51	Philippians	
8:3	51	1:1	108–109 n. 223
10:17	108–109 n. 223	1:13	108–109 n. 223
12:2	108–109 n. 223	1:14	108–109 n. 223
12:9	51	1:23	110
12:12	51	1:26	108–109 n. 223
12:19	108–109 n. 223	2:1	108–109 n. 223
13:4	51	2:5	108–109 n. 223
		2:5–11	91 n. 86
Galatians		2:19	108–109 n. 223
1:22	108–109 n. 223	2:24	108–109 n. 223
2:4	108–109 n. 223	2:29	108–109 n. 223
2:17	108–109 n. 223	3:1	108–109 n. 223
3	83	3:3	108–109 n. 223
3:5	51	3:10	51
3:14	108–109 n. 223	3:14	108–109 n. 223
3:26	108–109 n. 223	3:21	49
3:28	108–109 n. 223	4:1–2	108–109 n. 223
4:5	54, 60 n. 171	4:4	108–109 n. 223
4:4–5	122 n. 350	4:7	108–109 n. 223
5:6	108–109 n. 223	4:10	108–109 n. 223
5:10	108–109 n. 223	4:19	108–109 n. 223
5:13–26	96	4:21	108–109 n. 223

Ephesians		Colossians	
1:1	108–109 n. 223	1:2	108–109 n. 223
1:3	108–109 n. 223	1:4	108–109 n. 223
1:5	54, 60 n. 171	1:11	51
1:10	108–109 n. 223	1:15	103
1:12	108–109 n. 223	1:15–18	103
1:15	108–109 n. 223	1:28	108–109 n. 223
1:19	51	1:29	51
1:20	108–109 n. 223	2:20	110
1:21	51	2:22	68
1:22	49	3:10	46
2:6–7	108–109 n. 223	3:18	108–109 n. 223
2:10	108–109 n. 223	3:20	108–109 n. 223
2:13	108–109 n. 223	4:7	108–109 n. 223
2:21	108–109 n. 223	4:17	108–109 n. 223
3:6	108–109 n. 223		
3:7	51	1 Thessalonians	
		1:1	108–109 n. 223

1:5	51
2:14	108–109 n. 223
3:8	108–109 n. 223
4:1	108–109 n. 223
4:16	108–109 n. 223
4:17	108–109 n. 223
5:18	108–109 n. 223

2 Thessalonians

1:1	108–109 n. 223
1:11	51
2:9	51
3:4	108–109 n. 223
3:12	108–109 n. 223

1 Timothy

1:14	108–109 n. 223
3:13	108–109 n. 223

2 Timothy

1:1	108–109 n. 223
1:7–8	51
1:9	108–109 n. 223
1:13	108–109 n. 223
2:1	108–109 n. 223
2:10	108–109 n. 223
3:12	108–109 n. 223
3:15	108–109 n. 223

Philemon

8	108–109 n. 223
16	108–109 n. 223
20	108–109 n. 223
23	108–109 n. 223

Hebrews

7:25	124
9	61 n. 189
10:6	92 n. 95
10:8	92 n. 95
10:18	92 n. 95
13:11	92 n. 95

1 Peter

1:2	106 n. 207
1:20	106 n. 207
5:14	108 n. 222

2 Peter

3:17	106 n. 207

Revelation

21:1–22:7	68

1 Enoch

40:9	59

4 Esdras

3:4–5	43

4 Maccabees

18:3	59

Psalms of Solomon

14:10	59

Tobit

13:4–5	69

Wisdom

3–5	69
9:10	104, 122
9:17	104, 122

www.ingramcontent.com/pod-product-compliance
Lightning Source LLC
Chambersburg PA
CBHW072012110526
44592CB00012B/1273